Major European Ports

1783 - 1829

St. Petersburg

Glasgow • ENGLAND

• Liverpool

Cork •

Cardiff

London

Le Havre

• Paris

Plymouth

FRANCE

Trieste

Leghorn

SPAIN

St. Ubes

Gibraltar

Barbary

Azores
Fayal

Cádiz

Malta

Coast

Port of Portsmouth Ships and the Cotton Trade
1783–1829

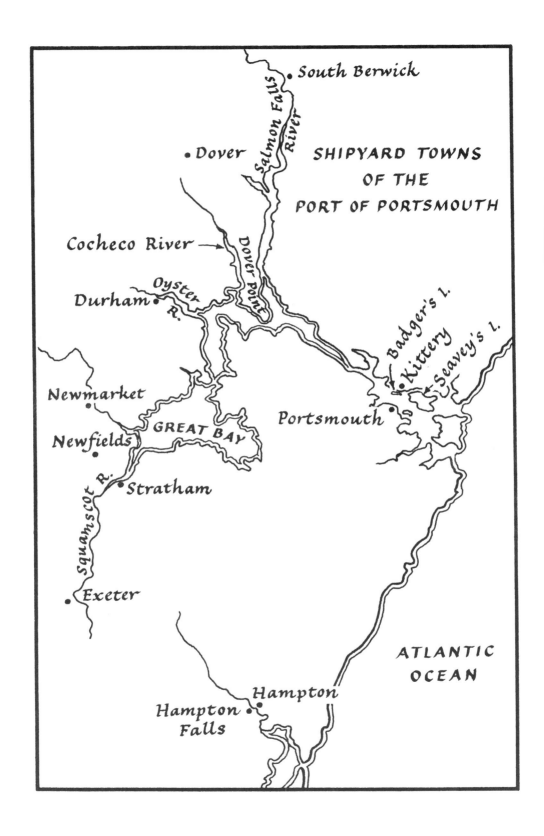

South Berwick

Dover

SHIPYARD TOWNS
OF THE
PORT OF PORTSMOUTH

Salmon Falls River

Cocheco River

Dover Point

Oyster
R.

Durham

Badger's I.

Kittery

Seavey's I.

Newmarket

GREAT BAY

Portsmouth

Newfields

Squamscot R.

Stratham

Exeter

ATLANTIC
OCEAN

Hampton

Hampton
Falls

Port of Portsmouth Ships and the Cotton Trade
1783–1829

by Ray Brighton

The Portsmouth Marine Society
Publication Ten

Published for the Society by
Peter E. Randall
PUBLISHER

To the memory of George Nelson,
collector in the Portsmouth Customs District,
1930–1942

© *1986 by The Portsmouth Marine Society*
Printed in the United States of America
Maps by Alex Wallach
Designed and Produced by Peter E. Randall Publisher
Box 4726, Portsmouth, NH 03801

A publication of
The Portsmouth Marine Society
Box 147, Portsmouth, NH 03801

Library of Congress Cataloging-in-Publication Data

Brighton, Ray.
   Port of Portsmouth ships and the cotton trade,
1783–1829.

   (Publication/Portsmouth Marine Society ; 10)
   Bibliography: p.
   Includes index.
   1. Shipping—New Hampshire—Portsmouth Region—
History. 2. Ships—New Hampshire—Portsmouth
Region—History. 3. Shipmasters—New Hampshire—
Portsmouth Region—History. 4. Cotton trade—
New Hampshire—Portsmouth Region—History.
I. Title. II. Series: Publication (Portsmouth
Marine Society) ; 10.
HE767.P7B75 1986   387.1′64′097426   86-27920
ISBN 0-915819-09-0

Other Portsmouth Marine Society Publications:
   1. John Haley Bellamy, Carver of Eagles
   2. The Prescott Story
   3. The Piscataqua Gundalow,
         Workhorse for a Tidal Basin Empire
   4. The Checkered Career of Tobias Lear
   5. Clippers of the Port of Portsmouth
         and the Men who built Them
   6. Portsmouth-Built
         Submarines of the Portsmouth Naval Shipyard
   7. Atlantic Heights
         A World War I Shipbuilders' Community
   8. There are No Victors Here
         A Local Perspective on the Treaty of Portsmouth
   9. The Diary fo the Portsmouth, Kittery
         and York Electric Railroad

Contents

Acknowledgments

THERE IS A COMPELLING REASON why this book should be dedicated to the late George Nelson: it couldn't have been written without him. During his years in the Portsmouth customs office, George Nelson had access to records from the founding of the district in 1789 down to his own day. But it is one thing to have access to records and quite another to do something about it. He read, edited, annotated, and transcribed them to typescript. It was a labor of love that went unremunerated. The results of his tireless efforts was a set of five manuscripts. These were photocopied a few years ago and bound into several sets of five, hard-cover volumes. The work was done by the Portsmouth Athenaeum under the guidance of Joseph P. Copley, then curator.

Without Nelson's work, this volume and any subsequent publications would not be possible since the originals are no longer in Portsmouth but stuffed in dusty cubbyholes in the National Archives in Washington, D.C. In writing this book and future volumes, the writer is obliged to honor Nelson's compilation of all the technical descriptions of the 203, three-masted, square-rigged vessels built in the Port of Portsmouth between 1783 and 1829. Furthermore, unless otherwise credited, ship arrival dates are from his Volume IV. Those interested in Portsmouth maritime history owe a debt to the late George Nelson that can never be paid.

Many others have helped in the preparation of this work. Special thanks must go to Richard E. Winslow, III, that tireless pursuer of details. Dick located some of the material used in this project, while doing research for his book on privateering. It was Dick who found the article on the whaling cruise of the *Ann Parry*. Although already mentioned, Joseph P. Copley produced other useful data. Robert Whitehouse of Dover, a student of Cocheco River history, was most helpful in the study of Dover and Berwick ships, including a field trip to the beautiful Jonathan Hamilton mansion in South Berwick. And, when it came to sorting out the multitudes of Ladds and Havens, Dorothy M. Vaughan kindly came to the author's assistance.

Librarians, from many ways and far apart, were more than helpful. One such was Elinor Mawson, archivist for the Charlotte County Historical Society, St. Andrew's, New Brunswick. Another was Ernest J. Brin, a reference worker in the New Orleans Public Library. Then there was Dean Love of the Key West Marine History Society and the people in Appalachicola, Florida, who helped. Jean Sawtelle of New Castle took particular pleasure in seeking out and photographing the grave of Edmund Roberts in Macao.

Never to be forgotten is the patience and cooperation of Margaret Reardon at the Moffat-Ladd House and thanks also to Mrs. Reginald Frost of the National Society of Colonial Dames in New Hampshire who gave permission to photograph several portraits in Moffat-Ladd. We are appreciative also to the directors of the Portsmouth Athenaeum for permission to photograph some of that institution's treasures for use in this book.

Once again, many thanks to Betty J. Nelson of Burlington, Vermont, a severe editor. The only reason she suffers through these manuscripts is that she enjoys working again with "hard copy" instead of terminals.

And there are many others. The list is legion and I will close with special thanks to the Portsmouth Marine Society and its talented publisher, Peter Randall.

Ray Brighton
Portsmouth, New Hampshire

THE EMBARGO,

A SONG COMPOSED AND SUNG AT DOVER. *JULY* 4th, 1808.

by Henry Miller.

[*TUNE—Come let us prepare—*]

DEAR Sirs, it is wrong
　To demand a *New Song*;
　　I have let all the breath I can spare, go;
With the Muse I've confer'd,
And she won't say a word,
　　But keeps laughing about the EMBARGO.

I wish that I could
Sing in *Alegro* mood,
　　But the times are as stupid as *Largo*;
Could I have my choice,
I would strain up my voice,
　　'Till it snapt all the *strings* of EMBARGO.

Our great politicians,
Those dealers in visions,
　　On *paper* to all lengths will dare go;
But when call'd to decide,
Like a *turtle* they hide,
　　In their own pretty *shell* the EMBARGO.

In the time that we try,
To put out Britains *eye*,
　　I fear we shall let our own *pair* go;
But yet we'er so wise,
We can see with French eyes,
　　And then we shall like the EMBARGO.

A French privateer
Can have nothing to fear;　　[go;
　　She may load, and may hear or may there
Their friendship is such
And we love them so much,
　　We let them flip thro' the EMBARGO.

Our ships all in motion
Once whiten'd the ocean;
　　They sail'd and return'd with a Cargo;
Now doom'd to decay,
They are fallen a prey,
　　To Jefferson, worms, and EMBARGO.

Left Britain should take
A few men by mistake,
　　Who under false colors may dare go;
We're maning their fleet
With our Tars, that retreat
　　From poverty, sloth, and EMBARGO.

What a *fuss* we have made,
About rights and *free trade*,
　　And swore we'ed not let our own share go;
Now we can't for our souls
Bring a Hake from the *shoals*,
　　'Tis a breach of the *twentieth* EMBARGO.

Our Farmers so gay,
How they gallop'd away,
　　'Twas money that made the old mare go;
But now she wont stir,
For the whip or the spur,
　　'Till they take off her *clog*, the EMBARGO.

If you ask for a debt,
The man turns in a *pet*,
　　" I pay sir? I'll not let a hair go;
" If your officer comes,
" I shall put up my thumbs,
　　" And clap on his breath an EMBARGO."

Thus Thommy destroys,
A great part of our joys;
　　Yet we'll not let the beautiful fair, go;
They all will contrive
To keep commerce alive,
　　There's nothing they hate like EMBARGO.

Since rulers design,
To deprive us of wine,
　　'Tis best that we now have a *rare go*;
Then each to his post,
And see who will do most,
　　To knock out the blocks of EMBARGO.

Printed and for *sale* by *J. K.* REMICH, *at his Printing Office on Dover Landing.*

I *Once Upon a Time*

ALTHOUGH IT IS HARD to conceive nowadays, once upon a time, the Port of Portsmouth did indeed profit by a two-way, ocean-going commerce. This flourished for more than two centuries, finally peaking in the early 1830s. The reasons for the demise of this traffic were simple and still exist today.

In the first quarter of the nineteenth century, wharves of all descriptions were in operation from Rindge's on the edge of the North Mill Pond in Portsmouth to below the South Mill Pond. Moreover, there were busy wharves in the up-river ports as well. Most of them could handle any of the merchantmen of the time. This had been so since the earliest days and continued to be true until the hinterland ran out of exportable products.

In its heyday as a commercial competitor, timber of all descriptions from huge mast pines to clapboards was shipped out of the Port of Portsmouth. Important as wood products were, however, one of the port's basic exports was fish. Through the centuries, from the first settlements until after the Civil War, thousands of tons of fish were exported. How many thousands of tons is beyond calculation. Europe, except for Great Britain, was largely Catholic, and the demand for fish for religious occasions was insatiable.

With these great distances to be traveled, a primary concern was always preserving the fish. Refrigeration, as known in modern times, was unheard of, but before there were permanent settlements on the Piscataqua River, fishermen from Brittany, England and Portugal were coming to the New World to fish not only the Grand Banks, but also the George's Banks off New England. Their need to preserve their catches led eventually to a whole new shipping industry—the importation of salt. Various efforts were made to provide salt on the New England coast. For example, Judge Samuel Sewall in seventeenth century Boston invested in a salt works, but with indifferent success. In Eliot, Maine, a salt works was set up early on, with the idea of evaporating the water, leaving salt for a residue. Worthy as these schemes were, they simply didn't produce enough salt to preserve all the fish being caught and shipped to the West Indies and Europe. Because of this, salt was a major import from the earliest times. According to the observant Judge Sewall, salt was brought into Boston from the Dry Tortugas. In the nineteenth century, by an odd twist, Port of Portsmouth vessels were going to Europe to get salt to preserve the fish being shipped to Europe.

At first, New England's salt ships were content to go to Liverpool, England, where they loaded Cheshire salt. But other ports, like Cadiz, Spain, and St. Ubes, Portugal, became greater sources. And the shrewd New Englanders continued to exploit the salt islands such as Turks, Exuma and the Tortugas, in the Caribbean. Importation of salt lasted as long as Portsmouth had a credible fishing fleet. Imports tapered down in the years after the Civil War.

No matter how much change there seems to be, however, nothing really changes. Today, one of Portsmouth's few imports is salt. One shipload of salt arriving at the pier of Granite State Minerals on lower Market Street would be equal in tonnage to the cargo of dozens of the square-rigged sailing vessels which used to come into port with salt as their principal cargo. Granite State Minerals searches all over the world to find the salt it handles because some of the sources of a century ago are exhausted. Nevertheless, the use to which the salt is put has changed drastically over the years. Once a preservative for fish, it is now a preservative for human life in its winter use on New England's highways. A little salt, however, is used on the bait fish employed by vessels operating out of the Portsmouth Fish Pier on Pierce Island. And, after all, that use is also evidence that nothing really changes. Over the past decade, the Portsmouth fishing fleet has increased slowly, and fish are again being shipped to distant markets.

While salt was a major item of importation between 1783 and 1829, customs records make it obvious that the development of American manufacturing was far behind that of Europe. Manifest after manifest of the ships built on the Piscataqua during the period includes iron and steel manufactures, crockery, cloth, tableware and like goods in large quantities. Detailed analysis isn't possible within the limits of this work, but many Port of Portsmouth merchants made handsome fortunes. The amount of duty paid on imports over the years serves as a strong indicator of the growth and decline of the Port of Portsmouth. In

LAWS  OF THE
United States,
PASSED AT THE
FIRST SESSION
OF THE
TENTH CONGRESS.

[PUBLISHED BY AUTHORITY.]

EMBARGO.

An ACT laying an EMBARGO on all Ships and Veffels in the Ports and Harbors of the United States :—

BE it enacted by the Senate and Houfe of Reprefentatives of the United States of America in Congrefs affembled, That an EMBARGO be and hereby is laid on all fhips and veffels in the ports and places within the limits or jurifdiction of the United States cleared or not cleared, bound to any foreign port or place ; and that no clearance be furnifhed to any fhip or veffel bound to fuch foreign port or place, except veffels under the immediate direction of the Prefident of the United States ; and that the Prefident be authorifed to give fuch inftructions to the officers of the Revenue and of the Navy and Revenue Cutters of the U. States, as fhall appear beft adapted for carrying the fame into full effect. Provided, That nothing herein contained fhall be conftrued to prevent the departure of any foreign fhip or veffel, either in ballaft, or with the goods, wares and merchandize on board of fuch foreign fhip or veffel, when notified of this act.

Sec. 2, And be it further enacted, That during the continuance of this act, no regiftered, or fea letter veffel, having on board goods, wares and merchandize, fhall be allowed to depart from one port of the United States to another within the fame, unlefs the mafter, owner, confignee, or factor of fuch veffel, fhall firft give bond with one or more fureties to the Collector of the diftrict from which fhe is bound to depart, in a fum of double the value of the veffel and cargo, that the faid goods, wares and merchandize fhall be relanded in fome port of the United States, dangers of the feas excepted : which bond, and alfo a certificate from the Collector where the fame may be relanded, fhall, by the Collectors refpectively, be tranfmitted to the Secretary of the Treafury. All armed veffels poffeffing public commiffions from any foreign power, are not to be confidered as liable to the Embargo laid by this act.

J. B. VARNUM,
Speaker of the Houfe of Reprefentatives.
GEO : CLINTON,
Vice-Prefident of the United States, and Prefident of the Senate.
December 22, 1807.   Approved,
TH : JEFFERSON.

AN ACT

To appropriate money for the providing of an additional number of Gun-Boats.

BE it enacted by the Senate and Houfe of Reprefentatives of the United States of America in Congrefs affembled, That the Prefident of the United States be, and he hereby is authorized and empowered to caufe to be built, or purchafed, armed and equipped, a number not exceeding one hundred and eighty-eight Gun-Boats, for the better protection of the ports and harbors of the United States, and for fuch other purpofes as in his opinion the public fervice may require.

Sec. 2. And be it further enacted, That a fum not exceeding eight hundred and fifty-two thoufand five hundred dollars be, and hereby is appropriated for this purpofe, out of any monies in the Treafury not otherwife appropriated.

J. B. VARNUM,
Speaker of the Houfe of Reprefentatives.
GEO : CLINTON,
Vice-Prefident of the United States, and Prefident of the Senate.
December 18, 1807.   Approved,
TH : JEFFERSON.

1790, a year after the establishment of the Portsmouth Customs District, a grand total of $16,965.19 was collected in duties from 91 arrivals.[1] In the port's peak year of 1822, incoming vessels paid $156,609 in duties.[2] From then on, Portsmouth's path as an importing center led almost steadily downhill, to the point where, in 1849, only $84,854 was collected. There were ups and downs in this general pattern, however, and the merchants did have some good years.

For example, in the year before the enforcement of the Embargo Act, the customs office collected $177,505 from 80 arrivals. But the next year, 1808, revenues were only $60,956, of which only $1,521 was collected from vessels arriving from Europe. The total was even less the next year, $54,503, although trade with Europe had picked up. Records for the years of the War of 1812 aren't available, but, with the coming of peace, the duties in 1816 were $62,596, and, with infrequent dips, kept rising until 1823, when the downward trend began. According to one account of the time:

> The lifting of this ban [the Embargo Act] on our ocean trade was like the end of a long nightmare to the people of the seaboard. All the way from Maine to Georgia there was frank rejoicing. The Repeal Bill received on March 1 the signature of President Jefferson, whose executive career was closing [1809], and the embargo ended for the most part on March 16...
>
> But these bright hopes of a reviving commerce were destined to fade away like a mirage. The embargo indeed was an acknowledged failure. It was abandoned. In its place, however, came forward the Non-Intercourse Act, and there was no relaxation in the fierce hostility of England and France toward the merchant ships of the republic.[3]

It is impossible within this work to discuss the depredations against American merchants by the two powers. Much of it is touched on in the stories of the ships themselves, but the trickery and treachery exercised against a young country is almost unbelievable.

Of more lasting significance to those who fought so hard to keep Portsmouth a viable commercial port was the fact that the value of exports never came close to matching imports. And nothing has changed in that respect. Oil tankers, coal barges, salt ships and package freighters come into Portsmouth low in the water but go out riding high and empty. Again comparing the peak year of 1822: total imports were $446,419; exports $199,699. In 1829, the last year of the period under study, exports totaled only $10,740, and, with minor exceptions, that trend also continued downward.

Coal was another of the Port of Portsmouth's imports. Even before the Revolution, the colonists demanded this long-burning fuel. And when peaceful commerce with England was restored, importation of coal resumed. How much coal was brought in isn't known. Coal was measured then in chaldrons (and still is in England), which was an old unit of dry measure equal to 36 bushels. In the 1830s, coal importations came more from Nova Scotia than England. But coal remained an important import until the post World War II era, when oil replaced it as the major fuel. But once more, nothing really changes since coal is again being brought into the Port of Portsmouth.

While coal was beginning to be used to heat homes, the products of sugar cane including rum also became major imports. It has often been said that New England's famed stone walls were built by the liberal use of bull sweat and rum. Port of Portsmouth merchants were substantial importers of rum, known in early colonial days as "Kill Devil." There's little doubt that those who fancy the delightful rums of the exotic Caribbean Islands, such as Barbados and St. Croix, would find the heavy, black rum of an earlier day a bit much.

Port of Portsmouth vessels trading in the West Indies also brought back other sugar cane products: sugar (white and brown) and molasses. Just as rum was marketed directly in whatever quantity the purchaser wanted, molasses also went directly to consumers, although some of it was made into rum by local distillers like William Torrey, who operated the Sugar House.[4] The finer sugars were put to the same use as they are today. In the years before the War of 1812, the importation of sugar cane products showed a steady increase. Rum, for example, went from 74,332 gallons in 1790 to 313,349 in 1801, then showing a slippage until 1807 when 351,620 gallons came in.[5] How the thirsty working class got along when the Embargo Act reduced importation in 1810 to 88,837 gallons can only be guessed. Sugar, too, showed some vagaries in amounts, but exceeded two million pounds in 1804.

Coffee and cocoa were other commodities on the Portsmouth list of imports, along with tea. Here again, the Caribbean Islands, plus Brazil, were the main sources of coffee and cocoa. Until early in the nineteenth century, most of the imported tea came by way of England, but American merchants were soon exploiting markets in the East Indies.

Another facet of Portsmouth's commerce developed as the Industrial Revolution gripped Europe. The invention of machinery which could process raw cotton stirred the demand for this fiber in ever-increasing quantities. Cotton mills on the Mersey River at Liverpool, England, and around Le Havre (called "Havre" at that time) in France were insatiable in their demands. Importing of cotton from southern ports in the United States began in 1785. To meet the ever-increasing demand for shipping to transport it, the Cotton Triangular Trade came into being. In pre-Revolutionary days, merchants had to ship their exports south to British islands, and from there, the goods made their way to Great Britain. The triangle was completed when English merchandise arrived on the wharves in the Port of Portsmouth. This is a simplification, of course, but, in the main, the cotton triangle worked in that manner. A Port of Portsmouth merchant loaded his ship with whatever goods he could muster for sale, and this became more difficult as the years went by. Timber products were the favorites, but also marketable were fish, hay, potatoes and apples. Once loaded, the ship sailed to one of the southern cotton ports: New Orleans, Louisiana; Savannah, Georgia; Charleston, South Carolina; Mobile, Alabama; or Apalachicola, Florida. In one of those ports, the ship unloaded, and hundreds of bales of cotton were stowed on board; then it was off to Liverpool or Havre. After unloading the cotton, the masters sought return cargoes. Sometimes they brought back immigrants, but the bulk of the entries into the Port of Portsmouth were of ships carrying salt, coal or merchandise, and often all three. Fairbairn wrote of the triangular trade in *Merchant Sail*:

> Generally, northerners took all of the financial risk of this export business, and there were occasions when they not only lost heavily, but were also driven into insolvency by the European market on cotton, with its depressions and panics (and long periods of time required for news conditions in Liverpool or Havre to reach the shipping ports of the South or northern cotton factors in inland southern towns).[6]

There were, of course, many variations in the cotton trade. Quite often a Piscataqua ship, after unloading cotton, would take on a cargo and head right back to the southern port it had sailed from. These ships were absent from their home port for months at a time. Not infrequently, Portsmouth-owned ships would start out on the triangle, but on return go into Boston, New York, Philadelphia or Baltimore with cargoes. At times, such ships would bring some part of their cargoes to Portsmouth before heading south again. Yet another variant in the cotton trade developed when northern capitalists constructed and operated cotton mills of their own. New England towns, like Lowell, Massachusetts and Manchester, New Hampshire became great manufacturing centers. And cotton became an important import in the Port of Portsmouth when mills were established on the Cocheco and Salmon Falls Rivers. Edward F. Sise became a major importer of cotton, acting on behalf of the Cocheco Manufacturing Company in Dover. On the Salmon Falls River, the Portsmouth Manufacturing Company flourished in South Berwick, and its office building, "The Counting Room," is now occupied by the Old Berwick Historical Society.

That the Port of Portsmouth enjoyed the large volume of commerce that it did was something of a miracle in itself. Between the end of the Revolution and the end of the War of 1812, American merchants operated in perilous times. Modern-day newspaper readers are constantly reminded of terrorism throughout the world; again nothing changes. The newspapers of 180 years ago were also filled with terrorism stories. Other than the pirates on the Barbary Coast, the chief perpetrators of terrorism on American shipping were, ironically, England and France, two of America's strongest allies today. The American colonies won their independence from Great Britain in 1783, but it wasn't confirmed until the United States fought England again in the War of 1812. At every opportunity, the British did their utmost to make life tenuous for the young republic. It is a story too long to be unfolded here, but it has many ironic touches. British merchants wanted trade with the United States; it was a lucrative market for manufactured goods. They wanted trade, however, on terms little different from those of the profitable pre-Revolution days.

Complicating matters was Britain's almost constant embroilment with France. Despite what some history books may contend, France hadn't come to the aid of the struggling American colonies because of belief in political freedom. France wanted to hurt England, and the loss of the thirteen colonies proved a heavy blow. Shortly after the Revolution, France itself went through a traumatic change. When the United States tried to keep out of "entangling alliances," the new regime in France saw it as ingratitude bordering on open hostility. So belligerent were the French, the new nation began building up a navy, and there came into being famous warships like the *Constitution* and the *Constellation*. Throughout the Quasi War in the late 1790s, American merchantmen were continually begin (sic) captured and taken into French ports for condemnation. Because it was in their interest to do so during this period, the British gave tacit support to the Americans.

An additional problem for American merchants was the constant harassment their ships took from the Barbary Coast pirates. One warship, the *Crescent*, built in Portsmouth in 1797, was presented to the Dey of Algiers as part of the bribery necessary to keep American shipping safe. But the Algerines were by no means the menace that the French privateers were. The results of all the captures became the French Spoliation Claims, a tedious mess of litigation which dragged on for more than 100 years, long after all the original claimants had left the scene. The *Portsmouth Chronicle*, on May 23, 1874, published an article on the claims:

> Among the list of seventeen hundred American vessels
> and cargoes, estimated at fifteen million dollars, which were

illegally captured by the French, prior to the convention with France of July 31, 1801 . . . we find the following belonging to this port, together with their captains and their owners at the time they were taken.

The *Chronicle* then listed all the vessels taken by the French, running to a total of 40. Ten ships, 21 brigs, eight schooners and one sloop. The article continued:

> These vessels were generally laden with breadstuffs and provisions, and were light, tonnage and moderate value [sic]. The entire list of 1,700 vessels and their cargoes now on register is estimated at nine thousand dollars each, or, in the whole, fifteen million dollars. The indemnity for these captures was arranged with France by a mutual set-off in the final ratification of the convention of 1801, by which the United States became responsible to their citizens for their property. The above aggregate sum is now due the claimants—whose memorials, about 5,000, are now on the files of Congress, praying for relief . . . Portsmouth—at least some of her people—would be richer than now if these claims were allowed.

Thirteen years later, on November 4, 1887, the *Chronicle* reported:

> A Washington dispatch of the 2d inst. says: "Judge Davis of the Court of Claims has prepared a very elaborate opinion covering the contested questions raised in fifty pending cases of French Spoliation claims . . . The opinion will probably be announced next Monday. It is very confidently expected the decision will favor the claimants." A large number of these claims are held by persons in this city and vicinity.

Congress, however, didn't rush into action. Fifteen years later, on March 2, 1902, Congress passed the Spoliation Act, setting up a system of payments of money owed by the United States for 101 years. The Sheafe family heirs were still pushing to get their claims paid in 1904, and a descendant of Thomas Sheafe was finally awarded $3,880.

While the French pushed their vendetta against American shipping, the British, too, were displeased by the neutrality the United States was trying to maintain. As the intermittent wars with France waxed and waned, British warships preyed on American vessels. More than 6,000 American seamen were impressed into the Royal Navy, kidnapped from the decks of American merchantmen under the pretext that they were British citizens, even if born in Portsmouth, New Hampshire. Concerning the period after the signing of the Treaty of Tripoli in 1805, Fairbairn wrote:

No. *1160*

I, Joseph Whipple,

Collector of the District of Portsmouth, in the State of New-Hampshire,

DO hereby certify, that *Waymouth Lydston*
an American Seaman, aged *Forty* _____ years
or thereabouts, of the height of about *five* feet *8* inches
dark ____ complexion, *dark* ___ hair *dark* ___
eyes *has a wart on his left side just above*
the hip _____

was born in *Kittery* _____ in the State
of *Massachusetts.* ___

has this day produced to me proof in the manner directed in the
Act, intitled, " *An act for the Relief and Protection of American*
Seamen," and pursuant to the said act, I do hereby certify that
the said *Waymouth Lydston* ___
is a citizen of the United States of America.

In Witness whereof, I have hereunto set my hand and Seal
of office, this *15th* ___ day of *June 1803.*

Joseph Whipple

PHS, document #101.

9

... American foreign commerce had fared badly not only at the hands of Britain and France... but also by the lack of national unity and far-sighted, constructive and courageous policy and by the injury wrought through the embargo and "peaceful coercion" program of President Jefferson. The total export trade of the United States, which was $138 million in 1807, dropped to $22 million in 1808; it had risen to around $50 million just before the hostilities commenced with Britain, and the war drove it down to $7 million in 1814.

... Prior to the War of 1812, the United States enjoyed benefits flowing to it as the principal neutral ocean carrier; yet it suffered greatly from the restrictions placed on its commerce by the belligerent powers. On the basis of "rights flouted and injuries inflicted" to its shipping and commerce, it was a toss-up for years as to whether or not the United States should make war, in defense of its honor against France or Britain... During the period 1807–1812, the French (under Napoleon) confiscated 558 American ships, and the British seized 389...[6]

The preceding describes the climate in which Port of Portsmouth merchants operated from 1783 onward. In subsequent chapters, the stories of Piscataqua-built ships caught in the squeeze between the superpowers will be told. As if all of those problems weren't enough, merchant vessels sailing to the south were frequently the prey of pirates. Most of these sea robbers had their genesis in the revolutions that tormented Latin America and still do today.

One of the minor mysteries in Portsmouth's status as a seaport is why it didn't become more of a whaling base. The present volume won't include a discussion of whaling per se, but the fact is that it was never of major importance in the Port of Portsmouth. A firm, the Portsmouth Whaling Company, with no less a personage than Ichabod Goodwin as a moving spirit, was formed. The company's minute book is in the library at the Portsmouth Historical Society, but its pages are few, since the company didn't last long. Several whalers operated out of Portsmouth for a few years. One was the *Pocahontas*. She was quite successful, but her story isn't told in this volume because she wasn't built on the Piscataqua. The *Pocahontas* had had the misfortune to pile up on the Whale's Back but was later repaired on the Portsmouth Marine Railway. Two others, the *Triton* and the *Ann Parry*, made whaling voyages out of Portsmouth.

In summarizing the status of the Port of Portsmouth in the first four decades of the Republic, it has to be stressed that a viable two-way merchandising operation prevailed. It lasted as long as the merchants had cargoes to ship out. One of the main problems was that Portsmouth was difficult to reach from the interior of the state. Attempts were made to alleviate that situation by the construction of a bridge across Little Bay and the building of the New Hampshire Turnpike to Concord in the early 1800s. This helped, although there was a strong tendency in the Merrimack Valley towns for commerce to follow that stream south.

The death knell of Portsmouth as a commercial center was sounded by the hiss of escaping steam from a railroad locomotive. Boston, and to a lesser extent, Portland, became centers of northern New England's commercial traffic. By the time the Portsmouth & Concord Railroad was constructed in the 1850s, it was too late.

The Port of Portsmouth continued to build commercial ships, but, increasingly, they tended to go out empty, and the larger they were built the less apt they were to return. All that was in the future, however, as Port of Portsmouth merchants were sustained by a prosperity over four decades that has never yet been equalled.

In the matter of ship construction in the Port of Portsmouth, it was almost as if the year 1829 marked a transition from the dominance of the up-river yards. Out of the more than 200 square-riggers built between 1783 and 1829, only 14 were built in the Town of Portsmouth and 38 across the river in Kittery. All the others came from tributary streams of the Piscataqua. A few more ships would be built in the up-river yards after 1830, but the last was launched in 1837. By then, a whole new generation of master shipwrights were plying their trade in Kittery and Portsmouth, but that's a story that must be told in a later volume.

The " cabaliftic number'' of

6257

As it is denominated by the Brit'fh faction, cannot be too often brought to public recollection. In addition to this monftrous number of American feamen ftolen by Britifh prefs gangs, we have now to complain againft her, that, in conjunction with the faction whofe necks are faved from the halter by the mildnefs of our laws, fhe has fought to overthrow the government and again annex the New England States to the Britifh provinces. What will Yankee fpirit fay to this? O fays Gen. Tim. it is *no effential injury.* Do you think fo Americans?

NHG, March 24, 1811

Henry Ladd,

Ship-Chandler,

MARKET-SQUARE,

Has juſt received by the Criterion, *from LONDON,*

LARGE, Middle, & Small
ſize Herring Nets ; 9, 12, 15,
and 18 thread Fiſhing Lines ; Chalk,
Squid, Log, Hand-Lead, and deep
Sea, do. Sewing, Salmon and Whip-
ing Twine ; Fiſh Hooks, of all ſizes ;
5, 10, and 20 inch Red, Blue and
White Bunting ; Mahogany, Acany
and Ebony frame Quadrants, with
braſs and wood Indexes ; 28 and 14
Second Time Glaſſes ; Hour & half
Hour, do. Patent Shot ; Sheet Lead.

Alſo for Sale,

Cordage and Boltrope, of
all ſizes ; Worming ; Marline ; Ra-
vens Duck ; Ruſſia, do. do. Sheeting ;
Sheet Copper ; Copper Hand Pumps ;
Nails, of all kinds and ſizes ; Black
and Bright Varniſh.

Spirits of Turpentine ; Sper-
maceti Oil, of the firſt quality ; a few
Bbls. Powdered Brown, do. Yellow
Ocre ; Boxes Candles ; do. Choco-
late ; caſes Florence Oil, 30 Flaſks
each ; Cheſts Hyſon-ſkin Tea, of the
Hazard's cargo, at a reduced price ;
White Spaniſh Sugar, ſuitable for
Family's uſe, in Bags of Cwt. Phila-
delphia refined Loaf do. per Cwt.
St. Ubes Salt, &c. &c.

NHG, May 25, 1802

Portſmouth, May 25, 1802.

II *Port of Portsmouth Merchants and Captains*

FROM THE FIRST SETTLEMENT in 1623, entrepreneurs in the Port of Portsmouth gave primary consideration to commerce. They were traders, fishermen, merchants, mariners and shopkeepers. Shillings and pence were always uppermost in their minds. Like other mortals of their time, they did pay some heed to the care of the soul, but business was equal to godliness.

In the years before the Revolution, businessmen worked in the face of difficulties created by bureaucrats in London who had little or no understanding of colonial problems and no desire to learn. Like merchants in other colonies, those in the Port of Portsmouth did their best to navigate around the restrictive Navigation Acts, devoting much effort to hoodwinking the revenue officers appointed by the home government. Despite the problems, many of them became wealthy and maintained themselves at luxurious, almost princely, levels. One such was Peter Livius who had a mansion on the North Pond with the privilege of operating a grist mill there. Another was George Boyd, who rose literally from rags to riches in the years before the Revolution. Although he had no sympathy with the rebellious spirit of the 1770s, Boyd clearly understood that the British government was forcing the colonists to defiance. A letter he wrote to his English agent, Thomas Fraser, on January 11, 1774, shows it:

> . . . As to particular news about the East India Company exporting tea to America &c the papers are full to which I refer you —There is the greatest Spirit of freedom and unity in America at this time perhaps that was ever known. - what will be the Consequence time must bring to light — for my own part

I believe a Civil War will ensue. If the Mother Country should be strenuous in Imposing her Tax on any of your exports to favor the Oppression—they will never submit to be taxed by a British Parliament, which they have no voice in . . .[1]

George Boyd knew whereof he spoke, but few people were listening, at least not in King George III's government. Boyd himself sat out the war in England and died at sea a few days from home after the conflict was over. His son, William, took over his father's role and became an important member of the Portsmouth business community.

Before presenting a series of sketches about the men who were the commercial leaders and master mariners in the Port of Portsmouth, it should be pointed out that the eight years of the Revolutionary War were damaging to trade. Great Britain and her other colonies, ever prime markets for American goods, were cut off, and no subtantial trade with France was built up. Early in the war, some merchants tried to continue trade but the risk became too great.

Many American merchants owed heavy debts to their English agents, and the years after the Revolution were particularly difficult as American businessmen sought to rebuild their lines of credit. That American merchants survived at all was due largely to the need of the former mother country for the goods they had to sell. Moreover, the Americans were building ships that could deliver those goods. Britain herself was hard up for shipping because the French wars continually diverted craftsmen and materials from the construction of civilian vessels. Vessels built in the Port of Portsmouth were often sold to English shippers as soon as they were unloaded.

This economic background is important to keep in mind when considering the merchant princes who dominated the commerce of the Port of Portsmouth from the end of the Revolution in 1783 and on into the 1830s, although this volume arbitrarily closes with the year 1829. While the democratic instinct is to treat all of those long-ago businessmen on a basis of equality, some were more equal than others. The first of them, Eliphalet Ladd, had his beginnings before the Revolution. The Ladd genealogy sets the scene:

> At the early age of 23, in 1767, he was captain and part owner of a brig in trade to the West Indies. Later he was a merchant and ship-builder in Exeter, N.H., where he rapidly accumulated property...He removed to Portsmouth, N.H. in May, 1792, and interested himself mainly in the welfare of that then growing and prosperous town...He enjoyed a high credit in England, by the aid of which his business and commerce were largely extended and very profitable; but he suffered severely from the French spoliations prior to 1800, and also by the great

fire by which the town was desolated in 1802. But at the time of his death, which occurred Feb. 24, 1806, he was one of the wealthiest of the many wealthy merchants of Portsmouth.[2]

Eliphalet Ladd's name lives on in Portsmouth by virtue of Ladd Street, where the family business was centered. His residence was at Bridge and Islington Streets in the Buckminster House, which, ironically, takes its name from the man, Joseph Buckminster, who married Ladd's widow. One of Ladd's great civic acts came in 1797 with the Portsmouth Aqueduct, the town's first water system. Ladd continued to be associated with shipbuilding in Exeter. Perhaps the most notable vessel built by him was the *Archelaus*, a 500-ton merchantman, the story of which is in Chapter VI.

Eliphalet Ladd's greatest achievement, however, came in being the sire of a merchandising family that might have become a dynasty if the commercial world hadn't turned its back on the Port of Portsmouth. Eliphalet Ladd married a Berwick girl, Abigail Hill, and they had ten children.[3] Three of the sons became prominent in Portsmouth's business community. The eldest of these brothers was William:

> He was educated in the public schools, prepared for college at Phillips Academy in his native town, and entered Harvard University, Cambridge, at the age of 15...He had an honorable appointment in his class when he graduated ..When William came home one of his father's ships was lying at the wharf ready for sea. He applied for permission to go in her as a passenger...[4]

For William Ladd, that was the beginning of a seafaring career which ended when the War of 1812 drove commercial vessels from the oceans. The Ladd genealogy makes no mention of the difficulties William ran into when he tried to end a voyage without paying duties which Customs Officer Joseph Whipple believed due. That contretemps is discussed in the story of the ship *Eliza*. When he left the sea, William turned his back on it completely by becoming a farmer in Minot, Maine. Later in life, he became president of the American Peace Society. He died at the age of 62 while on a visit to his family in Portsmouth.

It was the next brother, Henry, born May 1, 1780, who did the most to keep the Ladd firmly established as a leading commercial family. After receiving some education at Phillips Academy, Henry went to work in his father's counting room.

> At the age of 21 his father gave him an interest in one of his vessels and sent him as supercargo to Europe, to make his own business acquaintances and connections. In person Mr. Ladd was a trifle over six feet in height, with an erect carriage, light wavy

Eliphalet Ladd
HAS REMOVED
To his Store in Market-ſtreet,
AND HAS FOR SALE,

NEW Superfine and
fine Flour ; ſhip and pilot Bread;
Philadelphia and Ruſſia Iron ; hallow
Ware ; Canvas and Cordage ; W. I.
and N. E. Rum ; Sugar ; Molaſſes
and Salt by the Hhd. or ſmaller
quantity ; Fiſh ; Grindſtones ; Oil
and Painters Colours ; Tea ; Coffee ;
Dry Goods, &c. &c.
Caſh given for FLAX-SEED.
☞Said Ladd wants to hire a good
able bodied Man, by the year.
January 8.

NHG, January 9, 1779

☞ *NOTICE.*

THE Subſcribers have formed a
co-partnerſhip in trade, under
the firm of

Henry & Alex'r Ladd.

They occupy a commodious fire
proof Brick Store, Merchant's Row,
N° 14, and will advance on conſign-
ments.   HENRY LADD.
Jan. 1.   ALEX'r LADD.
For Sale as above,
50 puncheons W. I. RUM ;
300 Hhds. Cadiz SALT ;
60 Boxes 6 by 8, and 7 by 9 Window
Glaſs ; 15 barrels meſs PORK.
Exchange on London & Liverpool.
Alſo to be LET,
Store No. 10 Merchant's Row.
February 9, 1808.

NHG, February 9, 1808

hair, large blue eyes, clear complexion, and a calm, dignified and intelligent expression, which at once won for him respect and confidence. In England his striking appearance and bearing earned for him the sobriquet of "Prince Harry."[5]

The third Ladd brother was Alexander, born in Exeter, May 9, 1784. The Ladd genealogy makes no mention of Alexander's educational background, passing immediately to the fact that on December 29, 1807, he married Maria Tufton Haven, "daughter of Hon. Nathaniel Appleton and Mary Tufton (Moffatt) Haven, and granddaughter of Col. John Tufton Mason, who in 1745 sold the title to New Hampshire to the Masonian Proprietors." Like Henry, Alexander became interested in business and in October 1807 was advertising goods he had received by the ship *Liverpool Packet* (q.v.) commanded by Captain James Place. The articles he offered ran the gamut of manufactured goods imported from England:

> Eighty crates, 5 Hdds. earthern Ware, cream colored, blue and greed edged, enameled, gold and white, per crate or hogshead; 3 table setts blue printed ditto complete; 20 casks best English plain and cut Glass, per cask, 1 elegant table sett cut Glass complete.[6]

The listing went on to include such variant items as BB shot; sheet lead; ingredients for paint, like dry white lead, red lead, dry yellow ochre, and 10 hogsheads of paints of various hues, described as "composing a complete assortment of Painters colours." In the same consignment, he received 3,000 bushels of coarse Liverpool salt and 800 bushels of coal, "very suitable for grates." As of January 1, 1808, within days after Alexander's marriage, he and Henry announced their partnership. They were selling West India rum and Cadiz salt, and one shipment included, "60 Boxes 6 × 8, and 7 × 9 Window Glass; 15 barrels mess pork."[7] The partnership endured for 24 years, when Alexander withdrew to manage the estate of his father-in-law. Alexander died in 1855. George Nelson wrote of the Ladds:

> One of Portsmouth's leading concerns dealing with England, the West Indies and South America, from 1806 to 1829, Henry carrying on to 1840. Some of the highlights were 43,000 gallons of molasses in 1812, 34,000 pounds of sugar in 1825, 46,000 pounds of coffee in 1826, 20,000 pounds of raisins in 1817, 112,000 pounds of hemp in 1818 and 270,000 pounds of Swedish steel in 1829.[8]

With connections to the Ladd family, the Haven family was also significant in this period. Nathaniel Appleton Haven's obituary in the *Portsmouth Journal* of March 19, 1831, was only nine lines long, a gross understatement of what the man stood for in Portsmouth during the first three decades of the nineteenth century. Perhaps as much, if not more, than any Portsmouth resident since, Haven was the complete citizen. According to his meagre obituary:

> Mr. Haven has been one of the first merchants in this town, has held various municipal offices, for several years represented the town in the State Legislature, and has represented the State in the Congress of the United States.

Few words indeed for a man who was a factor in state politics, a ranking merchant, and a leading figure in the town's genteel society. Born in Portsmouth, he was a son of the Rev. Samuel Haven, pastor of the South Church, an edifice that stood on Meeting House Hill. His basic education was at the hands of the Rev. Nathaniel Appleton, his maternal grandfather. The schooling enabled him to enter Harvard and graduate with the class of 1779. In 1786, he married Mary Tufton Moffatt, the adopted daughter of William Whipple, a signer of the Declaration of Independence.[9] After Harvard, he studied medicine under the tutelage of one of the town's physicians but eventually found merchandising much more to his taste. It's quite possible that this change in careers came from a medical source. An advertisement in 1784 shows him selling medicines he had received "by the last vessels from Europe."[10] Some of the medicines he was offering in his shop on present-day State Street would baffle a modern pharmacist. Among the items were "Flor Sulphur, Fol. Sennae. Gum Arabac, Manna, Myrth, Glycrrhiz, Mirab, Glauber, Essence Burgamot," to name only a few. The advertisement also announced that he was selling teas (Hyson, Souchong and Bohea), sugars, rum and brandy, olives, almonds and raisins, and various seasonings. The advertisement had one further note:

> N.B. He [Haven] further wishes to acquaint the public, that having made the Theory and Practice of Physick and Surgery, the object of his particular attention; he now offers his services to all such, who may choose to employ him, in either branches of his profession.

When he began selling items other than drugs, Haven was making a move toward merchandising, and he, apparently, had ceased activity as a physician by 1798 when a yellow fever epidemic swept the North End; at least, he isn't mentioned as one of the doctors fighting the outbreak.[11] At some time, he formed a partnership with his brother John. Nelson wrote:

> Nathaniel and John were so closely related in business affairs that it is practically impossible to show each separately. They began their activities in 1792 and for 38 years, they were amongst Portsmouth's leaders in commercial circles. In 1806, they imported 306,000 pounds of sugar, 26,000 gallons of rum, 597,000 pounds of coffee and various items, After the War of 1812, they changed from the produce of the West Indies to articles from England.[12]

It was undoubtedly the closeness of their association that enabled Nathaniel to turn to politics, with John always on hand to "mind the store." At the time he was elected to the United States House (1808), Nathaniel Haven, as an importer, had intense interest in any legislation involving trade. But he served only the one term. Nathaniel's death ended the partnership. John lived until 1845, dying in his 80th year. His obituary affords a bit more information about the Havens:

> Mr. Haven occupied so conspicuous a place in our community, that we cannot afford to suffer him to pass away without some record of his numerous claims upon general respect and reverence. The son of a clergyman of very limited pecuniary means, and one of an unusually large family, he was early cast upon his own resources, with a good school education for those times... He served his apprenticeship with the late Joshua Wentworth, and at an early age made one or more voyages as supercargo in a vessel belonging to him, and afterward several

voyages as supercargo and master on his own account. For the last half century he has been largely engaged in navigation and foreign commerce, and for a considerable period, in connection with his brother, Hon. N.A. Haven, conducting more extensive mercantile operations than any other individual or firm in New Hampshire.[13]

While John and Nathaniel Haven were leaders in commercial enterprises, they weren't the only ones in the Haven tribe to follow mercantile careers. John's obituary said he was "one of an unusually large family," and this was true. Old Samuel Haven was a prolific sire, begetting a multitude of children by two wives. The family homestead was in present-day Haven Park on Pleasant Street. With funds to purchase the Parry house next door, the property was left to the city by two Haven sisters who were the last of Samuel's children. Across the street from his father lived Joseph, a shopkeeper. Then there was Joshua, who "traded with the West Indies from 1804 to 1817. His [big] year was 1806 when he imported 15,000 gallons of rum, 70,000 pounds of sugar, 4,000 gallons of molasses and 1,000 pounds of cocoa. In 1817 he brought cotton goods in from Calcutta."[14] Joshua also had a hand in building some of the ships used by his fellow merchants. He lived on the site of the present Knights of Columbus building on Islington Street.

Another merchant brother was Thomas who "dealt with the West Indies from 1798 to 1812 and with the West Indies and England from 1816 to 1821."[15] Thomas was also a large investor in privateers in the War of 1812. He made his home on Middle Street in a house on the site of the present Lafayette Apartments. Across Middle Street from Thomas lived brother William who "dealt with the West Indies from 1804 to 1830 and had one large cargo from Calcutta in 1817."[16] John made his home on the site of the present Farragut Apartments. The house was razed in 1903 to make way for the city's second high school. Nathaniel built a mansion on High Street which is now the Haven Apartments. Other brothers, such as Alfred, Washington and Henry, were scattered around the town, engaged in other lines of endeavor. Then there were sisters, one of whom was married to the prominent merchant, Samuel E. Coues, the son of Peter, who lived where Rosa's restaurant is today on State Street. Coues was an importer and often associated in ventures with his brother-in-law, Thomas Haven. Coues was a major importer of salt between 1825 and 1844. His home was on Livermore Street on the eastern edge of Haven Park.

Still another of the leading merchant families in the Port of Portsmouth were the Sheafes. Jacob was the senior of them, born in 1745 and dying in 1829. His obituary read in part:

Mr. Sheafe was an eminent and complete merchant. He
was distinguished for industry, energy, perseverence, independence
of mind, and the most strict and unimpeachable integrity of life.—
At the solicitation of Gen. [Henry] Knox, he was for several years
the Navy Agent for this station, and superintended the building of
the Frigate *Crescent*, that was sent to Algiers, as part of the
ransom to liberate some of our fellow countrymen from Turkish
bondage;—the Frigate *Congress*, that has been pronounced to be
one of the best vessels in our Navy;—and the Sloop of War
Portsmouth.[17]

Jacob Sheafe was "a heavy dealer in molasses, rum and sugar from
the West Indies and South America; and salt, coral and various merchandise from England and other European countries. Some of his
large cargoes were 25,500 gallons of rum in 1806; 26,500 pounds of
coffee in 1798; 23,500 pounds of sugar in 1790 and 12,000 gallons of
brandy in 1804. He was active between 1790 and 1827."[18]

His will, on file in the Probate Office, Exeter, lists ten children.
Unbelievable as it may seem, his estate wasn't finally settled until early
in the twentieth century, when his descendants were paid their shares
in the final settlement of the Spoliation Claims. At one time, Jacob
Sheafe had five warehouses on the waterfront. No. 3, which was at the
foot of Mechanic Street, is now located in Prescott Park where it serves
as a museum. The others are long gone. There were few major Portsmouth projects in which Jacob Sheafe, along with his brothers, Thomas
and James, wasn't involved. As often as it is told, the story of Jacob
Sheafe and Daniel Webster in the perilous moments of the Great Fire of
1813 serves as testimony to the imperturbability of the former. They
were having a quiet glass together when it was realized that the fire
was sweeping Webster's house and would shortly reach Sheafe's.
Webster started to rise and make his erring way home. But, no, his host
insisted, "Mr. Webster, we will take another glass." Black Daniel wasn't
a man to spurn such an invitation. Later Jacob Sheafe wrote to a friend
to say he had lost $50,000 in property and "my faithful dog Trim."

Another of the Sheafe brothers, Thomas, with Jacob, owned Rindge's
Wharf in Portsmouth's North End. The ship *Mentor*, docked at that
facility in 1798, had a lethal cargo of mosquitoes loaded in her bilges.
The winged killers attacked any and all. Victims of the onslaught of
yellow fever were two of Thomas Sheafe's children: daughter Sally, 17,
and son Thomas, 14; along with more than 50 other persons. Another of
Thomas' sons, Charles, lost his life at sea; a daughter, Mehitable, married
Charles Coffin, a sea captain who was closely associated with Thomas
Sheafe in mercantile enterprises. Coffin's son, Thomas Sheafe Coffin,
was master of vessels owned by his father and grandfather. One of
these, the *Lycurgus*, is listed in an 1831 inventory of Thomas Sheafe's

estate, "as she came from the sea" and was valued at $2,100. Thomas Sheafe invested heavily in manufacturing in addition to his shipping and banking interests. His inventory shows 114 shares of the Pittsfield Manufacturing Company, $14,250; 10 shares of the Salmon Falls Manufacturing Company, $10,000; five shares of Exeter Manufacturing at $650 each, $3,250. The total inventory, including various farms and other land holdings, was $88,878, a large sum for those days.

Still another of the brothers in this remarkable family was James Sheafe. In pre-Revolutionary days, James Sheafe was a Loyalist. When the war came, his political beliefs landed him in jail at Exeter. There he stayed until he gave his word he would remain quiet if released. When the Revolution ended, he bought a store on Congress Street.[19] He was one of the early venturers in the Chinese trade. James Sheafe, along with another Loyalist and former crown officer, Jonathan Warner, are evidence of the healing of political wounds from the Revolution. They served on the committee to welcome President George Washington when he visited Portsmouth October 31, 1789. So well did James Sheafe accommodate himself politically that he had the distinction of serving in both houses of Congress.

As an importer, James Sheafe "dealt heavily in the produce of the West Indies and Europe. In 1796, his total importations consisted of 22,000 gallons of gin, 1,900 gallons of wine, 2,000 gallons of brandy, 900 gallons of porter and 6,200 bushels of salt. In 1802, be brought in 119,000 pounds of coffee, 86,000 pounds of cotton and 200 gallons of wine; in 1803 [the year he went to the United States Senate], 536,000 pounds of sugar, 6,000 gallons of rum, 11,000 pounds of coffee, 1,200 gallons of wine and 3,200 bushels of salt; in 1804, 232,000 pounds of sugar, 13,000 gallons of rum, 52,000 pounds of coffee and 800 gallons of brandy."[20] James died on December 5, 1829.

John Sheafe was still another of these merchandising brothers, but on a lesser scale, and apparently was associated in the ventures of his brothers. Perhaps he kept James' business going while the latter was in Congress. Theodore Sheafe, a son of Jacob, was an importer of sugar products between 1817 and 1828. William Sheafe, yet another of the brothers, "at various times between 1790 and 1835 combined with John Sheafe, Thomas Sheafe, William Rice, Samuel Rice and John Wardrobe to import sundry articles from the West Indies and Europe."[21] He had interests in many different vessels, most of them brigs or smaller. He died March 2, 1839, at the age of 81.

Although they may never have attained the wealth and social prominence of their contemporaries, the Ladds, Havens and Sheafes, no discussion of Port of Portsmouth master mariners and merchants would be complete without members of the Blunt family. It would appear that they leaned a bit more toward seafaring than merchandising, and their importations were frequently the captain's privilege of bringing in goods freight free.

Captain Charles E. Blunt was born August 3, 1768.[22] He made his home at 4 Gates Street in Portsmouth and went to sea at an early life. In his 55 years of life, Charles Blunt packed far more adventure than ordinary men. In 1799, while master of the schooner *Diana*, Captain Blunt and his crew were taken by a French privateer off Trinidad. The French put a prize crew on board and took off the mate and a seaman for their own use. Blunt and the remaining seamen played ill and so caught the prize crew off guard. They recaptured the *Diana* and arrived home in her on August 30, 1799. A newspaper account of the incident reported:

> The French gang whom Capt. Blunt so gallantly conquered had a large quantity of Johannes [Portuguese gold coins] with them, the spoils of many an honest fellow. It was mentioned by some that Capt. Blunt should seize enough of this ill-gotten gain to pay for his long boat. No, says the manly seaman; it is none of my business how they came by their gold. It appears to be theirs and I will not touch a farthing.[23]

Time finally ran out on Captain Blunt in 1823. He was master of the brig *Alert* when she was captured by pirates at Matanzas, Cuba, on April 10th. After a desperate struggle in which Captain Blunt was stabbed to death and thrown overboard, the brig was looted. One of the crew was thrown into the hog pen on deck and nearly eaten before being pulled to safety.

Another member of this family was George F. Blunt, who dealt in crockery, earthenware, pewter and brass from 1791 to 1799. In that year, he was captured by the French and taken into Cherbourg, France, and had to ransom his vessel. One of his ships, the *Brutus*, was captured by the British in the War of 1812. In the 1820s, he went heavily into the salt trade with Europe.

Before the War of 1812, Mark S. Blunt was both a ship master and an importer. Between 1796 and 1804, he "dealt moderately in rum, coffee, sugar and molasses... His biggest year was 1804 when he imported 42,000 pounds of sugar and 6,000 gallons of molasses. His last registered cargo was 17,000 pounds of sugar, which arrived in Portsmouth, September 18, 1811."[24] He was master and owner of the schooner *Franklin* when it foundered in 1804, but he was still going to sea in 1813.

Oliver Cromwell Blunt, named for the seventeenth century Puritan leader in England, combined importing with his duties as master mariner. His biggest year was 1825. He, too, experienced capture. In

Abraham Shaw was one of Portsmouth's leading merchants and privateer owners during the War of 1812. The painting is attributed to Samuel F. B. Morse. PA.

Eliphalet Ladd was a merchant and ship builder in Exeter and Portsmouth about 1800. ML.

Abigail Hill of Berwick, Maine, became the wife of Eliphalet Ladd and the mother of their merchant sons. ML.

William Ladd, oldest son of Eliphalet and Abigail, was a ship captain.
He later founded the American Peace Society and became known as the
"Apostle of Peace." ML.

Dr. Nathaniel A. Haven was a physician who devoted himself to commerce.
He was the father of Maria Tufton Ladd. ML.

Jacob Sheafe, Jr., was a member of the enterprising Portsmouth family of merchants and ship owners. PA.

1800, he was master of the brig *Betsies* when she was captured by the British. He was captured again by the British in 1812 when master of the brig *White Oak*.

Still another of the family was Robert Blunt, who was more a shipmaster than importer. In a two-decale span between 1792 and 1810, he was master of eleven different vessels.

Other Merchants and Captains

In the course of his detailed compilation of the customs' records, George Nelson touched on the activities of many merchants. The effort here will be to recognize as many as possible, although realizing some worthy names may be passed over. In his work, Nelson followed an alphabetical arrangement which will be used here, although some of the minor figures must be passed by. Before going any further, let it be pointed out that the customs' records, so religiously pursued by Nelson, reflect only what the captains and ship owners reported. Only the Great Revenue Collector himself knows the difference between what they reported and what they really imported. With that cautionary observation, it is time to look at others among the merchants between 1783 and 1829.

Abbott, John
Primarily an importer of coffee, in partnership with Langley Boardman, he prospered between 1820 and 1828. At one time or another, he held interests in nine deep-sea vessels.

Akerman, Joseph
As an importer, Akerman brought in small quantities of salt, wine, rum, molasses and sugar from the West Indies.[25] He was also an unsuccessful speculator in privateers in the War of 1812. His home was on Islington Street.

Amazeen, John
A dealer in rum, coffee, molasses, and cocoa from the West Indies between 1819 and 1831, John Amazeen's home was in New Castle. He was master of 22 different vessels, including George Raynes's brig, the *Planet*, between 1819 and 1837.

Appleton, William
A cousin of the Havens, William Appleton traded with the West Indies from 1791 to 1803.[26] For nearly 20 years, he was a trader with Russian ports, and among his employers were William Boyd and William Sheafe. He was master of seven different vessels in his career, and his last eight voyages were for John and Nathaniel Haven. In

August 1830, while a passenger on a packet ship between Buenos Aires
and Montevideo, he died a miserable death. The packet was upset in a
hurricane. A news item reported:

> ...Her passengers were Naltiro Frazier, Esq., Capt.
> Appleton, Mr. Cooper, Mr. Lyons, and Mr. Stewart. Two or three
> of the passengers were in the main cabin when she capsized, all
> of whom reached the companionway, except Capt. Appleton. He
> was distinctly heard to rap on the vessel, and the master
> requested him to dive for the companion way. Capt. A. replied
> that it was impossible, the water being up to his chin; his
> companions being unable to render him any assistance, he was
> necessarily left to linger and perish. Capt. Appleton was master
> of the ship *Hamilton* [q.v.], of Portsmouth, N.H. His loss was
> deeply regretted by the citizens of B. Ayres, among whom he was
> extensively known as an excellent shipmaster...[27]

Ayres, Joseph S.

Ayres was another merchant dealing heavily in molasses, rum and
sugar from the West Indies and South America from 1804 to 1824.[28].

Barnes, Lewis

One of the more unusual men in the Portsmouth mercantile circle,
Barnes was born in Sweden as Ludwig Baarhelm and came to America
in the 1790s as the protege of Hasket Derby of Salem, Massachusetts.
He anglicized his name into Lewis Barnes and was trained in seafaring
by Derby. His obituary said in part:

> ...About the year 1800 he came to this town in command
> of a ship owned by Captain Nathaniel Cutter, and from that time
> until his death, remained a most valuable citizen among us...

Barnes made his home at what was then 20 Islington Street in a
house that is now occupied by an auto parts service. The remodeling of
that house into apartments and a garage was used in the 1950s as an
example of the manner in which Portsmouth was allowing its heritage
to die. Captain Barnes frequently commanded his own vessels, returning in them with merchandise consigned to himself. He traded to the
West Indies for coffee and sugar in his early years and, after the War of
1812, went into the salt business, largely with Europe. Barnes died
June 27, 1856, at 80.[29]

Beck, Michael

Beck was a frequent trader to the West Indies, mostly in the brig *Triton*,
which he commanded for Clement Storer. Captain Beck took the
schooner *Almira* to the West Indies in 1815, a vessel owned by Reuben
Shapley and Reuben Shapley Randall. "On his return...the vessel was

wrecked at Salisbury Beach, Massachusetts, and the frozen body of Captain Beck was found in the long boat."[30]

Bell, Andrew W.

During his career as an importer, Bell had interests in 22 different vessels, ranging in size from the ship, *Niagara*, 343 tons, to a schooner, *Enterprise*, 38 tons. His trading was extensive, importing coal and salt from Liverpool and sugar products from the Caribbean and South America. His son, Andrew Bell, Jr., was closely associated with him.

Billings, Richard

An importer on a small scale in the years right after the Revolution, he was master of the ship *Adolph* on at least one voyage. During the Revolution, he had worked for John Hancock, and that worthy, on occasional trips to Portsmouth, always visited his former clerk.

Boardman, Langley

An importer on a small scale, Langley Boardman was primarily a cabinet maker. Many of his shipping ventures were unlucky, but, supposedly, he recovered some of his losses by an investment in the privateer *Fox*. Boardman built the Boardman-Marvin House on Middle Street. He was one of the partners in building the original Franklin Block on Congress Street and served on the Governor's Council. He died at the age of 58.

Bowles, John

A skilled mariner, John Bowles, like so many of his fellows, dabbled in merchandise. Born in 1755, he was already a captain in 1791 when he brought in the brig *Elizabeth* from Bideford, England. Later the Champney brothers, Richard and Joseph, had him as master of their brig *George* in 1792. Customs entries establish that Bowles' major importation efforts came in the early years after the Revolution. Over a span that ended in 1803, he brought in earthenware from Bideford and Dublin, Ireland; feathers and salt from Lisbon; stone mortars from the Isle of Wight; hair powder, muskets and goat skins from the Isle of May. Other highlights in John Bowles' career are related in later chapters.

Boyd, William

In the years right after the Revolution, William Boyd was one of Portsmouth's leading merchants. The son of George Boyd, a merchant prince in colonial days, he used his father's English connections and traded with England from 1790 through 1792. Two years later, he began to trade instead with the West Indies and South America, building up a huge business, only to be ruined by the Embargo and Non-Importation Acts.[31] In 1793, for example, he advertised receiving, via the ship *Nancy*, "150 whole and half Barrels new superfine and common flour. 50 barrels of good ship-bread. 20 Anchors high proof and good flavor'd Cogniac brandy [The Oxford English Dictionary defines an anchor as 8½ imperial gallons.] 15 Whole, half and Quarter chests Bohea tea..."[32] This listing was, of course, only part of the shipment Boyd had brought in. He continued to prosper in that manner for years, being a major importer, auctioneer and shopkeeper. In 1816, he decided his future rested in the South, and he moved to New Orleans. The New Hampshire Historical Society has voluminous files of his correspondence after 1816, but he sold out his Portsmouth interests in one big auction on August 15, 1816, with Samuel Larkin as auctioneer.[33]

Briard, Samuel
One of the first of the post-Revolutionary importers, Samuel Briard flourished from 1790 to 1805, with rum his major import. It's possible that Samuel Briard could have expanded his business had he lived longer, but he died at 44, on April 20, 1806.

B. Brierley,
BEGS leave to inform his friends and the public, that he has just received by the late arrivals from England, A VERY EXTENSIVE ASSORTMENT OF
Fall and Winter
GOODS,
which he is now opening, and will sell at a low advance for cash, or approved credit, by Wholesale or Retail.
Portsmouth, October 12, 1802.

NHG, October 12, 1802

Brierley, Benjamin
Two Englishmen, William Lang and Benjamin Brierley, came to Portsmouth in the mid-1790s to seek their fortunes. They set themselves up in business under the firm name of Lang, Brierley & Company. They advertised in the *New Hampshire Gazette*, on February 20, 1796, that they were located in "the westerly apartment of the New Brick Store in Ladd Street, where they have just received, and are now opening in addition to their former stock, a large quantity of fresh goods..." Within a year, they were in a new location on Pleasant Street.[34] They advertised goods brought in by the ship *Mayflower*. Lang and Brierley dissolved their firm 18 months later, and Lang went to Boston. Brierley then advertised that he had "just arrived from Europe, with a generous assortment of Fancy, Fashionable and Staple goods..."[35] His location

was then in the Spring Hill area, and he was an active merchant and ship owner for 18 years. He held shares in the *Elizabeth Wilson, Thomas Wilson* and the *Islington*. Brierley married Margaret, the daughter of Captain Thomas Thompson, and lived in the house at 179 Pleasant Street after Thompson's death. But the pull of England was too much for him. In 1818, he sold out and moved his family to England for good.

Brown, Thomas
In partnership with his brother, Elihu D. Brown, Thomas imported sugar cane products for years. Like his brother, Thomas also worked as a ship master.

Champney, Richard and Joseph
From their advertising, it appears as though the brothers operated separately for a time before merging their interests. The peace treaty ending the Revolution was barely signed before Joseph was advertising the arrival from London of "An assortment of Piece Goods, and hard ware, which is for sale at the store opposite the Post Office. . ."[36] At the peak of their prosperity, the brothers owned various ships, some of which they had built in Durham. Joseph eventually returned to Britain, but Richard stayed on. A few years after Joseph left, Richard's luck ran out. In 1801, he was advertised as bankrupt.[37] After his death in 1811, at the age of 71, all the furnishings in his house on Court Street were sold at an auction.

Chase, Theodore
His importations were chiefly coal, salt and merchandise from Europe after the War of 1812 until 1827. He owned extensive interests in several ships.

Chauncey, Samuel
His importations were on a small scale in the early years when he served as master of several different vessels for Eliphalet Ladd. In 1793, he brought in 3,400 gallons of molasses and 3,700 pounds of coffee, probably under his privilege as master. He later became a shareholder, at different times, in five ships.

Clark & Conner, Jonathan and Benjamin
This Exeter firm was among the most prominent in the Port of Portsmouth after the Revolution. At one point, they had a Portsmouth outlet for their goods. "During the years 1791 to 1801, they were the consignees of some large cargoes, among them being one of 25,000 pounds of sugar; 6,400 pounds of coffee and 2,800 gallons of rum in 1798; one of 10,700 gallons of rum and another of 45,500 pounds of cocoa in 1799; and one of 40,000 pounds of sugar and 1,000 bushels of salt in 1800."[38]

Coffin, Peter

A major importer before 1800, Peter Coffin was a believer in the power of advertising, and he spent a lot of money to buy space in the *New Hampshire Gazette*. "He was active between 1798 and 1806, importing sugar, coffee, molasses and cotton from South America and the West Indies; linens from Holland; earthernware, woolens, etc. from England, and cotton and bananas from Calcutta."[39] Some of his advertisements in the *Gazette* were nearly half a column long. In one of the shorter ones, he said he had "just received per the ship *Mentor*, Captain [John] Flagg, from Liverpool, an additional Supply of goods; among which are the following: A Great Variety of Mock Sable, red and gray Fox, Goats beard and Bear Muffs and Tippets; White Angora, and grey Ermine..."[40]

Coues, Samuel E.

This man's connections to the powerful Haven famiy have already been mentioned. As an importer, he occasionally partnered with Thomas Haven. He was also heavily involved in shipping and at one time, he was a partner with one of the Blunts.

Cushing, Charles

In the latter part of the period from 1783 to 1829, Charles Cushing was one of the most prosperous of Port of Portsmouth merchants. He operated out of South Berwick until 1821, but the completion of the bridge between Portsmouth and Kittery made Piscataqua navigation more difficult, so Cushing shifted his business to Portsmouth. Perhaps another factor in his move to Portsmouth was his marriage to a daughter of Jacob Sheafe. Cushing bought the one-time mansion of Governor Benning Wentworth at Little Harbor in 1817.

> Molasses and sugar were the items around which he built his foreign trade; to which he added at various times rum, coffee, tobacco, cocoa, earthenware, crockery, salt, coal, etc. The year 1827 was his best, and during that one year, he imported 190,000 gallons of molasses, 76,000 pounds of sugar, 25,000 pounds of coffee, 100 gallons of rum, 3,250 cigars, 2,300 ox horns, 1,750 bushels of coal and straw carpeting.[41]

Cutter, Daniel and Jacob

The Cutters were in the forefront of Portsmouth importing for more than 30 years, starting in 1792 and continuing until 1828, with Daniel redominating before the War of 1812, while Jacob continued the business after 1815. Dealing almost exclusively in the produce of the West Indies, their biggest year together was 1798, during which they brought in 16,788 gallons of molasses, 76,104 pounds of sugar, 2,187 gallons of rum, 8,047 pounds of coffee, 1,887 pounds of cotton. After the war, Jacob specialized in salt and coffee. His biggest year was his last, the year 1828, importing 15,535 gallons of molasses, 187,477 pounds of sugar, 24,441 pounds of cotton and 3,673 bushels of salt."[42]

Cutts, Edward
The next few entries will deal with members of the multi-branched Cutts family; descendants are legion throughout the Piscataqua Valley. The Edward Cutts was an importer from 1794 to 1819. "In 1802, he brought in 36,000 pounds of sugar, 17,700 pounds of coffee and 4,000 gallons of rum. He never equalled this record."[43]

Cutts, George
Another moderate importer between 1797 and 1803, George Cutts made a few investments in ships. He was master of the ship *Intercourse* (not Piscataqua-built) in 1807 and later had a financial interest in her.

Cutts, Richard
Although not a major importer, he brought sugar products from the Caribbean into the Port of Portsmouth between 1807 and 1825.

Cutts, Samuel
For all his wealth, Samuel Cutts offers an ugly side of the merchandising business in the Port of Portsmouth. As a ship owner, Samuel Cutts betrayed the trust of one of his captains, Thomas Leigh. Cutts was a trader before and after the Revolution. The ship Leigh commanded was captured and put up for ransom. Captain Leigh finally had to leave his mate and a seaman as hostages while he came home to raise the money to free them. Captain Leigh constantly importuned Cutt to send the money to gain the freedom of the men. Cutts's indifference to their plight drove Leigh to distraction, and, when it was learned that William Bennett, the mate, had died in captivity, Captain Leigh became insane.[44] Bennett's companion, who had less faith in the integrity of merchants, escaped.

Dennett, William
As informed citizens of the Piscataqua Valley know, the name William Dennett still flourishes today. This earlier member of the distinguished family was an importer for about a dozen years, ending with the War of 1812. He was a master and commanded the ship *Two Brothers* on a voyage to Portugal in 1810.

Drisco, James, senior and junior.
Today the name is more familiarly Driscoll, but in 1813, the town map showed a "Drisco's Wharf" about where the iron gates to upper Prescott Park are located. Father and son traded with the West Indies from 1793

to 1809. "Their best year was 1805, during which they imported 4,872 gallons of molasses, 120,072 pounds of sugar, 2,623 gallons of rum, 11,782 gallons of brandy, 19,845 gallons of wine, 495 gallons of claret, 10,314 pounds of candies, 10,774 pounds of soap, all from the West Indies, and other articles from Marseilles, France."[45]

Ferguson, Timothy

One of the important merchants in South Berwick, Timothy Ferguson imported goods for two decades, beginning in 1818. He dealt "most extensively in coffee, sugar and salt. In 1820, he brought in 19,000 pounds of coffee and 15,400 pounds of cocoa. Two years later he reported 56,000 pounds of sugar, 30,000 pounds of coffee and miscellaneous goods to the value of $3,000."[46] Ferguson died in 1840.

Flagg, John

During his relatively short life of 50 years, John Flagg utilized his master's privilege to the utmost. His trading spanned two decades from 1790. Through no fault of his, John Flagg's fame will endure because he was the master of the ill-fated ship *Mentor* when she brought in the yellow fever epidemic of 1798. (See Thomas Sheafe and the ship *Mentor*.)

Folsom, Nathaniel

Although he never attained top rank among the port's importers, Nathaniel Folsom prospered. From 1820 to 1824, he "brought in fair quantities of molasses, rum and sugar. In 1824 he concentrated on coffee and from that year to 1830, averaged 70,000 pounds a year."[46] His merchandising career may have begun before the Revolution, and he was an active Patriot during that struggle. His first vessel was the *Nancy*, which he owned outright between 1786 and 1792. Folsom almost died during the yellow fever epidemic. He was naval officer at the Portsmouth Customs House (corner of Penhallow and Daniel Streets) between 1812 and 1816. During the War of 1812, he was an investor in various privateers, including the *Fox*.

Gilman, Stephen

A member of a leading Exeter family, Stephen Gilman was an active importer in the early years of the nineteenth century. In 1805, he brought in 34,244 gallons of molasses, 21,000 pounds of sugar, 1,400 gallons of rum and 776 pounds of coffee. For the most part, Gilman used small vessels in his trading ventures.

Goddard, John

Like Nathaniel A. Haven, John Goddard trained as a physician but finally abandoned medicine for a life in trade. Goddard was an extensive advertiser and, in 1793, ran a quarter-page advertisement in which he announced the arrival of hardware from England "which he will positively sell at Boston prices"[47] For some time, he was associated with Jonathan Goddard. When the yellow fever epidemic struck, John Goddard was in the forefront of the doctors fighting it. In fact, the periodic health reports published in the Gazette were signed by him. When the town built the Brick Market in Market Square in 1800, Goddard was on the committee. He was active in politics, serving in town offices and the General Court. To John Goddard goes the unusual distinction of having refused to serve in the United States Senate after being duly elected to that body. Dr. Goddard died in 1829 at 73.

Goodwin, Ichabod

The influence of this man and activity as a master mariner and merchant extended far beyond the limit of the period under study. A native of South Berwick, Goodwin moved to Portsmouth early in life to begin business training under Samuel Lord, also a native of South Berwick. Lord first sent Goodwin to sea as a supercargo; later he commanded the ship *Elizabeth Wilson*. On his own as an importer, he dealt extensively in salt, importing an average of 14,000 bushels between 1826 and 1836. Later he went into whaling and other investments. He was also New Hampshire's governor during the first part of the Civil War. He died in 1882 at the age of 88.

Hale, Samuel and William

The Hales were among the most active of up-river importers. Over the years, they brought in vast quantities of salt and other goods from Liverpool. Their store in Dover was built in 1783, taking the place of one wiped out in a Cocheco freshet. They took over the building in 1806, and William Hale used it for more than a half century. Ultimately the building was sold to the Cocheco Manufacturing Company. Several of the Dover-built ships were constructed to their order.

Hall, Elijah

A Revolutionary War hero, Elijah Hall prospered after the end of the war, at first as master of the brig *Betsy*. Later he had shares in full-rigged ships. Hall owned the building that had been Stoodley's Tavern on Daniel Street. His service as an officer of John Paul Jones's ship *Ranger*, gave him high stature in the town. In 1790, he imported from London 1,300 pounds of hemp, 16 casks of paint, two bundles of brushes, 40 quarter barrels of gunpowder, 80 boxes of window glass, six boxes of glassware, 40 cases of gin, a barrel of oilcloth and 24 bundles of steel. "In 1793, he had a cargo consisting of 176 casks of whale oil valued at $5,000, being the first importation of this description after the Revolution."[48] He came into possession of the Stoodley property by marrying a daughter of James Stoodley. The old building still stands but on a new foundation at Strawbery Banke. Throughout his life, he was active in state and local politics. He died in 1830 at age 84.

Ham, Samuel

Trading mostly with the West Indies, Captain Samuel Ham built a fortune. He was also active in public matters and was one of the founders of the New Hampshire Fire and Marine Insurance Company, which built the building which is now the home of the Portsmouth Athenaeum. His prosperity gave him the chance to build one of the town's more stately mansions off Woodbury Avenue. Tradition has it that after Captain Ham had staged a house-warming party, he went upstairs and hanged himself. Later the house was occupied by the famed Levi Woodbury for whom the avenue is named. A few years ago the house was razed to make way for Woodbury Manor, a housing unit for the elderly.

Hamilton, Jonathan

If he achieved nothing else, Jonathan Hamilton left behind him on the banks of the Salmon Falls River, South Berwick, one of the finest of the early Federal-type houses in the entire Piscataqua Valley. Hamilton started his climb to riches by operating a small village store. When the Revolution ended, Hamilton moved into importing and, by 1787, was able to erect his mansion. A few rods from it, right on the river bank, was his wharf, warehouse and counting room. Timbers still protruding from the bank testify to this. "In 1799, he imported 5,000 gallons of molasses, 1,600 pounds of sugar, 23,000 gallons of rum, 11,000 gallons of wine, 200 boxes of raisins, 2,500 bushels of salt and sail cloth. Three years later he ended his career by bringing in 2,800 gallons of rum, 18,000 pounds of coffee, 7,000 bushels of salt, 11,500 gallons of wine and sail cloth."[49]

Hamilton married a Mary Manning (Perhaps connected to the Portsmouth family) in 1771. They had two sons. After Mary's death on November 23, 1800, Hamilton married Charlotte Swett of Exeter. She returned to Exeter after Hamilton died and married John Gilman.

Although a visitor can imagine Hamilton enjoying solitary splendor by the tidal river, he was extremely community conscious, being one of the founders of Berwick Academy, where the previously noted Ichabod Goodwin attended school. The *New Hampshire Gazette* reported on September 28, 1802:

> Departed this life on Sunday evening [September 26], at his house in Berwick, Jonathan Hamilton, Esq., merchant, aged 56; he was at meeting [church] the same day in health apparently as usual, but was taken with a paralytic complaint at 5 and died at 12 o'clock...

About a half mile from his mansion, Jonathan Hamilton rests in a quiet pine grove not far from the banks of the river. He reposes there, under a table-type monument, beside his first wife. The stone is fast-yielding to the elements. He died intestate and his property was scattered to the four winds.

Harris, Abel and Robert
They were closely associated as importers, beginning operations in 1790. Abel Harris died in 1829 at the age of 67. Both he and Robert were investors in the privateer *Fox*. The largest vessel they owned was the ship *Bristol Packet*, 249 tons.

Hart, Richard
After the Revolution, Richard Hart went into the West Indies trade, dealing in "large quantities of molasses, coffee, salt, rum, and sugar."[50] In 1795, he switched to trading with England. He was affluent enough to be an organizer and incorporator of Portsmouth Pier in 1795. Built in 1796, the pier was almost an extension of State Street into the river. Frequently used by shippers, the pier was 340 feet long and 65 feet wide, with a row of stores on one side.

Hill, Samuel
Prominent in the early post-Revolutionary period, Samuel Hill traded with both the West Indies and England. He apparently came to Portsmouth from Rochester while still a minor and apprenticed to the trade. By 1773, he was advertising in the *New Hampshire Gazette* that he had a "neat assortment" of coffins for sale. One of his advertisements in 1790 was one column by eight inches, and he said he had "imported in the last vessels from London and Bristol a general assortment of Fall and Winter Goods."[51] The listing included "Gentlemen's best furlined, and unlined Beaver Gloves. Ladies leather and silk ditto. Fur hats . . . Chintzes and calicoes." Other items in his advertisement indicate that American manufactures at that time were far from competitive with British imports. Hill was selling knives and forks, shears, scissors, warming pans, frying pans, locks and hinges and brass kettles.

Huntress, Daniel
For thirty years, Daniel Huntress traded with the West Indies. He was a heavy investor in shipping of various classes. When he died in May 1820, he left a fair estate.[52]

Hussey, Andrew
"Traded with the West Indies and South America from 1811 to 1826. On May 8, 1825 arrived at Portsmouth the brig *Margaret* with a cargo, included in which were 615 pounds of horsehair, 1,000 horsehides, 53

tiger skins, 95 pieces of gold totalling $1,420 and 6,000 Spanish dollars."[53] The *Margaret* was owned by Nathaniel and John Haven, with Hussey serving as master. So it's probable that his share in the cargo was limited to a captain's privilege. Hussey died in 1861 at the age of 78.

Jackson, Clement
In the early days of the republic, there were no health insurance plans to guarantee a doctor could make a comfortable living. Dr. Clement Jackson, like his colleagues, Nathaniel A. Haven and John Goddard, indulged in trade to make ends meet. While an importer on only a small scale, Dr. Hall Jackson, Clement's son, had an apothecary shop to eke out a living. Dr. Clement Jackson owned shares in various vessels and imported goods in them. His trade was mostly in the West Indies.

Jewett, Theodore
Grandfather of the famed author, Sarah Orne Jewett, Theodore F. Jewett operated in what is now South Berwick in the early years. His first ventures were in conjunction with the Rollinses; later he was associated with Thomas Haven, and still later with Thomas Brown. His ownership interests involved many Piscataqua-built vessels. Jewett was master of a privateer, the *Dart*, and he was captured with that vessel, February 17, 1804.

Jones, William, Jr., and son William
This partnership came late in the period and did little significant importing before 1830. They began acquiring vessels in 1824, and before the Civil War had been owners of 20, most of them Piscataqua-built.

Kennard, Nathaniel
One of the leading practitioners of a master's privilege, Kennard prospered, although he never set himself up as a merchant. In early manhood, he served a year with troops besieging Boston in the Revolution. After that he went privateering, but his ship was captured, and he was held for two years in the notorious Mill Prison in England. In 1779, he was exchanged, went to France and enlisted on John Paul Jones's ship *Bon Homme Richard*. After taking a prize, Kennard was one of the men put on board. Again bad luck was stalking him: the prize was captured by the English, and Kennard was impressed into the Royal Navy on *HBM Unicorn*, a frigate. He escaped from the *Unicorn* in Jamaica and made his way back to the United States. With peace, he became a shipmaster and launched his own limited trading career. During the War of 1812, he commanded a revenue cutter, and then became an inspector of Customs. He died in July, 1823, at the age of 68.

Kennard, James

This man deserves mention if only because he was, at the time of his death, president of the original Portsmouth Marine Society, the predecessor of the present organization which sponsors research on Portsmouth marine history. His death came in 1856, when he was 76 years old and had been retired from the sea for more than twenty years.[54] Among the vessels he commanded were the ships *Alexander, Maria Tufton* and *Ann Parry*. After he left the sea, he engaged in commerce in a small way.

Lake, John

For the most part, John Lake's merchandising was confined to small vessels, with only two of them, both brigs, in excess of 200 tons. Between 1800 and 1822, he imported molasses, sugar, rum and coffee. He took the brig *Columbus* on a voyage to Liverpool in 1824 and brought in a load of salt from St. Ubes in 1826. His home was on Austin Street at the corner of Summer.

Langdon, John

Portsmouth's leading citizen from the opening of the Revolution until his death in 1819, John Langdon was never a trader on the Ladd scale. His forte was politics, although he owned and operated merchant vessels all his life. His long career can't be detailed here, but it should be noted that he was one of the few in the Port of Portsmouth to applaud the Embargo Act, and he made no bones about his stand:

> WHEREAS, a report has been industriously circulated in the Country, that Governor Langdon is opposed to the Embargo Laws; and has remonstrated with the President of the United States against certain regulations, necessary for carrying the same into effect; and has even sent a vessel to sea; and whereas it is the duty of every man to establish truth; therefore, I feel it incumbent on my self to declare, that the above reports, are founded on falsehood; and that, so far from disapproving of the Embargo Laws, I am *firm* in the opinion that they originated in the purest patriotism, are founded in wisdom, and are the only measures that could be adopted to preserve the honor and peace of the United States.
>
> *John Langdon*[55]

Such a strong statement from such a strong leader must have really upset the merchants and captains along the Portsmouth waterfront who were spending their waking hours bewailing the Embargo Act. But John Langdon was ever his own man, even daring to oppose Portsmouth mobs when necessary during the Revolution. His graceful mansion, once visited by French royalty and the first president of the United States, still stands on Pleasant Street.

Larkin, Samuel

His activities as an importer were limited, but Samuel Larkin played an important role in many mercantile ventures. After the death of Abraham Isaac and the departure of William Boyd, Larkin came to the fore as an auctioneer. His training had taken place during the War of 1812 when it was he who sold off the cargoes of prizes brought in by privateers:

> Soon after passing out of his minority, he came to this town [Portsmouth], and for about ten years was engaged in the book business. In 1807 he changed his business for that of an auctioneer and commission merchant, and continued serving the public in that capacity with undiminished vigor and ability, to the close of the last year [1849]. So distinguished was he as an auctioneer that in the War of 1812 he was employed to sell many of the prizes which were brought into Massachusetts, and nearly all that were brought into Maine and New-Hampshire. His sales in that war amounted to over three millions of dollars...[56]

Samuel Larkin died on March 10, 1849. His continuing memorial is the Larkin House at 180 Middle Street, the home of Lt. Col. Arthur H. Rice.

Leavitt, Gilman

An Exeter merchant, Leavitt was active in the first years of the nineteenth century. His trading was chiefly in the West Indies, and, other than a share in the ship *Hampshire*, his vessels were small.

Leigh, Thomas

A South Berwick merchant, Thomas Leigh was the son of the Captain Thomas Leigh who went insane over Samuel Cutts's refusal to ransom a hostage. Leigh imported 10,000 gallons of rum in 1810. When the War of 1812 ended, he resumed importing West Indian products.

Long, Edward J.

As early as 1796, Edward J. Long was importing "a general assortment of West-India goods and groceries."[57] At the same time, he informed "his friends and the public that he has removed to the new store in Market Street, directly opposite *Judge Pickering's* house," which would put the store about where Peavey's hardware is today. Five years later, an advertisement indicated he was then associated with Jonathan Hamilton of South Berwick.[58] The partners had "imported in the ship *Harriot* from Bristol, a general assortment of goods in the ship chandlery line." This merchandise was being sold in their store on Fore Street, a thoroughfare that was an extension of Market Street north of Bow Street. Dozens of items as well as West Indian goods were included in the listing. Hamilton's death in 1802 ended the partnership but Long continued. He made his home on Livermore Street and commanded the 1st Brigade of militia.

Long, George
"George Long was born July 4, 1762, the son of Col. Pierse Long, who won his rank in the Revolution. Long went to sea at a young age, became a captain and retired from the life in 1789 to become a merchant. At Portsmouth Pier [of which he was a founder] he had shop No. 3. There were few ventures in town in which he did not have a share, and he took an active role in the operations of the Portsmouth Aqueduct..."[59] At one time, Long owned what is now known as Four Tree Island and had a wharf and warehouse on it. He made his home at 1 Auburn Street (Richards Avenue) but died in Exeter, April 8, 1849, at the age of 87.

Lord, John
A member of a prominent Berwick family, John Lord was a heavy trader in West Indian goods. In 1798, he imported 12,000 gallons of molasses; 110,000 pounds of sugar in 1802; 174,000 pounds of sugar in 1806; 24,000 pounds of coffee in 1801; and 22,000 gallons of rum in 1807. To facilitate his ventures, he invested in shipping and owned shares in the ships *Hitty*, *Alligator* and *Elizabeth Wilson*.

Lord, Nathan
Another of the Berwick Lords, Nathan traded with the West Indies between 1789 and 1800 for sugar products and with England for salt, crockery and porter. He was master for some years of John Lord's *Hitty*.

Lord, Samuel
A native of South Berwick, Samuel Lord was more involved in financial and insurance aspects of business than in trade. He invested, however, in large-scale importation of salt between 1822 and 1827. Lord was a leading banker, a founder of both the First National Bank and the Portsmouth Savings Bank. He ran both institutions with an iron hand. For many years, he lived in the building now known as the John Paul Jones House, home of the Portsmouth Historical Society.

Lowe, John
John Lowe became master of the brig *Elizabeth* at the age of 21. That was in 1817, and for the next half-dozen years, he made repeated voyages to the West Indies. With Joseph Lowe, John Lowe invested in brigs and schooners. In 1838, Captain John Lowe sailed from New York to Gonaives, Haiti. He was never heard from again. He was 42.

Manning, Thomas
During the Revolution, Thomas Manning was master of two privateers, and probably from that pursuit earned the funds that enabled him to

own and sail the brig *Kitty,* the first of a long list of vessels he owned. In July 1776, after the Declaration of Independence had been read in Market Square, Manning won instant immortality by proposing that the name of King Street be changed to Congress Street.[60] His commercial ventures resumed after the Revolution, and he came in from the West Indies on August 26, 1785. From that time on, until 1818, Manning was engaged as a master mariner or merchant, and sometimes both. Prior to his first recorded entry from the West Indies, he was trading for English goods. He advertised that he had for sale the "Best New-Castle sea coal by the chaldron [2,500 to 2,900 pounds] or bushel, Lignumvitae, by the hundred or ton—Porter in hampers or cask, or by the Dozen—Cheese by the hundred or single pound. Cod-lines and twines of all sizes;—Cordage and hausers, from 3 to 7½ inches...and sundry other articles; Which we will sell at a low advance."[61] Manning did business out of a shop in his home near Liberty Bridge." Manning Street was named for him, and although he never quite reached the aristocratic level of the great merchant class that dominated the town, he was on the periphery, often with a sharp verbal needle to jab into the hides of his complacent social betters. His epitaph read, "An Honest Man."[62] He died March 24, 1819.

Manson, Joseph

As a ship master, Joseph Manson was employed by owners like Jonathan Hamilton, Joseph Lowe, Joseph Salter and Daniel Cutter. In the few years he was active, Manson imported a master's allowance of Caribbean products. Eventually he owned his own vessel, the brig *Polly,* 179 tons.

NHG, September 8, 1801

FOR SALE BY
Matthew S. Marſh,
Superfine and fine Baltimore FLOUR, and middlings.
—*A L S O*—
A quantity of
Smith's COALS.
July 28, 1801.

Marsh, Matthew S.

Some years ago, a restaurant prospered on State Street in Portsmouth under the name of Matthew Marsh House. Few of its patrons ever realized that a man by that name had been an active merchant in Portsmouth 150 years earlier. In some of his ventures, Matthew Marsh was associated with Jacob Sheafe. They had the ship *St. Cuthbert* built for them on Pierce Island by Enoch Bagley. Marsh was on the committee that planned the construction of St. John's Church.

Martin, Thomas

Some writers have a predilection for garbing all who lived in the eighteenth century with the purest of patriotic robes. Only few deserve such treatment, and Thomas Martin isn't one of them. When General Washington was begging in 1776 for Portsmouth merchants to sell their rum stocks to his army in Cambridge, Martin was one of several who refused. Time, however, has a way of cleansing; in 1798, Martin was able to wangle the collectorship in the Customs House, a post he held until 1801, when the Jefferson Administration came in. In an advertisement, Martin gave a good description of his store and its location.

> He has in his occupation that Large and convenient store on Church Hill belonging to the Hon. Mark Hunking Wentworth, Esq. where a vessel of almost any common burthen may come under the end thereof, and discharge a cargo of casks with the convenience of a crane, and without the expence of either wharfage or truckage, or deliver a cargo of salt, corn, coals, &tc. from the Vessel into the door; together with a small but convenient wharf for receiving lumber and laying it secure from thieves : Any person wanting storage room for a shorter or longer time, may find this convenience on reasonable terms.
>
> He has scales and weights capable of weighing draughts of more than a ton in weight, where persons may be accommodated at any time in the day.[63]

Another advertisement indicates that Martin offered a wide spectrum of goods imported from Europe, including such odd items as "Playing Cards and Jews Harps."[64] Martin served in the Legislature and was active in town and social affairs. He died in 1805 at 73.

McClintock, John

To John McClintock goes the distinction of being the last survivor in Portsmouth of the Revolution. He died November 13, 1855, at 94. Born on August 28, 1761, Captain McClintock went to sea at 16, serving on the privateer *Alexander* under Captain Thomas Simpson. Within a year, he was master's mate and given command of a prize. An obituary said in part:

> After the peace, John McClintock entered the merchant service, and was, before the close of the last century, shipmaster and owner, He met with losses by the French Spoliations in 1797, of over $10,000, for which his government received a remuneration, but none ever reached him—nor did he ever dispose of a dollar of his claims to anyone. After leaving the ocean, he followed mercantile pursuits in this city...
>
> Under Harrison's administration he was appointed Naval

Officer of this port, and when his term of office expired in August, 1854, President[Franklin]Pierce renewed his commission. We met him in the Athenaeum on one morning in that week, perusing, as was his custom, the papers of the day. Speaking of his appointment, he said,—"Some may regard me as old and worn out, and the office given to me as a mere sinecure. But such is not the case. *For five years I have never been absent from attending to the duties of office but one day, winter or summer.*"[65]

The first merchant command listed to him was the brig *Lucretia*, owned by Supply Clapp, a former associate of George Boyd. He made three voyages to the West Indies in her and then took the larger brig *Arethusa*, owned by William and Thomas Sheafe. The first full-rigged ship he commanded was the *Fame*, owned by Elijah Hall. With the exception of one voyage to Cadiz for salt, all his early cruises were to the West Indies. In 1794, Jonathan Hamilton sent him to Liverpool in the ship *Cato*; two years later, he went to Cadiz in the *Fame*. He was also master of the *Randolph* for Elijah Hall. McClintock invested largely in shipping, and, as noted above, suffered some losses. He was part owner of the ship *Janus* when captured by the British in the War of 1812.

Moore, John
John Moore brought in earthenware and salt when he came from Liverpool, cotton and cotton cloth from Bombay, and sugar products from the West Indies. During his nearly four decades at sea, Captain Moore was master of only two full-rigged vessels, the Apollo, for James Sheafe, and the *Jacob*, also for Sheafe. Moore married Sarah Chauncey, a daughter of that maritime family.

Moore, Samuel
Samuel Moore was a major dealer in rum, sugar, molasses, coffee and cotton from the Caribbean and South America. Again, as happened so often, Samuel Moore apparently limited himself to the master's privilege. None of the vessels he commanded were full-rigged. At one time, he was master of Clement Jackson's brig *Polly*. He also worked for John Lord and George Long. His last voyage, in 1806, was in the brig *Betsy* for Abner Duncan.

Neal, Joshua
For nearly 30 years, Joshua Neal "dealt extensively in sugar, rum, molasses and coffee from the West Indies."[66] He commanded the *Cato* for Jonathan Hamilton in 1799. Before commanding the ship *Watson* in 1805, he was the master of brigs and schooners. His last ship was the *Trajan*, which was owned by Samuel Sheafe, sailing in 1818, and in which he had a share.

Neal, William

As master and owner, William Neal was involved in shipping for almost 40 years. He traded with the West Indies and Europe. Most of the vessels he commanded were small, but from 1830 onward, he shared in ownership of full-rigged vessels.

Noble, John

Noble's Island, with its brick condominium structures, each named for a Portsmouth-built clipper ship, honors this man's family. John Noble was born in 1735 and had his best years as a merchant between 1795 and 1802, usually trading to the Caribbean. The vessels he commanded were small; among them were some owned by John Langdon, Jr., and George Long.

Norton, Winthrop P.

Prior to the War of 1812, Winthrop Norton brought in large shipments of sugar products, although the vessels he used were all below 200 tons burthen.

Odiorne, Samuel

Under the ownership of Jonathan Hamilton, Samuel Odiorne was master of the brig *Joseph*, 1801–1802, on voyages to the West Indies. He later worked for Jacob Cutter and made two voyages to the island of St. Vincent's for John Moore. Odiorne was in command of the schooner *Hero* when she was lost at sea in 1803. Earlier he had been third mate of a revenue cutter stationed in the Port of Portsmouth.

Oliver, Thomas E.

One of the progenitors of the Oliver-Marvin family, Thomas E. Oliver of New Castle traded with the West Indies, mostly in small schooners, for more than a half century.

Orn, James

A highly respected shipmaster, James Orn was at sea between 1791 and 1815. In the span of two years, he made an importation from Germany and three from St. Ubes. The ship *Elizabeth*, owned by Jonathan Warner, was his first command on record. In between that and his last, the brig *Susan* for John Lord, he had steady employment. He was master of the ship *Nancy*, 220 tons, for Reuben Shapley, for five years; later was master of the *Montgomery* for John McClintock. His obituary said of him:

> The last *Gazette* contains the following notice of the character of Captain Orn, whose death in Italy was noticed in our last.
> Capt. Orn, for a great length of time, sailed from this port, and was considered one of our most able navigators. In his

integrity, perfect confidence was reposed, and his nautical skill and great experience rendered him valuable as a shipmaster, and highly useful as an instructor to young seamen.[67]

Parrott, Enoch G.

Like so many other Portsmouth merchants, Enoch G. Parrott started out as a seaman, rose to master and later owner. The first command listed to him was the brig *Hitty*, owned by John Lord. Later, he combined his efforts with those of his brothers, John F. and William. They were importers of rum, sugar, coffee, molasses and cocoa for over a quarter century from 1800. Enoch Parrott bought the privateer *Fox* after the War of 1812 for $2,400.[68] She wasn't a commercial success, but Parrott had profited from investments in her and other privateers during the war. He was one of the few local men to make money out of privateering. Enoch G. had a son, also Enoch G., who invented the Parrott rifle, an artillery piece that changed the course of the Civil War. Enoch G., the elder, died June 3, 1828.

Parrott, John F.

Unlike brother Enoch, John F. Parrott apparently served no time at sea but did some importing on his own before joining with Enoch. John Parrott was naval officer at the Custom House from 1816 to 1818. In the latter year, he was elected to the United States Senate where he served for six years. He was later Portsmouth postmaster.

Parry, Edward

Parry apparently arrived in Portsmouth late in 1793. In an advertisement, he said, "Edward Parry, from London, begs leave to inform the public in general, that he has received from London, and has for sale at his store in Market-Street, at the sign of the Lamb & Flag, a complete assortment of fall and winter goods..."[69] Parry's listing of available merchandise was similar to that of other merchants, but included one odd item: "...a large quantity of French guns with Bayonets."

A memorial to Edward Parry hangs high over old Market Street, set in the brick wall above the present-day A&M paint store at No. 46. Edward Parry, the second of the name in Portsmouth, had the building put up after the fire of 1802 leveled the previous structure. Parry had a house in present-day Haven Park. It was razed to make way for the park. On the South Mill Pond boundary of his property, Parry created a fort, complete with cannon. Admittedly, there wasn't anything to defend, but for Parry, a Welshman, his Fort Anglesey, honoring an island in Wales, was a source of pleasure. This was especially so on the Fourth of July. Although Parry was of British origin, he celebrated the Fourth with fervor. He usually timed his fusillades for the hours when members of an opposing political party were holding exercises in a

Edw'd Parry,

Has received at his Store No. 10 Market street, a very extensive supply of

Spring and Summer

GOODS,

AMONG WHICH ARE,

Real superfine Broad Cloths.	Cotton & silk Hosiery
do. Cassimeres,	Stuff Goods of all kinds,
London printed Cambrics,	Black and yellow India Nankeens,
New fashion Chintzes from 1s6 to 5s per yard.	Fancy vesting of the latest fashion,
New fashion Furnitures,	Blk. Modes and Sarsnet, of all colors.
a large assortment of	Black and color'd silk Shawls,
New fashion silk and cotton Chambray Muslins,	India and Florence Silks,
Sarsnett Cambrics,	Silk Umbrellas and fashionable Parasols, with walking sticks and fringes,
Black, purple, blue, pink, buff and other fashionable cottons,	Cotton Umbrellas & walking Canes,
White Cambric from 2s6 to 8s6 per yd.	Sewing and tambore Cotton,
Collonade and sprig'd lace Muslins,	White and colored Thread,
Japaned and India cobweb Muslins, some very elegant,	Thread Laces, some very wide & cheap,
5-4, 6 4, 7-4 white and colored laced and silvered muslin Shawls, from 5s3 to 42s.	Black and white silk Laces,
	Ladies & gentlemens silk & cotton Hose,
Hair striped 6 4 cambric Dimities,	Ladies long silk and kid Gloves,
Corded & tape stripe do.	Black and colored Crapes,
Border'd and figur'd pocket Hkfs.	New fashion ladies Hats and Bonnets.
Black and cotton Cassimeres,	Mens & youths London made Hats,
Do. twill'd Nankeets of all colors.	India Cottons per ps. or bale,
Velvets & Corduroys,	Irish Linens, of the best fabric.

And other GOODS as usual, which will be sold at such prices, as shall be satisfactory to purchasers for Cash, or good Tow Cloth, &c. *May 27.*

NHG, May 27, 1806

nearby church. Despite his joy in being a practical joker, Edward Parry was a serious importer, with ownership in three ships and a brig. Parry moved to Philadelphia after the War of 1812 and died there.

Parry, Martin
Fast on his way toward becoming one of Portsmouth's leading citizens, Martin Parry was struck down in the little publicized yellow fever epidemic of 1802. "He had left a disconsolate widow [Ann Simes Parry], and an only daughter to bemoan their loss."[70] The daughter became the first wife of merchant William Jones mentioned above. Parry was only 44 when he died. His store was on Portsmouth Pier, and he was a member of the committee to build the Brick Market.

Parsons, Isaac D.
Coming on the mercantile scene long after the War of 1812, Isaac D. Parsons was an important dealer in coffee from 1824 to 1848. Among his large consignments of coffee was one of 44,000 pounds in 1825, and another of 59,000 pounds in 1826. For the most part, Parsons employed schooners in his trading ventures. At one time, he did have a share in the ship *Olive & Eliza* (1826). He died at sea in 1850 on passage from St. John, New Brunswick, to Bristol, England.

Penhallow, Hunking and Benjamin
While not attaining the success of some of their contemporaries, the Penhallows were prosperous in the late eighteenth and early nineteenth centuries. They had a store on Market Street and were advertising hardware in 1793. Four years later, they again advertised the importation of hardware by the ship *Commerce* from Amsterdam and other goods newly arrived from London, Bristol and Liverpool.[71] The brothers were the sons of John Penhallow and nephews of the magistrate Samuel Penhallow. Their place of business was in the same locale as where they were born, and their back boundary ran along the west side of the street that presently bears their name.

Pinkham, Daniel
An importer on a small scale, Daniel Pinkham brought in sugar products and coffee between 1817 and 1826. His shipping investments were in small vessels, the largest of which was the schooner *Martin*, 97 tons.

Prescott, Henry and William
How the Prescott brothers, both of New Castle, managed to get into financial trouble isn't clear. A guess would be that they were small operators who over-extended themselves and were forced into bankruptcy when they couldn't meet their obligations. Their importing began after the Revolution, with Henry in the role of merchant and William as master of some of the vessels involved. They confined their trading to the Caribbean, except for one voyage to Cadiz. In 1803, a commission in bankruptcy was issued against them jointly, and they

were ordered to appear for hearings on three different dates, at which time they were supposed to expose their assets. Apparently they were able to satisfy their creditors because they continued in business until the War of 1812.

Randall, Reuben Shapley

With a name like that, it would be expected that the bearer would be a relative of the merchant Reuben Shapley. They were close but not kin. That is spelled out in Reuben Shapley's will in a clause in which he said:

> I give and bequeath to my friend Reuben Shapley Randall, as a token of my regard for him, my India reed Ivory headed cane, and all my wearing apparel.

Not only did Randall and Reuben Shapley have a close friendship, but there was also an employer-employee relationship. Captain Randall commanded Shapley's ship *Wonolansett* on four voyages between 1800 and 1810. On those voyages, Shapley purchased goods in ports like Calcutta and St. Petersburg [Leningrad], Russia. Randall traded with such places and the West Indies until 1818.

Rice, Robert

A younger generation started merchandising in Portsmouth after the War of 1812. Beginning in 1816, Robert Rice brought in rum, sugar and molasses from the Caribbean. In 1820, although still in the molasses trade, Rice's emphasis shifted to the importation of salt and for two decades was the Port of Portsmouth's major importer of that item. His investments in shipping were extensive, but he also gave his attention to manufacturing and banking. He was a founder of the Portsmouth Steam Factory and an incorporator of the Rockingham Bank. Rice married the widow of another merchant, Jonathan Goddard, in 1807, and was the father of a daughter, Arabella. His home was at the corner of Park and Islington Streets. He named one of his vessels in honor of his daughter. Arabella Rice reciprocated by providing, in her will, funds for the Rice Public Library in Kittery in honor of her father.

Rice, William

A successful investor in War of 1812 privateers, William Rice began his merchandising career in the 1790s by importing European goods. He then shifted his interest to the Caribbean trade, importing sugar products and coffee. Like cousin Robert, he went into the salt trade, staying with it until 1841. William Rice made his home on Deer Street, and the building still stands, despite the ravages of urban renewal. He married a daughter of Robert Parker of Durham, and one of his ships was the *Robert Parker*.

Riley, John, Jr.

One of Dover's most successful mariners, Riley, like other captains, dabbled in trade. His first command of record was the brig *Endeavour*, which he brought in from the West Indies in April 1785.[72] Who owned the *Endeavour* isn't known, but after four voyages in her to the West Indies, he shifted to the brig *Elizabeth*, owned by George Turner of Portsmouth. He worked as a master for Eliphalet Ladd and Joseph Chase, became part owner of the ship *Montgomery* and was master of her. He was master of the ship *Franklin* for six voyages to England. As late as 1842, Riley was still going to sea, master of the ship *New Hampshire*, in which he had a share.

Cemetery where Edmund Roberts is buried, Macao, Jean Sawtelle photograph.

Roberts, Edmund

The full story of Edmund Roberts ought to be told. For the purposes of this narrative, however, it suffices to mention that he was the son of Edmund and Sarah Roberts, and, like his father, became a mariner early in life. After following the sea for some years, Edmund Roberts was appointed consul in a South American port and later was the United States representative in Siam, where he negotiated a treaty which improved trade conditions for American merchants. Roberts owned several vessels, including the ship *Roberts*. He died in Macao, a Portuguese colony near Hong Kong, and is buried there.

Rollins, George

The Town of Rollinsford honors this up-river family. For a short period, 1801–1805, George Rollins imported rum, molasses and sugar, working out of his warehouse in Somersworth. The vessels he commanded were all brigs.

Rollins, Ichabod

In his early years, Ichabod Rollins was master of vessels owned by Samuel and William Hale. The ships *Ossian* and *Hantonia* were two of them. In 1827, he brought in 43,000 pounds of coffee and spent the last part of his career as an importer of salt. It was said of him:

> Ichabod Rollins, in 1840, was one of three Ichabods in town and all of them were directors of the Piscataqua Bank. The other two were Ichabod Goodwin and Ichabod Bartlett. Rollins was partnered with Samuel Hale, the son of the old schoolmaster, as a merchant. As might be suspected, Rollinsford was his home town. Born there on January 12, 1792, Rollins came here [Portsmouth] as a clerk. Early in the next century, such are the odd quirks of fate, he was sent on a trading mission to the Baltic as a supercargo and was away during most of the War of 1812. When he did return, he settled into the familiar Portsmouth business groove...[73]

Salter, Titus

Although one of the most important of Portsmouth's seagoing families, the Salters figured in only a small way in the mercantile business of the town. For several generations, they were the respected masters of deep-water vessels, but, for the most part, if they did any trading, it was by captain's privilege. Titus Salter's importations, from 1792 to 1805, were described as "earthenware, paints and nails from England, pewter and glass from Rotterdam, sail cloth, duck, wine and candles from St. Petersburg; sugar and rum from the West Indies."[74] Although he commanded three ships for Jonathan Hamilton, he was chiefly employed by a relative, John Salter. In 1806, he was master of the brig *Maria Jane*, the vessel being named for the daughter of his employer. An account of the *Maria Jane's* last passage reports:

> Arrived here on Wednesday last, passenger in the brig *Montezuma*, Capt. Titus Salter of the brig *Maria Jane*, which belonged to Capt. John Salter of this town. On his passage from Amsterdam to the Isle-of-May, Capt. Salter was cast away on the coast of Barbary in the night of the 27th of May. The next morning the captain and crew gained the shore and were employed during the day in getting provisions, &etc. ashore from the vessel which was not bilged. The next day a number of Moors (about 15) appeared on the beach, and proceeded immediately

to plundering, After robbing Capt. S. of all his provisions, and 800 dollars in specie, and his seamen of their clothing, these savages used the utmost violence to them. Having resisted for some time and sustained considerable injury to their persons, Capt. S. and his men escaped in the long boat in the evening, and put to sea in great danger from the breakers. The number in the boat was nine, and their whole stock of provisions was four or five pounds of bread, and about three gallons of water for a voyage they knew not of what length.[75]

Fortunately, Titus Salter and his men were able to endure. On the ninth day of their suffering, the first mate, Lang, couldn't stand thirst any longer and drank seawater until he died. They were driven ashore the next day, and the boat upset. John Nudd, second mate, and a seaman were lost. Captain Salter and the survivors made it ashore near Senegal and thence home. Adventures of others in the Salter clan of mariners are related below.

Shackford, John

Shackford was another well known Portsmouth maritime family, although John Shackford was an importer only on a captain's scale. One of the Shackfords, Josiah, founded Portsmouth, Ohio. A relative of John Shackford, William Shackford, was president of Portsmouth Savings Bank between 1844 and 1869. John Shackford was a master of vessels owned by Samuel Smallcorn, William Sheafe, John Lord, Nathaniel Haven, Henry and Alexander Ladd, and Edmund Roberts. He was captain of the ship *George* when it was lost at sea in 1812.

Shapleigh, Richard

Going to sea as a youngster, Richard Shapleigh rose rapidly in his chosen trade but died before he could amass the wealth that should have been the lot of a first-class shipmaster. In the early days, what he accumulated came from a captain's privilege. He did well enough to be master and owner of the ship *Granville*, built in York, Maine, in 1811. Yet what happened to Richard Shapleigh emphasizes that a sailor was never free from peril, although a few miles from home, as the following news account in 1813 testifies:

> Shipwreck...On Wednesday morning last at about 4 o'clock the ship *Granville*, Captain Richard Shapleigh, master, from Cadiz for this port, ran on Lock's Ledge near Rye Beach. A strong southerly wind and heavy sea soon dashed her to pieces. The perilous situation of the crew, soon aroused the humane feelings of the citizens of Rye, several of whom at the greatest risk of their own lives ventured in boats to the wreck, and were the fortunate instruments of rescuing 13 of their fellow creatures from a water grave... But the Captain, a worthy and respectable

man, was swept from the wreck while attempting to cut away the mizzen mast and drowned...

Her cargo consisting of salt, 800 boxes of raisins, and a quantity of lemons was lost...some part of the rigging only was saved.[76]

Shapley, James
Early in his career as an importer, James Shapley traded in the Caribbean for coffee, rum, sugar and molasses. In 1819, customs' records show, he switched to the salt trade with Europe, continuing until 1829.

Shapley, Reuben
A leading figure in New Hampshire's commercial circles, Reuben Shapley's activities covered the gamut of maritime ventures. He maintained two shipping facilities. One was a wharf at the foot of Court Street, and the other a wharf, with a warehouse and a shipbuilding facilities, on Shapley's Island. He brought his cargoes into the wharf off Water (Marcy) Street. "In 1791, he imported 272 gallons of molasses, 16,000 pounds of sugar, 9,000 gallons of rum, and 15,000 pounds of coffee, 1,600 pounds of cotton and 500 gallons of wine. Another big year was 1796 when he brought in 107,000 pounds of sugar, 3,500 gallons of rum and 70,000 pounds of coffee...and merchandise from Europe valued at $14,000. He reached his height in sugar in 1811 when he imported 275,000 pounds. After the War of 1812, he traded with the West Indies until 1824, but did not reach his former place."[77]

One bit of local legend has it that Shapley bought both Boat and Shapley's Island for two hogsheads of Tobago rum.[78] This, however, is not borne out by a study of the deeds at the Registry in Exeter. They show he paid Charles Henzell 200 pounds sterling for the islands. A later well-known shipwright, William Hanscom, worked on the island for Shapley for several years. Two years before his death in 1825, Shapley built the merchant ship *America* on his island. He died childless, and his executors lost little time in dismantling his property. An advertisement said:

Chance for Speculation
FOR SALE

That valuable Real Estate Called

SHAPLEY'S ISLAND

with all the privileges appertaining thereto and excellent Building-Yard, and Dock which holds 200 tons of timber; three houses; a Barn, Wharf and Store; situated between Portsmouth and New Castle; and capable of great improvements

> Also for sale or lease–the WHARF & STORES
> belonging to the estate of the late Reuben Shapley
> Esq. deceased.[79]

Shaw, Abraham and Thomas

Abraham Shaw's fortune was based on his success as an investor in War of 1812 privateers. He held shares in the *Thomas, Fox, Nancy* and *Portsmouth*. The mansion he built with the proceeds stands at what was once the northwest corner of Chestnut and State Streets. His portrait hangs in the Portsmouth Athenaeum. The Customs records indicate he was an irregular importer of West Indies products but usually on a large scale. For example, on one occasion he brought in 69,000 pounds of sugar; on another 28,000 pounds of coffee. On January 23, 1816, the *Gazette* reported the arrival of the ship *Farmer* from St. Pierre, Martinique, with rum and molasses consigned to Abraham Shaw. Shaw wasn't content with having his vessels plow the seas; he also plowed the land. When he died in 1828, he was the owner of a farm, of which an advertisement said:

> It is generally conceded that this is one of the best Farms in this vicinity; and for pleasant situation, fertility of soil, and proximity to a good market, it is inferior to few, if any, in this state.
> It lies about 2½ miles from the Parade, and contains, according to a late survey, 278 acres; viz. 85 of thrifty wood, about 70 of mowing, the rest tillage, pasture and orchard, comprising about 700 fruit trees, many of them engrafted. The several fields are separated by a good stone wall, of which there is about 1300 rods [about four miles].[80]

Closely associated with Abraham Shaw was his brother, Thomas M. Shaw, one of the most successful privateering captains in the War of 1812. While commanding the privateer *Thomas*, owned by Abraham and himself, Thomas Shaw took two prizes worth $528,000. After the war, Thomas Shaw continued to do the sailing while Abraham did the selling. On one passage in Abraham's ship the *Izette* (named for his wife), Thomas had a Rebecca Sampson, 28, a milliner, for a passenger. The Atlantic breeze fanned romance, and Thomas married Rebecca after the *Izette* docked at the Shaw Warehouse in Portsmouth, a building that is now the headquarters of Prescott Park. Thomas went on to win acclaim for his heroics as commander of the U.S. Revenue Cutter *Portsmouth*, and later was master of the Revenue Cutter *Madison*. He died April 6, 1836.

Sherburne, John N.

Teamed with John N. Blunt, Sherburne & Blunt were hardware

dealers. One of their advertisements shows the pressure that Boston merchants were beginning to have on the Portsmouth market, when they offered "Hardware Goods, Paints, Etc. at the lowest Boston prices."[81] That competition, in the form of outlets and malls, faces today's downtown merchants in Portsmouth. Sherburne & Blunt kept on trying, and advertised a bit more than a year later: "Have just received per ship *Marion*, direct from the manufacturers at Sheffield [England], their Spring supply of cutlery & tools...By the near arrivals they expect warranted cast and blistered steel, and an extensive assortment of Birmingham shelf goods."[82] Sherburne & Blunt's advertisement demonstrates the continued dependency of the United States on British manufactures.

Simpson, Andrew
Operating out of Durham, Andrew Simpson prospered both as a merchant and shipbuilder. As an importer between 1805 and 1809, he dealt with the West Indies. He owned some of the vessels which carried his imported goods. As will be seen in the chapter on Durham vessels, he was a competitive builder.

Sise, Edward F.
The family name is perpetuated by the insurance firm, John Sise & Company, founded by one of Edward's relatives. Edward F. Sise was an aggressive importer, dealing with the West Indies between 1824 and 1832, then switching to Liverpool and Canada for the importation of salt up to 1859. Sise also brought many shipments of cotton from the South into the Port of Portsmouth destined for the mills on the Cocheco and Salmon Falls Rivers.

Many more of the family were involved in maritime ventures. Among them was Shadrach H., a topnotch shipmaster. Shadrach later commanded the *Nestor*, taking her to sea under Samuel Pray's ownership.

Stoodley, Joseph
Heir to one of Portsmouth's best known maritime names of the eighteenth century, Joseph Stoodley dealt with moderate success in West Indian goods for a decade, early in the nineteeth century. During most of the time, he was master of a brig, the *Olive*, 107 tons, owned by Jonathan Hamilton, a post he held until Hamilton's death. The only square-rigged, three master he commanded was the *Zephyr*, built in York in 1802, by Enoch Hutchins.

Tarlton, John
Although he never owned a full-rigged ship, John Tarlton of New Castle was an importer for some years. Born in 1780, Tarlton was active

in Masonry and the town politics of his day until his death in 1866. "He engaged in the West India trade...commanding his own vessels at times. As he prospered he became part owner of many vessels..."[83]

Thompson, Ebenezer

Perhaps as well as anyone in the Port of Portsmouth, Ebenezer Thompson exemplified those who were involved in all aspects of mercantilism. Thompson built ships; he imported goods; he was a master mariner. In 1804, he was selling teas at a shop on Bow Street. At another time, he offered for sale the hulls of three vessels.

Thompson, Thomas

Of no known connection to Ebenezer Thompson, Thomas Thompson was an English immigrant before the Revolution and entered trade. He was master of several vessels, trading on his own account. During the Revolution, he was, briefly, sixth ranking officer in the Continental Navy. After the war, he returned to commercial activities, working for Thomas and James Sheafe. In what appeared to be an effort to establish regular sailings between England and Portsmouth, the Sheafes advertised in 1786 the sailing of the ship *Hope* under Thompson, and, later on, Thompson advertised in London for return passengers.[84] Thomas Thompson's home is 179 Pleasant Street, next to the John Langdon House.

Tibbetts, Richard Salter

Kin to the famed Salter family, Tibbetts turned early to seafaring. The ship *Mary* was his first listed command. In her, Tibbetts made four voyages to the West Indies and one to London between July 1789 and March 1792. While still working for Sheafe, he began importing and continued until 1817. His biggest year was 1806 when he brought in 1,000 gallons of molasses, 88,000 pounds of sugar, 6,000 gallons of rum and 14,000 pounds of coffee.[85] He died in the West Indies in 1831.

Treadwell, Charles

The grandson of Mary Kelley and Charles Treadwell, Charles Treadwell traded "moderately in rum, sugar, molasses, coffee and cotton from the West Indies from 1795 to 1811."[86] Another Treadwell, Richard, was master of the first Portsmouth vessel to sail to Calcutta after the Revolution. He made the voyage in a 95-ton brig, the *Augusta*, owned by Matthew S. Marsh. He made a later voyage to Calcutta in the ship *Murdock*, owned by James Sheafe.

Wardrobe, John

Dying at the youthful age of 42, John Wardrobe never enjoyed the full rewards of a promising career. A respected shipmaster from right after the Revolution, Wardrobe was one of the founders of the New

Hampshire Fire and Marine Insurance Company and secretary at the time of his death, November 1, 1804. His probate records indicate he was having fiscal problems at the time of his death.

Warner, Jonathan

Not only did he, through his marriage, acquire a house that today is a Portsmouth show place, but Jonathan Warner also came into a wharf that existed in the vicinity of the old Bow Street power plant. A pre-Revolutionary merchant and governor's councilor, he resumed trade with England after the war. Despite his early Loyalist sympathies, he suffered no reprisals at the hands of the Portsmouth mob.

Watson, Dudley

Based in Newmarket, Dudley Watson "imported coffee, cotton, sugar and molasses from the West Indies from 1791 to 1794."[88] The ship *Watson*, partly owned by him, was his namesake.

Wendell, Jacob

Making his home at the long-time residence of the Wendells, 222 Pleasant Street, Portsmouth, Jacob Wendell was an importer of West Indian products between 1817 and 1826.

Wheelwright, Ebenezer

An almost legendary name in Exeter, this Wheelwright was an importer of rum, sugar, molasses, and coffee for a couple of years in the 1820s and then went into the coffee trade full time.

Whipple, Joseph

Early in life, Joseph Whipple was associated in business with brother William. After Congress established the customs service in 1789, Joseph Whipple was appointed collector, a post that made him important to every merchant bringing goods into the Port of Portsmouth. The post was a difficult one:

> On the shoulders of the Collector of Customs was placed the responsibilities of collecting duties and tonnage taxes, of paying pensions, running the lighthouse [at Fort Point] and marine hospital, overseer of the fort [Constitution], in fact the collection and disbursement of all federal monies except that collected by the Post Office.[89]

Not the least of Whipple's problems was the innate dishonesty of those in mercantile circles. The battle of wits between the cheating merchants and the collector was never-ending. One dodge used by the smugglers was to bring their goods ashore in York or other Maine towns and then to bring the cargo into Portsmouth by road. Whipple held the post from 1789 to 1798, when he lost it in a political shuffle, but

Clearance Fees and Duties of the

	Dolls.	Cents.
Admeasurement,		
Register and Bond,		
Duties on Passports,		
Duties on Clearance,		
Clearance,	2	50
Bond for Passport,		
2 Bond for seamen, *1 ½ Dom*		80
Certified list of Seamen,		25
Endorsement,		
Sea Letter and Certificate,		20
Permits, Bonds, &c. for export- } ed Merchandize entitled to drawback. }		
Ditto for provisions exported } for Bounty, }		
Blanks,		55
Fees, &c. on Entry,	1	50
Dollars,	5	80

Custom House, Portsmouth, Aug. 13 1806

Received Payment,

J. Whipple

NHHS, Portsmouth Custom House Folder, 1985-(14)

was reappointed by President Jefferson in 1801. He held it until his death in 1815. Through all of these years, he was a constant foe of those who wanted to beat the government out of duties due on merchandise.

Woodward, Moses

An importer on a captain's scale, Moses Woodward gave his life in an effort to save his vessel. On November 8, 1802, he was on passage to Grenada when a storm struck. Captain Woodward was swept overboard but managed to grab a rope. A following wave wrenched the rope from his grasp, and he was gone.

Yeaton, Hopley

Yeaten was another Portsmouth seafarer and small trader whose story has been ofttimes told. After Independence, Hopley Yeaton became the first commissioned officer in what is now the United States Coast Guard.

MANIFEST

Of the CARGO, laded on board the *Brig Friendship*
William Lee Mafter, bound from the Port of Portfmouth in the
State of New-Hampfhire, to *Surinam*

B.F.

Thirty six Thousand Boards & Scantling	v.89	324.00
Six Thousand Staves	10.5	60.00
One Hundred Shooks with Heading	1	105.00
Two Thousand Hoops	.27	54.00
Fifty Hogsheads Dry Fish	40	2000.00
Twenty one Barrell Beef	10	110.00
Sixty half Barrell Beef	6	360.00
Nineteen Barrell Herrings	4	76.00
Thirty eight Kegs Butter cont 2000ᵈ	17	333.33
Seventeen Barrell Oil	9	153.00
Forty three Boxes Candle	8	344.00
Seven Boxes Soap	6	42.00
Four Barrell Flour	9.50	38.00
One Box Glass Weare		50.00
Two Boxes Castile Soap		135.00
One Box Linnens		200.00
One Box Ribbons		300.00
		$5279.33

January 4ᵗʰ 1798   *William Lee*

This Certifies that the above is a true copy of the Manifeft of the Cargo on board the American *Brig Friendship* on her prefent voyage to *Surinam* ; to the truth whereof the mafter hath made oath, and that faid Cargo is the property of Citizens of the United States.

Cuftom-Houfe, Portfmouth, New-Hampfhire.

January 4: 1799

J. Whipple Collr

III *Berwick*

NHG, January 18, 1803

THE ANCIENT TOWN OF BERWICK was the building place for 18 three-masted, full-rigged ships between the end of the Revolution in 1783 and 1829. This is said although it is realized that these vessels were really fabricated in South Berwick.

In the years 1783 to 1829, a total of 5,107 tons of these three-masters were built and launched. Before 1800, the master builders were not listed in the Customs Records. The first to be so recognized was an Isaac Bourne who built a brig, the *Frances Eliza*, late in 1800. Elisha Hill built a brig, the *Pallas*, 147 tons, in the same year, as did another shipwright, Josiah Weeks. In 1800, a prolific master builder, Samuel Cottle of Eliot, launched his first ship in Berwick. Two years later came a brig, the *Izette*, built by Stephen Paul who would continue to produce vessels for a number of years.

Not until 1803 did Nathan Nason of Berwick put the first of his six vessels in the water. In 1808, Joshua Haven of Portsmouth built his second ship, *Cato*, at Berwick. Haven built two other ships, plus a brig.

A really important builder in Berwick, and one who lent his talent to many of the yards in the upper Piscataqua Valley, was William Hanscom of Eliot, one of a ship-building family famed in the annals of the Port of Portsmouth. Hanscom worked for Reuben Shapley in Portsmouth before going to Berwick to build his first ship, the *Marion*, in 1824.

The identity of the master shipwright on Berwick's first full-rigged, post-Revolutionary War ship isn't known. But the Customs Records clearly show that the man financing it was Jonathan Hamilton. The *Cato* was his first ship and Hamilton's need for vessels increased constantly with his expanding mercantile interests.

Cato

Specifications: Built in 1790. Square stern, billet head. Burthen, 275 tons; length, 91.2 feet; beam, 26.4 feet; depth, 13.2 feet. Owner, December 29, 1790, Jonathan Hamilton.

At least two distinctions go to the first *Cato*. For one, the list of men who commanded her in the course of 12 years reads like a maritime who's who for the Port of Portsmouth. Included were men such as Samuel Rice, Samuel Parker, John Wardrobe, Titus Salter, Joshua Neal, John Parker and Perkins Salter. Secondly, she was once taken by a French privateer and released.

Samuel Rice was her first master, arriving in Portsmouth on September 29, 1791; presumably, she had already unloaded part of her cargo in Boston, a fairly common practice. Fifteen months later, Samuel Parker brought her in from Bristol, England. John Wardrobe was next, entering from Liverpool on October 23, 1794. She cleared out two weeks later, under Titus Salter, on the first leg of a triangular voyage. Salter returned in time for Christmas, 1796, having made a passage from St. Ubes, Portugal, in 53 days. On that passage, she was stopped by a French privateer. Salter reported that he was "very politely treated, and after a short examination acquitted."[1] The French captain was hoping to find the *Cato* loaded with English merchandise and thereby, in French eyes, a legitimate prize. The *Cato* wasn't as lucky the next time.

In November 1798, the *Cato* was in port and joined in saluting the launching of the new Federal frigate, *USS Portsmouth*. The news account described the *Cato* as an "armed ship" under the command of John Wardrobe. The *Cato* fired in response to a salute by the revenue cutter in honor of the occasion, her guns barking on behalf of the town.[2]

Joshua Neal returned from a voyage to Tobago on June 1, 1799, and turned the *Cato* over to Captain John Parker. She sailed for Europe and was captured by a French privateer. No explanation is available as to why, if she was indeed an armed ship, a privateer took her so easily. Captain Parker wrote to Jonathan Hamilton on January 24, 1800:

> I have the misfortune to inform you, that I have been captured by a French privateer of 14 guns and 75 men, on the 26th Nov...They came under my lee quarter and jumped on board like so many pirates; broke open my chest and trunk, took all my papers and cloaths from me, not leaving me a shoe to my foot; they threw me head foremost down the gangway, and told me she was a fine prize; they took us all out of the ship except three; they put on a prizemaster and 15 men, & ordered her for L'Orient [France], where the privateer belonged. 15 days we

lived upon six ounces of mouldy bread and a little raw beef, for 24 hours; but thank God, on the 29th Dec. we fell in with his Britannic Majesty's ship *Amethy*, Capt Cook who captured us and ordered us for Plymouth, and said he would take care of those Frenchmen, for the treatment we had received from them; he likewise informed me he had recaptured the *Cato*, and sent her into Cork. We arrived in Plymouth the 7th Jan. and have got to this place [Bristol, England] by land, to take the packet for Cork, which sails tomorrow, to join my ship. Mr. Evans my mate is with me.[3]

In this instance, Captain Parker fared well at the hands of the Royal Navy, but often, for American captains, it made little odds which side captured them. The *Cato* was at St. Ubes in August 1800 and arrived in Portsmouth in September with a cargo of salt. Her next master, Perkins Salter, brought her in from Lisbon with salt on April 7, 1802. The next year, she was sold in Norfolk.

George

Specifications: Built in 1793. Burthen, 216 tons; length, 87.1 feet; beam, 24.4 feet. Owner, January 2, 1794, Jonathan Hamilton.

Within a week after Jonathan Hamilton registered her, the *George* was cleared through customs for a passage to Virginia. She came back home at some point, although customs records don't show her entry, and in November 1795, she cleared for Philadelphia under the same master. Four years later, a news story appeared:

> Appeared here on Wednesday last, the ship *George* , Captain Titus Salter, in 72 days from St. Petersburgh [Leningrad, Russia], and 56 from Elsineur [Denmark]. He sailed in company with 19 sail of American shipping, under convoy of the armed ships *Rising States*...and the *Aurora*.
> Capt. Salter finds himself under great obligations to Captain Bickford, of the armed ship *Aurora*, for his kindness and politeness, in accompanying and protecting him...[4]

In January 1803, the judge of probate authorized the sale of the ship *George*, described as "well found with new sails and cables..."[5] It isn't certain from the records who bought her, but it appears to have been Nathaniel Haven. Her next few voyages were under James Greenough, and she worked mostly southern ports. On one passage, Greenough brought into Wilmington, North Carolina, the crew of a New York ship which had been captured "by a French pirate."[6]. The *George* was lost at sea in 1812.

Mary

Specifications: Built in 1794. Burthen, 238 tons; length, 84.6 feet; beam, 25.6 feet; depth, 12.8 feet. Owner, January 7, 1795, Jonathan Hamilton.

Five entrances into the Portsmouth Customs District are listed for the ship *Mary*. The first was on May 12, 1797, under William Rice, who came in from Hamburg. Twice Captain Titus Salter brought the *Mary* into the Port of Portsmouth, once from Liverpool, once from Grenada. John Hilton was her next master, entering from Liverpool on February 10, 1800. In June 1802, Captain Timothy Grow came in from the island of Nevis. The next terse note on her is "Lost at Sea."[7]

Ophir

Specifications: Built in 1795. Length, 78.9 feet; beam, 23.9 feet; depth, 11.95 feet. Owners, from outside the district.

On February 24, 1795, a Captain Stevens took the *Ophir* out of Portsmouth and headed for South Carolina. She was apparently named for the country in southeastern Arabia, which was the source of the treasure of King Solomon. It leads one to wonder if the *Ophir* ever sailed around the Cape of Good Hope to her namesake country.

Hitty Jane

Specifications: Built in 1796. Burthen, 199 tons; length, 80 feet; beam, 24.5 feet; depth, 12.25 feet. Owner, October 15, 1796, Peter Clark of Portsmouth.

Peter Clark had tough luck with the *Hitty Jane*. Her first master was Peter Turner, who took her to Virginia within a week of her date of registry. He returned in June 1797:

> Since our last arrived here the ship *Hitty Jane*, Captain Turner, 37 days from Liverpool, papers brought by him contain nothing later than we received by the last arrivals at Boston and New York...Capt. Turner said it appeared to be the opinion of the people in England that the Emperor [Napoleon] had included them in the peace with France.

Peter Clark sailed in the *Hitty Jane* on her next and last voyage out of Portsmouth. A news item tells the story:

> Mr. Peter Clark, merchant of this town, in a ship of his own, was captured within a few days sail of Charleston, S.C. by a

privateer from Guadaloupe [French] whither he was carried, and stript of all his property, papers, &c., his vessel and cargo condemned without form of trial—he and the Captain thrown into prison, allowed only a half pound of bread and two ounces of meat per day—what became of the crew they knew not. On the arrival of a Cartel for the exchange of prisoners, they were exchanged, and got down to Martinico, they took passage in different vessels bound to Newburyport—a few days after their sailing, Mr. Clark was seized with a fever, and on the 7th day of his sickness, he died![8]

Peter Turner survived the ordeal, and, later in 1798, took out the ship *Two Brothers* for Nathaniel A. Haven.

Two Sisters

Specifications: Built in 1800 by Samuel Cottle. Burthen, 235 tons; length, 85.7 feet; beam, 25.2 feet; depth, 12.6 feet. Owner, January 2, 1801, Jonathan Hamilton.

The *Two Sisters* was the first and smallest of four ships built by Samuel Cottle between 1800 and 1812. Cottle produced a total of eight vessels in that span of time.

A top-notch master, Titus Salter was on the quarter deck when the *Two Sisters* ventured on her first voyage. He brought her back into Portsmouth on November 24, 1801. Shortly before his death, Jonathan Hamilton sold his interest to Jonathan Clark and Samuel Ham.

George Nelson, the editor of the Portsmouth Customs Records, lists the *Two Sisters* as condemned abroad but gives no details. She could have been condemned as unseaworthy or, more likely, captured by a French privateer, thus becoming another item in the long, involved litigaton of the French Spoliation Claims.

Jane

Specifications: Built in 1803 by Nathaniel Nason. Burthen, 223 tons; length, 85.3 feet; beam, 24.5 feet; depth, 12.15 feet. Owners, February 11, 1802, Samuel Ham and Jonathan Clark.

Details as to the life of the *Jane* are lacking. During the first months of 1804, however, she changed owners often. Twelve days after being registered by Ham and Clark, she was bought by Peter Coffin and Daniel Rogers. They, in turn, were out by May 9th, when James Sheafe, Matthew S. Marsh and Robert Lenox became owners of record. She was sold in New York in 1806.

Miranda

Specifications: Built in 1805 by Nathaniel Nason. Square stern, billet head. Burthen, 296 tons; length, 94 feet; beam, 26.9 feet; depth, 13.45 feet. Owner, January 28, 1806, Jacob Sheafe.

All too little is known about the *Miranda*. Records indicate that Jacob Sheafe used her in the Baltic trade. Whether she was first sent to southern ports to load for Europe or went straight from Portsmouth isn't known. She did come into Portsmouth on September 15, 1807, under Captain A. Wadsworth. She made the passage from Russia in 62 days with a cargo of hemp, iron and duck. In July 1809, she sailed to New York under a Captain Thompson. In 1810, the *Miranda* was in Gothenburg, Sweden, On her return, she was sold in Boston. A Captain Place was master in 1811 when she was lost on Jutland Reef, en route to Gothenburg.

Thomas

Specifications: Built in 1806 by Nathanioel Nason. Square stern, billet head. Burthen, 236 tons; length, 86.9 feet; beam, 25 feet; depth, 12.5 feet. Built for parties in Newburyport.

Cato

Specifications: Built in 1808 by Joshua Haven of Portsmouth. Square stern, male figurehead. Burthen, 321 tons; length, 90 feet; beam, 27.2 feet; depth, 12.2 feet. Owner, June 8, 1809, Joshua Haven.

It isn't known whether Joshua Haven intended to honor the Roman statesman, Cato the Censor, or his great-grandson, Cato the Younger, when naming the second *Cato*. But in view of its being the second *Cato*, perhaps he had the great-grandson in mind, a man who committed suicide rather than surrender to Caesar.

The second *Cato* was launched in turbulent times, and it is hard to imagine that a highly successful Portsmouth merchant like Joshua Haven would take the time to oversee her construction but that is what the records say that he did. Because of the curb on shipping, brought about by the Embargo Act, it is impossible to tell when the *Cato* first went to sea. It would appear that Richard Phillips was her first master. He brought her into the Port of Portsmouth on July 6, 1810, from the West Indies with sugar and molasses. That was her last Portsmouth entrance for three years. A marine shipping note placed her in Liverpool on February 15, 1811.[9] Although running the risk of capture by the British, William W. Thompson brought the *Cato* in from Cadiz in 28 days with salt to Joshua Haven.[10] That was in May 1813, and Thompson was still master on a passage to Norfolk in August. Loaded with tobacco and/or cotton, Thompson arrived in Cork, Ireland, on January 6, 1816.[11] From Cork, the *Cato* went to St. Ubes for salt. In 1815, Thompson acquired an interest in her and when he arrived in June 1815, the cargo was consigned to him and Haven.

A Captain Lake commanded the *Cato* on her next voyage. She went to Martinique and was caught in a hurricane on September 25, 1816. She bilged on the high seas, lost her cargo of Portsmouth-dried fish, but managed to salvage the lumber she was carrying. In August, Lake again sailed from Portsmouth, but the *Cato* foundered.

Grotius

Specifications: Built in 1809 by Nathaniel Nason. Square stern, billet head. Burthen, 245 tons; length, 87.4 feet; beam, 25.4 feet; depth, 11 feet. Owners, September 30, 1809, Thomas Sheafe and Charles Coffin.

A question about the *Grotius* that can't be answered is whether or not she was named for Hugo Grotius, a famed Dutch jurist in the seventeenth century. No matter whence she acquired her name, the *Grotius* was a busy ship early in her career. Nason built her on speculation and had to advertise for buyers.[12] Sheafe and Coffin registered her on September 30, but she had already made one voyage to the West Indies under Charles Coffin, arriving August 30th in Portsmouth.[13] Francis Sheafe took her to the West Indies, returning on January 30, 1811; then went to Ireland, returning from there on December 5, 1811. Where she was for the next five years isn't known. The War of 1812 was well over when the *Grotius* entered Portsmouth on November 3, 1816, under Thomas Howland, with wine for Sheafe & Coffin. Her passage from Tenerife, Canary Islands, had taken 57 days.[14] On May 20, 1817, the *Grotius* was at Philadelphia, from Madeira, via the Isle of Sal. In January 1818 she was at New Orleans, along with the ship *Two Brothers*, also of Portsmouth, waiting for cargo. Her last entrance into Portsmouth Harbor was on November 29, 1819, and that year the *Grotius* was broken up, having become unseaworthy.[15]

Eudora

Specifications: Built in 1810 by Joshua Haven. Square stern, billet head. Burthen, 293 tons; length, 95.2 feet; beam, 26.5 feet; depth, 12.2 feet. Owners, April 4, 1810, Robert and George F. Blunt and Haven.

While the life of the *Eudora* was brief, she has enduring fame because of two paintings of her that hang in the Portsmouth Athenaeum. The paintings depict her being wrecked on England's rocky Cornish coast while on her maiden voyage. Captain Robert Blunt was master and had proudly taken her across the Atlantic. She was wrecked at 7 a.m. on December 21, 1810. Many years later, a news account said of the paintings:

> The ship is shown close in to a bold and rocky shore, in a tempest, and carrying a press of canvas in the endeavor to claw off; and the three masts are represented as breaking off near the deck, all going over the side together.
>
> The other picture shows the dismasted *Eudora* "on the rocks at Stratton, Eng., 221 miles west of London," with her people escaping to shore by means of a hawser, men on shore helping them.

The ill-fated *Eudora* carried a crew of 10, including Captain Blunt and the first mate, William Vaughan. There were three passengers. All made it safely to shore. The *Eudora* was on the second leg of a triangular voyage; she went from Portsmouth to Norfolk, then to England, with the intent to return to an American port.

Fabius

Specifications: Built in 1811 by James Tobey. Square stern, scroll figurehead. Burthen, 460 tons; length, 113 feet; beam, 30.3 feet; depth, 13.3 feet. Owner, March 13, 1812, Joshua Haven.

It could be debated whether the *Fabius* was named for Quintus Fabius, a Roman general who made life miserable for Hannibal of Carthage, or George Washington, known to some as the "American Fabius" because his harassment tactics against the British were much like those employed by Fabius against Hannibal. Whatever the source of her name, the *Fabius* was distinguished on two counts.

The first was her extraordinary size for a ship of her day. Only the *Archelaus*, built in Exeter in 1793, exceeded her tonnage when comparing ships built between the end of the Revolution and 1829. Two others built in Berwick in the early 1830s topped her, but not until 1833 did a ship, the *Rockingham*, built by George Raynes, exceed 500 tons burthen.

Secondly, despite the valor of the man for whom she may have been named, the *Fabius* suffered the ignominious fate of being captured on her maiden voyage by the British frigate *Shannon*.[16] The only really surprising aspect of the story is that Joshua Haven sent such a costly ship to sea in such perilous times.

Recovery

Specifications: Built in 1811 by Nathan Nason. Square stern, billet head. Burthen, 309 tons; length, 95.3 feet; beam, 27.3 feet; depth, 11.8 feet. Owner, April 20, 1811, Lewis Barnes.

Nine days after her registration, the *Recovery* left for New York with Lewis Barnes as master. Available records don't show where the *Recovery* was between that sailing and December 12, 1815, when she was reported as being at Bordeaux, France, under Barnes.[17] The *Recovery* arrived at New York on February 20, 1816, in 59 days from Bordeaux.[18] Although the shipping item doesn't say so, it is safe to assume she brought some passengers along with cargo.

Captain Barnes apparently elected to stay at home for a time because William Cox was master when the *Recovery* came in from Bonavista with 10,440 bushels of salt consigned to the owner. In December 1816, Barnes cleared out for New Orleans, the first leg in a triangular voyage. Not until the next October did Barnes return home. The *Recovery* came in from Liverpool in 40 days with salt and coal.[19] On her passage, she had supplied the British brig *Lion* with water; perhaps testimony that the wounds of the War of 1812 were healing. Two months at home and Captain Barnes was off again, this time for Matanzas, Cuba, where he loaded with rum, sugar and molasses for Europe. Barnes arrived at New York on September 6, 1818, after a voyage of 44 days from Liverpool.

In 1820, judged as unseaworthy, the *Recovery* was broken up, but she had well earned her keep for Captain Barnes.

Hitty

Specifications: Built in 1812 by Nathan Nason. Square stern, billet head. Burthen, 337 tons; length, 101.5 feet; beam, 27.45 feet; depth, 13.7 feet. Owners, December 17, 1816, John and Samuel Lord and William Haven.

Available records give no information as to where the *Hitty* was between her launching and her registration by the Lords. It is possible that her builder, Nathan Nason, had to wait out the War of 1812 before being able to sell his vessel. Whatever the story, the *Hitty* was quickly put to work under William Rindge, who brought her from Liverpool in 50 days with salt and coal consigned to the owners. In her next four voyages, which might have been triangular routes, Nathaniel Folsom was master. The homeward passages were from either St. Ubes or Liverpool.

Payment Receipt

Late in 1821, the owners turned the *Hitty* over to Ichabod Goodwin, their young protege to whom they had previously entrusted command of the *Elizabeth Wilson*.

Goodwin made three voyages in the *Hitty*, the return passages being salt runs from Liverpool. He then became master of the *Marion* in 1825. The *Hitty* was put up for auction in 1821, and Goodwin bought an interest, perhaps with the help of the Lords, to whom he may have been related. Customs records indicate the Lords still owned part of her as late as 1823. In 1822, the *Hitty* came from Liverpool in 47 days, bringing iron and salt for her master, Ichabod Goodwin. During her passage, she suffered from extensive damage to her rigging and was in constant danger from ice floes for five days. Even so, a vessel she met, an English ship carrying 250 immigrants to Quebec, was even worse off, needing supplies which the *Hitty* provided.

Under John Winkley, she sailed from Portsmouth on April 20, 1824, for Charleston, where she loaded cotton for Liverpool, and returned to Portsmouth in October, in a passage of 40 days from St. Ubes, with salt to Goodwin and Samuel Lord. Her triangular voyage had taken six months. That was her routine, although on July 8, 1827, she entered Portsmouth with 23 passengers, plus salt, iron and coal. The immigrants were mostly English. Among them were: James Argram, 50, a mechanic, and his wife, Betsy, 48; John Butcher, 25, a mechanic; Mary Busket, 38, a matron, with six little Buskets; Thomas Fearne, 48, a mechanic, from Ireland; Betsy Jepson, 55, and Betsy Jepson, 30, probably mother and daughter; and Mr. and Mrs. John Kay, with five children.[20]

Shortly thereafter, Goodwin sold his interest in the *Hitty* to William Neal, who brought her in from Liverpool on September 4, 1828, with salt and crates for himself. That was her last Portsmouth entry. In December, she arrived at Savannah, from Portsmouth, via Boston and Norfolk. She cleared there on January 10, 1829, for Liverpool. A news account reported:

> Savannah, Feb. 19—Ship *Hitty*, of Portsmouth, that went ashore on the Garden Bank, a short distance below the town, on 17th Jan. last, was sold with her three masts, on Wednesday, for $155, and 200 bales of cotton, yet in the hold under water, at 3 cents per lb. The H. was bound to Liverpool, and had a cargo of 930 bales of cotton, about 400 of which, damaged, were sold at an average of 3 cents per lb.; the sails, spars and rigging for $2000. The vessel was owned by Captain William Neil, and was insured.—*Georgian*[21]

Hamilton

Specifications: Built in 1815 by Joshua Haven. Square stern, billet head. Burthen, 322 tons; length, 99.3 feet; beam, 27.2 feet; depth, 13.6 feet. Owners, April 19, 1816, Nathaniel A., John, Joshua and Charles Haven, E.G. Parrott, and Henry and Alexander Ladd.

An advertisement strongly indicates that his family and friends had to bail Joshua Haven out of his costs in building the *Hamilton*.[22] Named in honor of the Berwick merchant, Jonathan Hamilton, the ship was without buyers until after Haven's advertisement:

> The hull of a good oak Ship, built about two years since, well calculated for the freighting trade, about 320 tons, iron fastened...

The *Hamilton* was without an owner for so long apparently due to the War of 1812. As far as the safety of vessels was concerned, the war didn't wind down until nearly the end of 1815, such was the state of communications. The Battle of New Orleans, for example, was fought on January 8, 1815, two weeks after a peace treaty had been signed at Ghent, Belgium. Ship commanders on both sides kept on taking prizes for months. With such uncertain conditions, Joshua Haven had to wait for a buyer for the *Hamilton*, the largest ship he built.

James Greenough took the *Hamilton* on her maiden voyage to India. She re-entered Portsmouth on March 6, 1817, in 110 days from Calcutta, "with a valuable cargo, consisting of 3,547 bags of sugar; 630 of saltpetre; 400 of tumerie; 37 bales of piece goods; 20 bales of goat skins; 1,000 gunny bags."[23] All of the cargo was consigned to the Ladds and Havens. The *Hamilton* went to Havana, June 1, 1817, and was in Leghorn, Italy, in November 1817 in quarantine. It took her 64 days to return to New York in April 1818. From New York, she went south and then to Europe, so it was not until August 16, 1820, before she came home taking 35 days from Cadiz and with a cargo including salt, iron and gin cases for the Havens and Parrott. Otis Falls followed Greenough as master and returned from a voyage to Russia, August 22, 1822. After that, she went to Havana, thence to Gibraltar and home. After her return, William Appleton became the master for several years. When the *Hamilton* came in from the West Indies on September 14, 1825, she brought the Spyers family, Dutch immigrants: The members were Maurice, 35, a merchant; Catharine, 25, his wife; three children, Rebecca, 3, Phebe, 1, and Henry, nine months.[24] They had embarked at Turk's Island. With them was the children's nurse, Rebecca Tilghman, already naturalized.

Oddly, for a ship of her day, the *Hamilton* seems to have only rarely

BRIGHTON. COTTON TRADE. - Period

17. August. lecture on plates, realism, Leeds lip ... ...

18. John Nelson - ... Nelson ... Clerk ... ... people
1792-1830
1912 M ... £5 ...   Not well ...
1945 ... Clerk ... contacts momentous ... by NH

14. Demand for Am. vessels. Ports built in England - New Jersey
Port ships ... in ... of E. Shipping engines reduced

17- NA18 bottling ... & RN ... Profits !

4-5. Saw Cotton from Bombay - going fast -

10 Ernest ? [illegible] - Spoolcotes, 1812

33-4 Cargo Marengo 1825 ~~Cargo~~ figures, slaves, horses / [illegible] [illegible]

58 George ship sold 1803 → NSW - [illegible]

66 Hamilton Longboat ship J Blair built Berwick. Act 2 yrs [unloaded]
1816 [illegible] [illegible]. [illegible] [illegible] Not J? Charles & [illegible]

visited southern American ports. She usually traded in places like Montevideo, Uruguay, from whence she came on October, 26, 1826, with hides and horns for her owners. She came in from Santos, Brazil, on February 21, 1828, with sugar and coffee for the Ladds and Parrott.[25] When she sailed on December 24, she had left the Portsmouth ship *Trajan* there, loading wood for a run to Montevideo. Besides cargo, the *Hamilton* brought with her Woodbury Langdon, whose brig *Gustavus* (built in Berwick in 1811 by Joshua Haven) had been sold in Montevideo. Captain Langdon brought with him news of fighting in and around Montevideo between guerrillas and Brazilian troops. The *Hamilton* sailed to Germany, to Russia, to Gibraltar; on one occasion went from Charleston to Europe. On another in May 1836, the *Hamilton* came into Portsmouth with 1,216 bales of cotton for E.F. Sise and the mills on the Cocheco River. She also brought three passengers, two from Salem and one from Boston.

That was the *Hamilton's* last visit to Portsmouth. She was sold to a whaling company in Sag Harbor, New York. In that capacity, she made six cruises in the next dozen years, bringing in catches worth a total of $138,659, or an average of $23,109 per trip.[26] Her last recorded whaling voyage was in 1848, and there is every reason to believe that she was sold into the California trade.

Marion

Specifications: Built in 1824 by William Hanscom of Eliot. Square stern, billet head. Burthen, 330 tons; length, 99.4 feet; beam, 27.5 feet; depth, 13.75 feet. Owners, December 17, 1824, Ichabod Goodwin, Samuel E. Coues, Timothy Ferguson and Theodore F. Jewett.

The *Marion* was the first full-rigged, three-masted vessel to be launched by William Hanscom, a progenitor of a generation of imaginative Port of Portsmouth shipbuilders. Hanscom put seven vessels in the water between 1814 and 1824, all of them at Reuben Shapley's yard on Shapley's Island, Portsmouth. The *Diomede*, a brig of 217 tons built in 1816, was the largest. To build the *Marion*, however, he went upriver to Berwick. He never again came farther downstream than his own yard in Eliot in the course of his next 26 years of shipbuilding.

Ichabod Goodwin took William Hanscom's first ship on her maiden voyage. Loading at Charleston, Goodwin sailed for Liverpool on February 17, 1825. In September, the *Marion* returned with salt and iron. Captain Goodwin took her on another triangular voyage and returned from Liverpool on September 11, 1826, with salt for the owners. Goodwin then turned the *Marion* over to Nahum Yeaton, who sailed in her on October 26, 1826, for Savannah. Captain Yeaton returned with her to Portsmouth on May 14, 1827, after 37 days. He brought salt for Goodwin & Coues, 95 crates of crockery for Taylor & Waldron, and iron railings for the still existing fence "at the new Stone Church" on State Street, an item of historical trivia in Portsmouth.[27]

In her next sailing, the *Marion* went to Richmond, Virginia, for cotton and tobacco; then to Marseilles, France. Leaving Marseilles in February 1829, she arrived at New York on May 5th—not a good passage. In June 1829, Goodwin & Coues advertised her as available for freight or passage to Havana; instead, as often happened, she went to New York, and later cleared for Marseilles. Not until February 1832 did the *Marion* return to her home port and immediately caused a tragedy. On her way in on February 23rd, she picked up her pilot, Ephraim Haley, who drowned while bringing the *Marion* into the harbor. News accounts said Captain Haley saw his pilot boat capsizing in the Piscataqua River. To save his boatmen, he jumped into the *Marion's* stern boat to go to their aid. The boat's falls hung up and dumped Haley into the river. His boatmen were saved but he wasn't. A native of the Isles of Shoals, Captain Haley had lived in Portsmouth for some years on Washington Street.

Among the more valuable possessions of the Old Berwick Historical Society are several ships' logs, including that of the *Marion* . The log is fragmentary and the work of two different masters, John Davis and Lyman D. Spaulding. Like most such documents, the log is a studied recital of weather conditions and touches little on ship life. Captain Spaulding was a man of few words, as his entries show. July 27, 1836, is an example:

> Comes in with fine breezes and pleasant
> At 7 P.M. sounded and got Bottom with 80 fathoms of line.
> Sand & Shells
> Midt. Light breeze & cloudy
> Ends light airs & pleasant weather
> Soundings 75 fathoms Sand & Shells

One of Captain Spaulding's in-port entries at Liverpool in 1838 illustrates the problems that faced shipmasters in dealing with their crews. It reads, in part:

> . . . William Davis, William Combs and William Roberts absent from the ship without leave.

The flesh pots of Liverpool were inviting, and Captain Spaulding decided he had at least one Bill too many because, on the next day, he logged the dismissal of William Roberts. William Davis and William Combs, however, were still AWOL, (absent without leave), and Matthew Gamble joined them in seeking out the sins of Liverpool.

Another log belonging to the ship *Marion* is in the Woodman Institute in Dover, New Hampshire. In recording life at sea, it is monotonous like the others of its kind. This log, however, provides information about the cargoes taken out of Portsmouth in the triangular trade. The *Marion* came into harbor on October 16, 1836, with the simple entry:

> Came to off the town. Hauled [winched] into the Wharf and moored ship. Ends fresh breeze and cloudy.
> So ends the voyage.

The *Marion* sailed again on December 2nd headed for Apalachicola, Florida, to load cotton. There was a bit of trouble getting into Apalachicola. After crossing the bar, she ran aground on the Western Land Bank but was taken off the next day. Once at the wharf, she began discharging her cargo: 394 bales of hay and 381 barrels of potatoes. As the workers brought out the inbound cargo, the outgoing cotton began coming on board. In all, 747 bales of cotton were loaded, coming in different lots, each with the marks of the consignors so that proper billings could be made. In the *Marion's* log, some of the bales were described as "square," and one of the last items of business was sending 3,000 feet of boards on shore. With that, the *Marion* took on a pilot and headed for New York. That was on February 15, 1837, and she was off Sandy Hook on March 3d. Her cargo was discharged by the 11th; she loaded hay, and headed back to Apalachicola on the 15th.

John Davis's handwriting is difficult to read, so quotations from his log entries will be brief. One entry while the *Marion* was lying in Charleston Harbor, December 7, 1835, is an example:

> This day comes in fine with Fine pleasant Weather the winds from the Southwest. Men employd at sundry jobs...

Events of all kinds were apt to take place on shipboard in sailing days. For example, at one time while in Portsmouth, the Rev. Moses Howe conducted divine services while the *Marion* was tied up at Haven's Wharf. In 1834, one of the ship's people died while visiting relatives in Somersworth. The *Portsmouth Chronicle*, on April 26, 1886, quoted an item that had been published in the *Kennebunk Gazette* of July 1, 1826:

> A seaman named John Kee of Saco, Me., belonging to the Portsmouth ship *Marion*, Captain Goodwin, from Charleston, who shipped in that port, unfortunately fell from the main yard to deck, at Savannah on Friday, 9th inst. He was carried to the hospital where he died the same night.

Sailing days were hard on both men and ships as seen by the death of William Cleaves of Portsmouth. He was only 17, a ship's boy, when he died. He was the son of Samuel, who was in the far-from-glamorous soap-making business.

The *Marion* did her job well, at minimum expense to her owners, the last of whom were Goodwin, Coues & Jewett. They had her when she was wrecked on the treacherous Florida Reef near Key West in 1843.

Olive & Eliza

Specifications: Built in 1825 by William Hanscom. Square stern, billet head. Burthen, 386 tons; length, 111.7 feet; beam, 27.7; depth, 13.9 feet; Owners, January 14, 1826, Ferguson & Jewett and I.D. Parsons.

The *Olive & Eliza* was William Hanscom's last ship built in Berwick for seven years. He returned in 1832 to build the ship *Berwick*, and the next year constructed the ship *Pactolus*, the last square-rigger built in Berwick. In the intervening years, Hanscom built three ships in Durham.

Theodore F. Jewett, one of the owners, was master of the *Olive & Eliza* on her first voyage, bringing her in from Liverpool on June 27, 1826, thus completing her first trip around the triangle. Charles Moody of York was her next master, sailing for the Chesapeake on July 22nd. She was gone for more than a year. When she did return, in 40 days from Liverpool, the ship and her people had to go into quarantine. The quarantine grounds in Portsmouth Harbor were between Clark's Island and Fort Constitution. Any vessel that had been exposed to various diseases was compelled to remain there until cleared by the health authorities. Shortly after the *Olive & Eliza* left quarantine, Isaac D. Parson sold his interest.

Round and round she went along the legs of the triangle, with occasional variations as to the ports she entered. Captain Moody was master until 1833, when he was relieved by Tyler F. Parsons. On February 26th, Captain Parsons wrote the owners from Matanzas:

> On my passage to this place, I had the misfortune to lose two of my seamen, viz. James A. Wanton, of Baltimore, 19, and Joseph Milne, of New Orleans, 17, who fell overboard from the main futtock shrouds, and were drowned.—The ship was going six or seven knots before the wind with the studding sails out. A royal yard was thrown overboard immediately, the first officer and two men were sent off in a boat, but after a half hour's ineffectual search, during which time the ship laid to, returned on board, and the ship proceeded on her voyage.[28]

Those last six words were the usual epitaph for seamen unfortunate enough to fall overboard in the days of sail. Many captains didn't bother to heave to—they could always get new hands. But the ever-present chance of falling from the yards made important the old slogan: "One hand for the ship, and one hand for yourself."

In 1834, the *Olive & Eliza* was out in the Far East but was in New Orleans by March 1835. James Kennard brought her up to New York and then went to Matanzas for sugar, thence to Europe. Always busy, she sailed hither and yon for a number of years as her orders dictated. In January 1839, she collided with a French ship, *L'Union*, near Poverty Point in the Mississippi River. She suffered little damage and continued on her way. She returned to her home port from Glasgow, Scotland, on February 17, 1840, and loaded with hay for a passage to New Orleans.

Back and forth she went, New Orleans or Apalachicola or Savannah or Mobile, wherever there was cotton for the fast-spinning bobbins in the mills of Liverpool.

In January 1842, she arrived at Apalachicola from Baltimore, then cleared for St. Joseph on the Mississippi. Apalachicola was at the mouth of the Apalachicola River, and cotton was shipped down it from the fields of southern Georgia. As in this case, eager captains were sometimes disappointed in finding cargoes, so they went on to other ports, as *Olive & Eliza* did under Edward Marshall. After loading, she headed for Liverpool. The *Olive & Eliza* was struck by lightning on March 11, 1842, which set her on fire. She limped into Fayal in the Azores on March 19, 1842. Holes were bored into her sides and deck, and water was poured into the hull. She was dismantled and towed into shoal water for lightening. When that was done, it was found the burned area wasn't excessive. The news item went on to say: "It was thought the vessel would be repaired. Great credit is said to be due Captain Marshall for his skill."[29] With a Fayal dateline of April 14, it was reported the *Olive & Eliza* was being repaired under the direction of another master. In May, the ship arrived at Liverpool, sailing for Boston on June 20th. She was either diverted or her orders were misunderstood, however, because, in August, she was at Fayal being loaded with whale oil for New Bedford. She sailed from New Bedford on October 19th and was in Portsmouth on the 24th. Over the next few years, the *Olive & Eliza* was operated in much the same fashion— working in the triangular trade. She was in Stockholm, Sweden, in 1845 and made it back to New York in 54 days, arriving on December 14.

In October 1846, the *Olive & Eliza* sailed from New Orleans on her last passage. Her cargo was 118,431 barrel staves intended for Bordeaux. Heading across the Gulf of Mexico, she was trapped on the quick sands of the Dry Tortugas on the night of the 18th. Only her anchors and chains were saved. The hull was sold to Key West wreckers for $43.30.

It is an oddity to note that the first two ships built by William Hanscom wound up their careers near Key West. Although the fates of the *Olive & Eliza* and the *Marion* had nothing to do with it, they were the last ships built in Berwick for seven years.

IV Dover

NHG, September 25, 1802

FROM THE END OF THE REVOLUTIONARY WAR until 1829, the shipyards in Dover produced 28 three-masted, square-rigged vessels. Their combined tonnage was 7,317. These ships ranged in size from the *Thomas Gordon* at 194 tons built in 1800 to the *James* at 332 tons built in 1810. As in the instance of Berwick, the records don't offer the names of the master shipwrights before 1800. The first to be credited was Richard Tripe with the *Aurora* in 1801.

The most prolific of the builders in Dover was Stephen Tobey who put nine ships in the water between 1801 and 1820. Another Stephen Tobey, in the mid-nineteenth century, became a prominent builder of much larger vessels on Noble's Island in Portsmouth. Stephen Paul was another top-notch builder in the upper Piscataqua region, although only two of his ships were built in Dover. The greatest volume of Dover shipbuilding was concentrated in the 20-year span between 1791 and 1811. After this period, only three more ships were built, one in 1818, another in 1821 and the last in 1837, a date outside the scope of the present work. A list of the Dover-built ships follows.

Industry

Specifications: Built in 1791. Burthen, 225 tons; length, 78.4 feet; beam, 24.4 feet; depth, 12.2 feet. Owner, November 19, 1791, Ebenezer Tibbetts of Portsmouth.

The *Industry* was one of the many Port of Portsmouth vessels captured during the Quasi War with France in the 1790s. William Twombley cleared Portsmouth for England soon after the *Industry* was registered and returned a little over a year later.[1] In March 1793, A Captain Moore sailed her to Tobago, but when the *Industry* returned, William Hanson was master. As often happened, it may be that Moore died of some tropical illness and was succeeded by the first mate. When the ship *Cato* arrived in Portsmouth in the week of December 10, 1796, she reported having spoken with the *Industry* and her captain, Robert Oram, 47 days out from Grenada bound for Portsmouth. The *Industry* had lost part of her crew and sails, had been twice blown off the coast by northwest winds, and "was making a third attempt to get into port."[2]

Ebenezer Tibbetts still owned the *Industry* when she was captured and confiscated before 1800, becoming yet another item in the list of French Spoliation Claims.[3]

Cleopatra

Specifications: Built in 1793. Burthen, 225 tons; length, 83.4 feet; beam, 25 feet; depth, 12.5 feet.

Some lover of the classics must have had a hand in the naming of the *Cleopatra* for the beautiful Egyptian queen who bewitched some of the leading Romans. The *Cleopatra*, however, was built for people in Boston and only sailed out of Portsmouth Harbor on her first passage.

Barrington

Specifications: Built in 1794. Burthen, 204 tons; length, 80.4 feet; beam, 24.3 feet; depth, 12.15 feet. Owners, December 23, 1794, William and Samuel Hale.

Obviously named to honor the neighboring town of Barrington, the *Barrington*'s time on the Piscataqua was brief. The Hales sold her in New York in 1796.[4] It is possible that she made one voyage for the Hales in the year they owned her, but there is nothing in the records.

Hazen

Specifications: Built in 1795. Burthen, 238 tons; length, 85 feet; beam, 25.5 feet; depth, 12.75 feet.

The *Hazen* was built under contract with William White of Boston, who registered her on February 6, 1795. She apparently sailed for Boston immediately. She came into Portsmouth early in 1800, however, cleared for Havana the week of March 19th under Benjamin Henderson. The day before the *Hazen* left, Captain Henderson advertised a $5 reward for the capture of a seaman, "John Calf, 23 years, five feet, six inches high, light complexion, light hair and light eyes, had on when he runaway, a blue jacket, red westcoat and coarse trousers."[5] The *Hazen* was then described as being from Salem and tied up at Rindge's Wharf in the North End.

Harriet

Specifications: Built in 1795. Square stern, billet head. Burthen, 208 tons; length, 81.6 feet; beam, 24.3 feet; depth, 12.05 feet. Owner, February 24, 1796, Abel Harris.

Very little is known about the *Harriet*. Captain Orn brought her from Cork on Independence Day, 1796, an indication that she had gone to Europe right after registration. Customs records show she was sold in Boston in 1801; quite possibly she had been sailing out of that port for a year or more.

Strafford

Specifications: Built in 1795. Burthen, 265 tons; length, 88.7 feet; beam, 26.3 feet; depth, 13.15 feet. Owner, William Hale.

To the first Dover-built *Strafford* goes the distinction of having more than four columns of newspaper space devoted to a mutiny staged on board. William Hale first sent her to sea under Benjamin Balch. She came in from St. Ubes on March 11, 1797, having gone around the triangle from Portsmouth to Charleston, thence to Europe and back to Portsmouth.[6] It was on her next voyage that the *Strafford* was the scene of a mutiny.

Captain Balch cleared the *Strafford* out of Portsmouth in the week of June 9, 1797, bound for Charleston. From there, she went to Liverpool, then to St. Ubes for salt. It was on the homeward passage that the mutiny took place. Captain Balch's deposition was filed with Thomas Bulkeley, American consul in Lisbon, Portugal, on February 15, 1799. Balch told his story to the newspapers, he apparently having only then arrived from St. Ubes without his ship.[7] In a preliminary paragraph, Balch declared:

TO THE PUBLIC

I feel myself constrained to address the public on a subject exceedingly interesting to the mercantile and maritime interests of the United States, and all descriptions of persons immediately connected with these.—Left in a destitute, distressed condition, by a company of base mutineers, who took advantage of my going on board a ship at sea, in order to obtain provisions and assistance; to run away with the ship *Strafford*; and further have cruelly injured me by their misrepresentations and aspersions of my character, made to cover their own villainy, on their arrival (during my absence), in the United States; I take the earliest opportunity after my return to lay the true, well supported state of facts before the Public...

Captain Balch's opening statement had many more lines, covering his appreciation to all concerned. He was forced into public comment because the mutineers had, as he noted, arrived in the United States ahead of him, which gave them the chance to tell their story first. A news item in the *Gazette*, datelined Providence, Rhode Island, January 19, 1799, shows the tack the mutineers took. The ship *Charles* of Boston, Captain Barnard, "on the 11th spoke the ship *Strafford*, Balch, late master, of Boston, from St. Ubes, bound to Norfolk in distress. Captain Balch had quitted the *Strafford* on the 28th of December, and went aboard a vessel bound for Oporto [Portugal], in consequence of his vessel leaking—mate and crew staid by her." Balch's former shipmates put their stake on those last six words to avoid charges of mutiny. The immediate effect was to put Balch in a rather despicable light. It is impossible to give Captain Balch's deposition in full, but excerpts paint a far different picture than that presented by the crew.

Balch testified that the *Strafford* sailed from St. Ubes "laden with a cargo of salt, bound to Portsmouth...; she being tight, staunch, stiff and strong, and well and sufficiently fitted, furnished and provided with every necessary, and a suitable crew for such an intended voyage..." Written in the third person, the deposition tells of the problems that arose about Christmas Day:

> ...He experienced a heavy gale of wind at different points of the compass, by the violence of which, and his mate and people's not exerting themselves with that energy which was their duty, his best sails were so much injured as to be unfit for service without undergoing great repairs, and the ship from laboring and straining caused to make about 150 strokes of water per hour...

With all these factors in mind, Balch elected to head south to avoid the worst of a North Atlantic crossing in winter. Further, he put the crew on short rations, not having any idea when he could make port. On November 30th, he fell in with an English brig, the *Nymph*, but she couldn't help because she was on short rations herself. The situation worsened as the weeks went by. The narrative continued:

> ...On the 23rd of December, the wind being S.E., he
> steered to the N.W. and had fine weather until 4 A.M. the wind
> hauling around to S.S.W. he close reefed his fore and main top
> sails and then left the deck, ordering the mate to call him
> immediately if the wind hauled away any further to the
> westward, or there was any alteration in the weather; at half
> past 6 A.M. finding the ship to go through the water very fast, he
> went on deck and as soon as he could reach the helm, got it up,
> every sail that was set blew from the ropes, the fore-yard broke
> off in the slings, and the main sail and mizzen that were furled to
> the yard, blew away likewise...

After that, the *Strafford* was a plaything for wind and waves,
shipping water and suffering severe damage. Balch exhausted the
crew by making them pump 300 strokes to the hour. For 36 hours, the
Strafford lay dead in the water before Balch could get a bit of sail set.
As if the *Strafford* didn't have enough misfortunes, the master found that
much of the ship's bread had been spoiled by flooding; what was left had
been improperly baked in St. Ubes. That was the *Strafford*'s plight on
Christmas Day, 1798, with the crew getting more surly every hour.

> ...Night approaching, he went forward to hurry them
> with the fore-yard, finding work went very slowly; when Samuel
> Huffman, boatswain, and Peter Snow, seaman, answered him
> with abusive language, called him a damned rascal, told him to
> go aft about his business, that he was starving them, and that
> they could not and would not do any more duty, that the ship
> might sink and be damned...[8]

Captain Balch tried to force the boatswain below, and they grappled,
with the boatswain trying to force the master overboard. Balch blocked
the effort, flattened the boatswain with his fist, and dragged him aft to
secure him in irons. The boatswain's cries of murder brought all hands
aft, with the intent of killing the captain. With no other recourse, Balch
had to beg for his life, while the mate stood by and let the crew do as it
wished. The odd part is that Balch never identified the mate, although
he pinpointed at least three of the crew. This hints that the mate had
strong Port of Portsmouth connections. Two days after Christmas, a
sail was seen, and Captain Balch was able to get a boat in the water and
row to the brig *Portland*. The most that came out of that was swap of
water for bread. The brig's captain had the decency to go to the *Strafford*
and assure the crew he had done all he could for them. Two of the
rebellious crew wanted to go on the brig but that was denied. The two
vessels parted, and Balch ordered the mate to get on what sail he could
but was cursed by the mate and told, "we will do as we please."

Despite his problems, Balch had found one man in whom he could confide, John Kelley, a seaman. Kelley told him the mutiny was led by the mate. So Balch moved Kelley aft to officers' country and kicked out the mate. Shortly after, a sail was seen and was hailed. She was a Danish freighter, the *Engehaden*, under Captain Hans Peter Molsen. Captain Balch went on board the *Engehaden* and arranged for supplies, only to find that while he was negotiating, the nameless, faithless mate had hoisted sail and run off with the *Strafford*.

Once arrived in Oporto, both Balch and the Danish captain were put through sharp grillings by various consuls. Captain Molsen stood firm under questioning, insisting that his cargo of grain barred him from coming about and pursuing the *Strafford*. How did it all come out? There is no sequel to be found in the *Gazette* files. The crew and mate made points by getting their story in first. By the time Balch's version reached the United States, the mutineers were scattered to the four winds. Portsmouth shippers must have believed Balch because he continued to command their vessels. Yet, the annoying question will always remain as to who that pusillanimous mate was.

The *Strafford*, once freed of legal tangles and restored to her owners, continued to sail the seas. A marine item noted her arrival from Ireland on the Delaware River in 1801 with between 400 and 500 passengers. One hundred others had died en route, such were the perils of passage in the days of sail.

Stockport

Specifications: Built in 1796. Burthen, 215 tons; length, 83 feet; beam, 26.3 feet; depth, 12.25 feet. Owner, William Jackson of Boston.

Hantonia

Specifications: Built in 1799. Burthen, 221 tons; length, 82.4 feet; beam, 25 feet; depth, 12.5 feet. Owner, February 19, 1800, William Hale.

There is little doubt that the *Hantonia*'s first voyage went around the triangle. From Liverpool, she came to Portsmouth on June 25, 1800. She had taken only 41 days from Liverpool, although her captain, John Moulton, had been ill for days before she sailed and had to be carried on board. Moulton's illness kept him from bringing any newspapers from England, essential for the *Gazette* in the dispensing of foreign news to its readers. Captain Moulton repeated the voyage in 1801, coming in from Liverpool on October 27th. The next year, William Hale was sharing ownership with brother Samuel, along with Thomas Sheafe and Charles Coffin. The listed master for the first *Hantonia* was Ichabod Rollins, who came in from Cadiz, August 7, 1805, with salt for the owners. With the Embargo Act in effect, she was sold in New York in 1807.

Thomas Gordon

Specifications Built in 1800. Burthen, 194 tons; length, 78.6 feet; beam, 24 feet; depth, 12 feet. Owner, January 9, 1801, James Sheafe.

Where the *Thomas Gordon* was between the time she was registered and February 7, 1807, when she came in from Portugal under James Place, isn't known and can only be a matter of speculation. She probably sailed out of ports other than Portsmouth, and it is possible that some Portsmouth entries were missed. In May 1807, with the Embargo Act restricting trade with France and England, the ownership of the *Thomas Gordon* changed to William Sheafe, Matthew S. Marsh and Jacob Pickering.

The new owners sent the *Thomas Gordon* to Europe, under Charles Treadwell. He returned to Portsmouth, September 21, 1807, from Rotterdam. Treadwell held the command three years. His last voyage was from the West Indies in 1810. Captain Thomas Savage took her to St. Ubes, returning on September 21, 1811. In January 1812, the *Thomas Gordon* was at Kingston, Jamaica. During the War of 1812, she apparently was one of the many American vessels that lay in port, gathering cobwebs in her rigging and barnacles on her bottom.

After the War, in November 1816, Captain Savage brought her from Rotterdam into Boston in 65 days.[9] Samuel Hobart was her next master. He sailed from Portsmouth in April 1817 for Savannah, and in September completed the triangle by coming home in 54 days from Liverpool.[10] Hobart made another voyage in 1820, the year *Thomas Gordon* was broken up.

On March 21, 1821, a few months after the *Thomas Gordon* was broken up, the *Portsmouth Oracle* published a poignant letter:

Information Wanted

To the Editor of the New York *National Advocate*, I observed in your Marine list, of the 28th of October last, that the ship *Thomas Gordon*, from Liverpool, had been spoken on the 21st of that month, on George's Bank, bound to Portsmouth, since which time I have regularly examined the marine news, but have seen no account of her arrival. Having a brother on board named *William Brown*, of whose fate I feel anxious to learn, the editors of the eastward will do a particular favor by giving, through the medium of their papers, such information of the above ship as they may possess; and also, that they will publish this paragraph, that in case the said William Brown has arrived in this country, that he may be induced to write to his disconsolate sister, who is anxious to hear from him.

The editor of the *Oracle* appended to the letter what information he had about the *Thomas Gordon* and a crew member, William Brown. After the *Thomas Gordon* came into Portsmouth on her last passage, October 25, 1820, William Brown took his discharge from her on November 10th, and, on November 14th, signed the articles on the ship *Frederick*, with John S. Davis, master, bound for Haiti, and she sailed on the 22nd. It can only be hoped that William Brown eventually was reunited with his "disconsolate sister", but the seamen of that day were a nomadic lot.

Aurora

Specifications: Built in 1801 by Richard Tripe. Square stern, billet head. Burthen, 243 tons; length, 86.9 feet; beam, 25.4 feet; depth, 12.7 feet. Owner, October 12, 1801, Elijah Hall.

It is hard to believe that a hard-bitten old seadog like Elijah Hall could have had a hand in giving his vessel the romantic name of Aurora, the rosy-fingered goddess who precedes the sun at dawn. But if he did, he lost no time in putting her to work. She made two voyages under his onwership. Robert Oram brought her in from Lisbon, September 25, 1802. Oram, a Portsmouth man, had previously commanded the *Randolph* for Hall. The *Aurora*'s second voyage was under John Bowles. Hall advertised the sailing, seeking freight or passengers to Charleston.[11] It was a triangular voyage, Portsmouth to Charleston, then to Europe and return to Portsmouth. Captain Bowles came home on July 27, 1803, in 37 days from the Isle of May (off Scotland), and Hall promptly advertised a thousand hogshead of salt, "good for country use."[12]

Elijah Hall sold the *Aurora* in Boston in 1805, and next, and last, word of her appeared in the *Gazette* on February 18, 1806. With a fortune—$45,000—on board, she had been captured by a British warship and taken into Gibraltar. The prize court condemned her, despite the fact she was bound from a neutral port to one in Britain. There was no way to appeal.

Sampson

Specifications: Built in 1801 by Edward Sargent. Square stern, dragon figurehead. Burthen, 236 tons; length, 85 feet; beam, 25.4 feet; depth, 12.7 feet. Owners, December 31, 1801, Jacob Sheafe and Richard Salter Tibbetts.

Richard Salter Tibbetts was master of the *Sampson* for three voyages; two were around the triangle. The third was to Demerara in 1803, bringing in a cargo of sugar for himself and Sheafe. They sold the *Sampson* out of the Portsmouth District in 1804.

Baltic

Specifications: Built in 1801 by Stephen Tobey. Square stern, billet head. Burthen, 262 tons; length, 88.8 feet; beam, 26.1 feet; depth, 13.05 feet. Owners, April 3, 1803, William Hale and George F. Blunt.

The *Baltic* was the first ship fabricated by the itinerant shipwright Stephen Tobey. Before launching the *Baltic*, Tobey had built two brigs in Somersworth. With Joseph Coe of Durham and Joseph Swazey of Exeter, Tobey was one of the leading builders on the upper waters of the Portsmouth District. In all, Tobey built nine ships, plus several other vessels of varying size and rig in four different up-river towns.

George F. Blunt took the *Baltic* on her first voyage, returning to Portsmouth on December 12, 1802, from St. Ubes. Blunt was master when the *Baltic* came in from Liverpool in October 1803. To the *Baltic* and Captain Blunt went the honor of transporting the United States envoy and his family to Spain. That was in May 1805.[13] The Embargo Act probably had an effect on the *Baltic*. In 1809, Blunt sold her out of the district. In 1811, a ship *Baltic* under a Captain Adams, perhaps the same vessel, went ashore at St. Mary's, South Carolina, but managed to get off without damage.

Triumphant

Specifications: Built in 1802 by Richard Tripe. Square stern, billet head. Burthen, 203 tons; length, 80.2 feet; beam, 24.3 feet; depth, 12.15 feet. Owners, January 29, 1803, Samuel Chauncey and Henry Ladd.

The *Triumphant*'s career in the Port of Portsmouth was short. Samuel Chauncey went south in her and returned home from Havana on June 4, 1803, in 17 days. She was sold in Boston in 1804.

Aeolus

Specifications: Built in 1803 by Stephen Tobey. Square stern, billet head. Burthen, 272 tons; length, 91.8 feet; beam, 26.1 feet; depth, 13 feet. Owners, March 4, 1803, Samuel and William Hale.

To give the name of Aeolus, god of the winds, to a wind-propelled vessel seems appropriate. The *Aeolus* made a few passages out of Portsmouth under Jacob E. Treadwell. The Hales put the *Aeolus* into the triangle trade. In June 1804, her namesake paid her a visit as she was sailing from Charleston to Elsinore, Denmark. Two days out, she ran into a wild gale.[14] One of the hands was killed by lightning. The next bolt hit the foremast, shivering it to splinters. So she called into her home port to repair the damage. Captain Treadwell, on another triangular voyage came into Portsmouth from Liverpool on December 1, 1807.

From a log kept on the *Aeolus* in 1809 comes a real glimpse into what a ship on the triangular trade routes did. The log is one of the treasures of the Old Berwick Historical Society, South Berwick, Maine. Although the captain isn't named and the log was kept by several different penmen, Jacob Treadwell was master. The log gets off to a bizarre start with a note on a Monday in September 1809 that John Gardner "the chief mate of the Ship *Aeolus* Deserted the Ship taking with him his baggage and the Ship's Log Book." As often remarked, ship's logs are rarely dramatic documents. At the time of the initial entry, the *Aeolus* was lying in George's Dock, Liverpool. There was no bewailing about the perfidy of the mate; the entries deal tersely with items of ship's business, with the weather understandably getting major attention. While in port, there were simply daily entries, telling of getting the vessel ready for sea, taking on cargo and the like. October 7, 1809, is typical:

> Those 24 hours pleasent with Light Ares from the Eastward Employd in taking in salt Recieved on bord 118 tuns finsh'd main top Gallant and bent it got up the yard.

On Saturday, October 14, Captain Treadwell ended these preliminary entries, saying, "This being the end of my harbour journal So I begin to Sea". *Aeolus* went to sea the next day, after a pilot had come on board. For the next 47 days of passage, the log is a weather report and a record of ship management. The 22nd day offers typical remarks:

> Those 24 hours begins with moderate Breezes and foggy wr At 4 am spoke the ship *Reaper* of & for Philadelphia...let one reef out of Each top sail & fore sail set Jibb main sail & mizzen top sail.

>Strong Breezes at 10 am took a reef in the top sails in jibb and main sail

>Latter part more moderate...So ends those 24 hours with Light Breezes & foggy wr.

John Hill Sick

On November 30 came the last entry of the passage:

>Those 24 hours begins with Light Breezes and pleasent weather Emplyd in turning to the windward between the Sholes & Rye Beach.

>Middle part Light ares variable...

>Latter part calm at 6 am got in and come too with the small bower [anchor] within the Light House [Fort Point Light] in 7 fathoms watter furld the sails & the Captain went to town At 11 am the Capt came on bord with a pilot waid and made sail

>So ends those 24 hours Light Area variable. I quit my Sea Journal & proceed to my harbour journal

For the next 17 days, the log is a daily account of getting out the cargo and doing routine work on board. The *Aeolus* tied up alongside the ship *Mars*, and one of the captain's first moves was to discharge the ship's people. On Sunday, December 17, the pilot came on board at 6 a.m., the sails were set "and at 8 cast off from the warf and Sails in company with several vessels bound out." The *Aeolus* was heading for New York where she had been sold, but there is no hint of that in the log. During the five days to New York, a sea journal was kept, and, after arrival, a land journal was kept until December 30, 1809, when the entries come to an abrupt end; presumably because the new owners had taken over.

India Packet

Specifications: Built in 1803 by Isaac Bourn. Square stern, billet head. Burthen, 286 tons; length, 95.1 feet; beam, 26.2 feet; depth, 12.2 feet. Owner, September 5, 1803, John Rindge.

John Rindge had the *India Packet* built for his own use and made at least one voyage in her as master. A shipping note reported that the *India Packet* was at Isle of France on February 27, 1804.[15] Presumably, Rindge came home in her and sold her the next year.

Piscataqua

Specifications: Built in 1804 by Stephen Paul. Square stern, billet head. Burthen, 323 tons; length, 97.7 feet; beam, 27.5 feet; depth, 13.75 feet. Owner, August 24, 1805, John Rindge.

John Rindge's short-term investment in ships like the *India Packet* and the *Piscataqua* leads to speculation that he was more a ship broker than trader. He did own a brig, the *Favorite*, for almost ten years, but other vessels in which he had an interest, like the ship *Alligator*, had short shrift at his hands. The first *Piscataqua* was sold by him within weeks after her registration. The new owners were in Philadelphia.

Laconia

Specifications: Built in 1805 by Stephen Tobey. Burthen, 263 tons; length, 89.1 feet; beam, 26.1 feet; depth, 13.05 feet. Owners, February 5, 1806, Samuel and William Hale.

One of the incidents in the story of the *Laconia* illustrates fully the hazards of a seafarer's life in the years prior to the War of 1812. Under Captain John Walker, the *Laconia* made several entrances into Portsmouth with salt from Liverpool, but one in October 1809 offered a dramatic tale. While on her passage, the *Laconia* was captured by a French privateer and taken to a French port. As quite often happened, the only way for Captain Walker to win her freedom was to have some of his people held as hostages until ransom was paid. Among the men he left behind was the mate Samuel Pray. Months later, notice of Samuel Pray was made in a news item:

> Letters have been received by the wife of Samuel Pray, late mate of the ship *Laconia*, Captain Walker of this port, and owned by Samuel and William Hale Esqrs of Dover, dated at Bayonne, March the 16, 1810, wherein he states he has suffered everything but death in prisons and hospitals, and just recovered from a severe sickness occasioned by unwholesome air and diet, and close confinement with which he is afflicted; that the Merchants which own the privateer which captured the *Laconia*, are determined not to release him, nor allow him any assistance until the money is paid, or security given for its payment, which was promised on the release of the ship; that he has applied to the American Consul there for assistance, who has afforded nothing for his relief, and that he depends for his daily support on charity from American vessels, which have been carried into France, and should they be condemned he expects no better fate than to

starve in prison, unless some better measures are taken than has been, to ransom him. The others of the crew that were taken out of the *Laconia*, are with him, and share the same fate.[16]

A few weeks later, another item was published:

> Mr. Samuel Pray, former Mate of the Ship Laconia, of this place, who was taken from the *Laconia*, on her passage from Liverpool, in November last...as hostage for the ransom of the Ship, has arrived at Baltimore, from France...[17]

Shortly after that item was published, there was a joyful reunion of the Pray family in their Deer Street home. The timing of Samuel Pray's release shows it was done as quickly as possible, although to Samuel Pray and his companions it must have been like an eternity. Even with that, Pray made out far better than William Bennett, the man the wealthy Portsmouth merchant Samuel Cutts left to die in a foreign prison. Pray didn't ship with Captain Walker when the latter took the *Laconia* to Havana in 1811. It was probably well that he didn't. Walker, his mate George Weld and a seaman, Joseph Bigelow, all died there of yellow fever.[18] Ebenezer Rowe brought the *Laconia* home and was given permanent command. Records are skimpy, but the *Laconia* was lost at sea in 1817.[19]

As for Samuel Pray: he died in Brooklyn, New York, on January 31, 1836, at the young age of 46. Perhaps the privations in that French prison took a deeper toll on his body than realized. His obituary said, in part:

> Capt. Pray was for many years an enterprising successful shipmaster; but has latterly been engagd in shipbuilding and mercantile pursuits...He desired not great wealth; he strove not for it...[20]

The editor knew Samuel Pray, so it may be true that he didn't seek great wealth. He did, however, acquire extensive shipping interests, thus laying the foundation for the holdings acquired by his son, Captain Samuel Pray.

Montgomery

Specifications: Built in 1805 by Benjamin Remick. Square stern, billet head. Burthen, 261 tons; length, 87.6 feet; beam, 26.3 feet; depth, 13.15 feet. Owners, December 13, 1805, John McClintock and Daniel Durell.

In all probability, the ship *Montgomery* was named to honor Brigadier General Richard Montgomery who had been killed 30 years before in a vain attempt to capture Quebec. As an old Revolutionary War veteran, John McClintock certainly would have been sensitive to such things.

Captain James Orne was master of the first *Montgomery* in her early voyages. Orne brought her in from Spain in September 1806, the eve of the Embargo Act. There are no Portsmouth records for her after that until 1810, when she came in from Ireland on October 6th. The Embargo could have been responsible for the hiatus, although she also could have been sailing out of other ports. In 1811, Captain Orne brought her in from Hull, England, in ballast. James Tibbetts was master the next time she came into Portsmouth from Cadiz, September 3, 1813. At that time, McClintock sold out his interest to the veteran shipmaster John Riley, Jr., of Dover.

In December 1813, State Street in Portsmouth was swept by a devastating fire that burned everything from the present Stone Church to the water's edge. Despite heroic efforts, there was some looting as the following advertisement shows:

> Taken from on board the ship *Montgomery*, soon after the late fire, a large spyglass, fixed over on the outside with twine, in a neat manner, forming various figures; one Hadley's quadrant with a chocolate-covered case; two bolts of raven duck, had been wet...If the above articles are in the possession of any person who shall return them, or any part thereof, or give information as to where they may be found, will be suitably rewarded for their trouble and receive the thanks of
>
> William Rice[21]

The last voyages of the *Montgomery* were under John H. Sise. She was broken up in Liverpool in 1821, having become unseaworthy.[22]

Brutus

Specifications: Built in 1806 by Stephen Tobey. Square stern, billet head. Burthen, 316 tons; length, 97.7 feet; beam, 27.2 feet; depth, 13.6 feet. Owners, March 2, 1807, George F. and Charles Blunt and Joshua Haven.

For the *Brutus*, there was the unhappy circumstance of being launched a short time before the Embargo Act paralyzed American shipping. But she made at least one voyage. George F. Blunt went to Russia in her in 1807. The next entry is a return by a Captain Macey in 1810 from Bonavista.

Nelson, in his customs records' compilation, dismisses the *Brutus* as having been captured by the British in the War of 1812.[23] Captain Blunt, however, was in command of a *Brutus* on a voyage to Russia in the summer of 1815, a vessel Nelson described as a brig of 236 tons.

Ships were sometimes cut down to the two-masted rigging of a brig and that may have happened in this case. The fact remains, the customs' records have only one *Brutus*, and Captain Blunt made many voyages in a vessel so named.

Ariadne

Specifications: Built in 1806 by Stephen Paul. Square stern, billet head. Burthen, 263 tons; length, 89.2 feet; beam, 26.1 feet; depth, 13.05 feet. Owners, March 25, 1807, James Shapley and Joshua Haven.

Often the names of sailing vessels show some romantic quality in the men who owned them. The original Ariadne was, in Greek mythology, the daughter of King Minos of Crete, who gave Theseus a clue to make his way out of a Cretan labyrinth, but he later jilted her.[23] The *Ariadne* that was built in Dover had little allure. She was typical of the era, only a bit more than three times her length as to width—almost a sailing washtub. She made at least one voyage before the Embargo crippled shipping. George Humphreys brought her in from Liverpool on January 20, 1808. She was sold in Philadelphia later that year. Humphrey was in command in 1811, however, when he brought her into New York with salt from St. Ubes. She had been dismasted and lost two men overboard.[24] With that, she disappeared from marine listings.

Ossian

Specifications: Built in 1808, under direction of William Hale. Square stern, billet head. Burthen, 286 tons; length, 90.7 feet; beam, 26.3 feet; depth, 13.15 feet. Owners, May 3, 1809, William and Samuel Hale.

Who would suspect that pragmatic businessmen like the Hales might have a touch of the poet in them? Such is evidenced by their naming their vessel after Ossian, a Gaelic bard in early Scotland.[25]

Poetic or not, the ship *Ossian*'s active life under Captain Ichabod Rollins was brief indeed. In one of his first trips on October 31, 1811, Captain Rollins brought the *Ossian* into Portsmouth in 60 days from Liverpool. Bound for Amelia Island, she was in distress and had been so ripped by storms that she had to put into the first available port. In a newspaper report, Rollins said the weather for the first 40 days had been "one continuous succession of gales, generally W to SW, during which the ship had been in a dangerous situation, owing to her not working."[26] Because of the usual contrary winter winds that prevail on this coast, it wasn't until the middle of January 1812 that the *Ossian* sailed for Amelia Island. Again, there is a paucity of records, but the *Ossian* was wrecked on November 3, 1813, on Turk's Island.[27]

Strafford

Specifications: Built in 1809 by Stephen Tobey. Square stern, serpent figurehead. Burthen, 266 tons; length, 92.5 feet; beam, 25.6 feet; depth, 11.5 feet. Owners, April 6, 1810, Jacob Sheafe, Stephen Patten, Jr., and Robert Rogers.

Second of the name, the *Strafford* was another vessel built in the Portsmouth District to suffer from the War of 1812. Her maiden voyage was under Robert Rogers, an owner, who brought her from Leith, Scotland, in November 1810. It took her 67 days, and then she had to put into Salem before coming on to Portsmouth. In February 1812, the *Strafford* was in Ireland, and returned to Portsmouth by way of St. Ubes. Through the war years, the *Strafford* either lay at her Portsmouth berth, gathering cobwebs, or worked out of other ports.

Once word of the end of the War of 1812 arrived in Portsmouth, the *Strafford* went into the cotton trade under a Captain Smith. Instead of going round the triangle, however, the *Strafford* came to Boston, then to Portsmouth on September 8th. Smith took her out again in November, sailing for Savannah. In January 1817, command went to Edward Shannon, but he was killed by yellow fever, along with two of his crew, David Ham and Richard Harvey. That was in Martinique, and John Briard brought the *Strafford* back to Portsmouth with rum and molasses for Jacob Sheafe.[28] A Captain Harman took her to Norfolk, but when she came in from Liverpool on September 24, 1818, Robert Rogers was again master. He took the *Strafford* to Havana and was there in January, reporting the loss of four men to yellow fever.

There are gaps in the customs' records, but the *Strafford* was commanded by John Dale for at least one voyage and was reported as coming in from Liverpool in 1823 with salt, coal and crates to Stephen Patten, and sheet iron and 50 packages of hardware to Pickering & Sherburne. Captain W. Cammett sailed her for Demerara in the week of February 24, 1824, returning in July. Cammett had one more voyage, finishing June 10, 1825, and command passed to Joshua Bailey. Bailey brought into Portsmouth, on July 20, 1826, 11 immigrants from the West Indies—the DeBritton family, listed in the records as John, 42, gentleman, Ann, 32, his wife; and their nine children, ranging in age from 2 to 17.[29] Besides the DeBrittons, the *Strafford* brought a cargo of molasses for Charles Cushing, by then one of the owners. Captain Bailey was master in 1828 when the *Strafford* ran into trouble. She had sailed for the River Platte in South America but lost rigging and deckload and sprang a bad leak. She put into St. Pierre, Martinique, where she had been the year before. A news item reported later that the *Strafford* had been condemned and sold.

James

Specifications: Built in 1810 by Joseph Smith and Rogers & Patten. Square stern, billet head. Burthen, 332 tons; length, 101.6 feet; beam, 27.7 feet; depth, 12 feet. Owners, April 17, 1811, Thomas Sheafe and Charles Coffin.

The first *James* had a short life under the Stars and Stripes. She was captured by the British in the War of 1812. The *James* did make one voyage around the triangle in 1811, and it could be she was captured on the return leg. A small mystery is posed by an advertisement in 1815 in which the ship *James*, 242 tons, was offered for sale.[30] Aside from Nelson's statement that she was taken by the British, there is a discrepancy of nearly a hundred tons.[31]

Hantonia

Specifications: Built in 1811 by Stephen Tobey. Square stern, billet head. Burthen, 299 tons; length, 96.8 feet; beam, 26.5 feet; depth, 12 feet. Owners, March 4, 1812, William and Samuel Hale.

Like so many other vessels built before the War of 1812, the second *Hantonia* was idled by the conflict. Because the two ships had the same owners in the Hales, it can be speculated that journeyman shipwright, Stephen Tobey, worked on the first in 1799. He became an accredited master builder in that year with a brig.

Where the second *Hantonia* spent the weary months of "Mr. Madison's War" can only be speculated. Her first recorded entrance into Portsmouth came on November 2, 1815, when she arrived from Exuma in the West Indies under James Adams of Portsmouth, with 1,300 hogsheads of salt. A news item said she was the "only American ship that has visited Exuma for several years."[32]

Ichabod Rollins, who had also commanded the first *Hantonia*, was the second master and stayed on her until 1820, when he apparently retired from the sea. Rollins' second voyage saw him coming in from Gothenburg, Sweden, with a load of iron for the Hales. In October 1817, the *Hantonia* arrived at New York from the Balize in 36 days with a load of cotton. Five had died on the passage, among them J.J. Lunt of Portsmouth; one of the seamen had fallen overboard. From New York, she crossed to Liverpool, finally returning to Portsmouth in September 1818 in 68 days with salt and crates for the Hales. The *Hantonia* arrived in Portsmouth in October 1820.[33] When she cleared out, she was gone until 1823. In that year, William Tisdale, a resident of Islington Street in Portsmouth, brought the *Hantonia* in from St. Ubes on April 1. Tisdale lost no time in a turnaround. He was back in home port by

September. Tisdale had *Hantonia* until the Shaw brothers bought her. The Shaws put Jeremiah Pike in as master, and he promptly took the *Hantonia* around the triangle. She arrived in Portsmouth from Liverpool on September 20, 1828, not only with the usual salt and coal, but also immigrants: Annabella Bird, 16, was from England; the other five were Irish. They included Nicholas Shaw, 23, a farmer; John White, 37, a farmer, and Betty, 34, his wife; Anastatia White, 30, also a farmer, and Mary, his wife. Carrying passengers was a familiar story with the *Hantonia*. In 1826, she brought 138 immigrants into Baltimore in 50 days from Belfast, Ireland.[35]

The *Hantonia* sailed from the Port of Portsmouth for the last time in 1829, having been sold in New York.

Orion

Specifications: Built in 1811 by Zechariah Beal. Square stern, alligator figurehead. Burthen 323 tons; length, 101 feet; beam, 26.9 feet; depth, 11.9 feet. Owners, February 14, 1812, Rogers & Patten and Joseph Smith.

Ignoring the mythology involved, what more appropriate name for a seagoing vessel than Orion, one of the great constellations seafarers constantly used for a guide. The ship *Orion* was one of three fabricated by Zechariah Beal, who was a stepson of Master William Badger and may have been apprenticed to him. Beal's other ships were the *Isabella Henderson*, built in Portsmouth, and the *Watson*, in Newmarket.

Unfortunately for the investors in the *Orion*, she was launched a few months before the outbreak of the War of 1812. Early in her career, she made a voyage. One of her owners, Robert Rogers, went to Alexandria, Virginia, then to Lisbon, where she arrived May 10, 1812, in 34 days from Alexandria.[36] The crossing was stormy, and the *Orion* lost two hands overboard. One, Thomas Young, apparently had family in Portsmouth because an item in the marine news said "his friends and connections may have his effects by applying to Joseph Smith or Rogers & Patten of Dover (N.H.)." The item showed no such concern for the other man lost, Benjamin Cain. When war came, the *Orion* ebbed out her days, rising and falling on Piscataqua's tides.

With the end of the war, Captain Rogers took the *Orion* south in 1816 and crossed to England. In 1817, there was a change of command. Under a Captain Thompson, she made a triangular voyage, arriving at Boston on October 6th with a cargo of salt, coal, crates and merchandise after 74 days at sea.[37] Not until December did she get home. In 1818, she was reported as being at Havre on February 13, 45 days from Portsmouth.[38] With that entry, she disappeared from marine news. Nelson noted she was condemned as unseaworthy in 1820.[39]

Janus

Specifications: Built in 1811 by William Jellison. Square stern, billet head. Burthen, 309 tons; length, 97.5 feet; beam, 26.9 feet; depth, 12.2 feet. Owners, December 25, 1811, John McClintock, O. Crosby and John Williams.

The unlucky *Janus* was named for the god in Roman mythology who provided the name for the first month of the year. Janus had two faces and, to the Romans, symbolized the end and the beginning. Whatever the reason for her name, the *Janus* was taken by a British warship early in the War of 1812.

Martha

Specifications: Built in 1818 by Stephen Tobey. Square stern, billet head. Burthen, 300 tons; length, 98.4 feet; beam, 26.3 feet; depth, 13.15 feet. Owners, March 24, 1819, Samuel and William Hale.

The launching of the *Martha* ended a seven-year hiatus in Dover ship-building, a period in which only eight vessels of any description had been constructed. These were the proverbial "seven lean years" and only two more three-masted, square-rigged vessels would be launched in Dover. The *Martha* was built in a shipyard at Squall Point on the Cocheco, where the Dover Public Works Department is located.[40]

Through her early years, Thomas Lunt of Lunt's Lane, Portsmouth, was master. Her departure on April 3, 1819, for Savannah, was noted, and she came home in mid-January.[41] On her next voyage, the *Martha* was gone 28 months, coming home from Liverpool on July 11, 1822, in 34 days with salt, iron and coal for the Hales. Before surrendering command to Andrew Hussey, Lunt made six more voyages in the *Martha*, several in the increasingly active cotton trade. When Captain Lunt left the *Martha*, he took command of the *Ann Parry*. Captain Hussey made the same kinds of voyages as his predecessor. On one of them, the *Martha*, sailing from Havana for Boston, had to put into Charleston on January 20, 1835. She had been struck on December 27th by a "tremendous gale, had the decks swept of everything but the long boat and sprung a leak. Half the crew were frost-bitten or otherwise disabled."[42]

Captain Hussey was master when the *Martha* was sold in Boston in 1835. Records fail to show any further commands for him; he was 52, and he lived another 26 years. Usually, when a vessel was sold out of the district, she vanished from local ken, but, in 1861, the same year as Captain Hussey's death, a for-sale advertisement in an English newspaper was published:

The United States Ship *Martha*, 274 tons English measurement:—Length 97 feet; breadth 25 feet; depth 19 feet; built at Dover (New-Hampshire) in 1818, of the very best materials; has since been rebuilt at very great expense, and was yellow-metalled in July 1860, and classed 3-4ths in French Veritas; carries 450 tons dead weight; sails well, and shifts without ballast. Now lying at Sheerness. For further particulars, apply to
David Brown
146 Leadenhall Street, E.C.

To this English item, the Portsmouth editor, Charles W. Brewster, appended the following:

Here still afloat is the good old ship "Martha, Capt. Lunt," as we used to put it in type when we first began to print in 1818—43 years ago! She was built on our river by Stephen Tobey, for Samuel and William Hale of Dover. We need no better evidence of the durability of our Piscataqua ships.[43]

Lydia

Specifications: Built in 1820 by Stephen Tobey. Square stern, billet head. Burthen 293 tons; length, 96.8 feet; beam, 26.2 feet; depth, 13.1 feet. Owners, February 9, 1821, Samuel and William Hale.

Considered the sister ship of the *Martha*, the *Lydia* was constructed in the same way in the Hales' shipyard at Squall Point. She was named in honor of William Hale's wife. When it came time to take her down the Cocheco, the riggers had to float her over the fish weirs by the use of empty water casks.[44]

On February 18, 1821, the "new and elegant ship *Lydia*" went to sea.[45] Her first master was George Humphreys, who brought her in from St. Petersburg with iron and hemp on December 22, 1822. Humphries was followed by several other Portsmouth captains, including William Parker, for whom she was his first command. Captain Parker's obituary noted he was born in 1804, and he took command of the *Lydia* at the age of 19. That doesn't check against customs records, which show Captain Parker first bringing the *Lydia* into Portsmouth from Liverpool in November 1829, which would make him 25.[46] Although mariners often became masters at young ages, 19 seems too youthful for command of a fair-sized merchant ship like the *Lydia*, so the Customs entry carries more weight than the obituary. Regardless, Captain Parker had a long career as a mariner, finally retiring from the sea in 1865 and dying 24 years later. Among the Port of Portsmouth-built ships he commanded were the *Pontiac*, *Arabella* and the clipper *Emily Farnum*.

Ebenezer Thompson had preceded Parker as master, making three voyages in the *Lydia*, arriving from St. Ubes in 1823, Gibraltar in 1825 and Liverpool in 1827. One of the *Lydia's* most important entries came on July 7, 1833, when Charles Flanders brought her in from Liverpool with 115 passengers—77 adults, 28 children—on board. It was one of the largest shiploads of immigrants ever landed in Portsmouth. They were mostly Irish nationals. One family, the Dimonds, was headed by John, 40, a mason; Margaret, 39, his wife, and eight children, 2 to 16. Others included Thomas Foley, 20 cooper; William Kane, 27, paver; James Kane, shoemaker. There was Margaret Lacey, 30, whose husband was in Boston. She brought with her seven children, 1 to 15.[47]

The *Lydia* went on the auction block on October 10, 1833, "to close a partnership."[48] Samuel Hale's advertisement read, in part:

> The ship LYDIA, as she came from the sea; 12 years old; 292 tons Burthen, Copper fastened, and new Coppered 20 months since.

> This vessel was built in Dover, of seasoned White Oak, under the direction of one of the present owners, and for his use,—sails fast, and carries a fair cargo, and is well calculated for a Whaler...

It should be noted that being "Copper-fastened" was a highly desirable quality in the days of wooden ships; copper spikes didn't rust out, iron ones did. When the advertisement spoke of her being "new Coppered 20 months since," it means the sheathing on her bottom had been replaced, copper being resistant to worms and harder for barnacles and weeds to gather on.

Samuel Cleaves, Elisha Crane and Captain Flanders bid in the Hales' interest, and Flanders took her to Charleston where she loaded for Liverpool. After unloading, the *Lydia* went to Rotterdam and returned to Portsmouth on November 1, 1834. In her came passengers: Wiss Dumbruff, 29, a lawyer from Germany; Philip Lynzing, 25, a physician from Germany; and Elizabeth, 24, Lynzing's wife. Sarah Jones and her son were also on the list of passengers, along with Eunice Blake of Ossipee, New Hampshire.[49]

Once again, the *Lydia* was sold. This time to a Salem whaling firm. An item from the *Salem Advertiser* was published locally:

> On stripping the whale ship *Lydia* of this port, now on the Railway, it was discovered that some rascal had bored five large auger holes in her run [part of a ship's bottom], evidently with the intention of sinking her at sea. It is supposed it must have been done the last time she was sheathed. The ship was purchased about three years ago at Portsmouth. Some explanation relative to this matter ought to be made by the late owners, or the person or person who put on the sheathing.[50]

It is doubtful that John Osgood, her Salem owner, ever learned who attempted the sabotage. The Hales apparently then owned her, but it isn't known where the sheathing job was done, at home or abroad. Prior to discovery of the auger holes, the *Lydia* had gone whaling, bringing in a cargo worth $42,620. After the holes were plugged, the *Lydia* went to the whaling grounds in the Indian Ocean. She returned to Salem, March 25, 1840, with a catch worth $25,672.[51] The *Lydia* was later owned in Fairhaven, Massachusetts, by F.R. Whitwell.

The *Lydia* was the last three-masted, square-rigged ship built in Dover for 17 years. A bark, the *Strafford*, 314 tons, was constructed in 1835, but the last and largest ship went down the ways in 1837. The builder of the *Oronoco*, 657 tons, was David Shiverick. But the *Oronoco's* brief story belongs in another volume.

V Durham

LITTLE INFORMATION REMAINS today to tell of the early importance Durham once had in Port of Portsmouth shipbuilding. Vessels of various kinds and sizes were being built there from the time of the first settlement. This was largely due to the fact that Durham, like Berwick, Dover, Exeter, Newmarket and Somersworth, was close to the forests wherein grew the majestic white oaks which were the source of the key timbers in framing the hulls of vessels. The rock maples, essential to the fabrication of sturdy keels, were plentiful, along with towering pines that went into masts, spars and planking. From the beginning, the craftsmen around Great Bay and the upper rivers exploited resources close at hand. In the earliest days, even the iron fastenings might have come from forges in Barrington.

Shipbuilding in Durham was concentrated below the falls in the Oyster River. Merchants throughout the Piscataqua Basin patronized these builders. An early instance is known in which Nathaniel Adams had the ship *Elizabeth* built there in 1756. A painting of that early ship is in the Portsmouth Athenaeum.

The period covered by this study, from the Revolution to 1829, probably spans the most active era on the Durham waterfront. During the course of those years, Durham's shipwrights built and launched 46 square-rigged, three-masted vessels, ranging in tonnage from the ship *Charlotte*'s 200 tons to 399 tons for the *Montgomery*. In the same span, 17 brigs (two-masted, square-rigged vessels), one bark (square-rigged on fore and main masts, schooner-rigged on the mizzen), 11 schooners and one sloop were built.

Then, almost as if cut off by an adze, shipbuilding came to an end in

Durham. The last ship was built in 1829, and from then on, only one brig and two schooners were produced. The last schooner was built at 78 tons by Stephen Paul in 1845.

There can be no doubt that the most prolific of the Durham ship-builders was Joseph Coe. To him goes credit for 11 full-rigged ships; he also built three brigs, one bark and four schooners. To top that, he went to Newmarket to build his largest vessel, the 403-ton ship *Nile*. All of these were built in nine years between 1818 and 1827.

More than 160 years ago, Joseph Coe was Durham's leading citizen. He was a selectman and the town's major employer. Joseph Coe grew up in Durham after his father, the Rev. Curtis Coe, was called to fill the pulpit there. Joseph Coe's burial place lies near the intersection of the direct road to Dover and the old New Hampshire Turnpike (U.S. Route 4). Tribute to Joseph Coe is found in the *History of Durham*. In those days, a section of Durham was known as Broth's Hill, where some of Joseph Coe's workmen lived. According to the lines of a poem:

> Broth Hill, the city of Seth;
> Were it not for Joe Coe,
> They would all starve to death.[1]

Another important shipwright in Durham was Robert Lapish, who put four full-rigged ships in the water between 1800 and 1808 and a brig, the *Hannah*, in 1810. The son-in-law of Robert Lapish, Andrew Simpson, became a builder in his own right, launching four ships in Durham, as well as investing in merchandising. Simpson's name is still well known in the area.

Oddly enough, the name Thompson, so commonly associated with Durham and honored by towering Thompson Hall on the University of New Hampshire campus, had little to do with Durham shipbuilding. Ebenezer Thompson did most of his stint in that field down-river in Portsmouth.

Stephen Paul, an itinerant builder, who fabricated ships in Kittery, Somersworth and Dover, launched six of his full-riggers in Durham. He started with the *Anglesey* in 1800. As previously noted, he also built the ship *Izzette* in Berwick in 1802 and rounded out a brilliant career with the schooner *Mary* in Durham in 1845, the last vessel to leave an Oyster River yard. Other shipwrights occasionally went to Durham to practice their trade. Their roles will be recorded in the stories of the vessels.

Charlotte

Specifications: Built in 1789. Burthen, 204 tons. Owners, April 20, 1789, Richard and Joseph Champney.

Why the Champneys went to the upper reaches of Great Bay to have a vessel built is explained by the fact that the top shipwrights were then congregated in that area. Prospective ship owners went where they could get their vessels built. Therefore, the *Charlotte* became the first square-rigger built in Durham after the Revolution. When the Champneys registered her, George Washington had yet to take oath as First President of the United States.

The Champneys didn't own the *Charlotte* for long. They sold her to William Tredick of Portsmouth in December, 1789. Under his ownership, the *Charlotte* was kept busy for four years. John Mendum was master on one voyage to Ireland, returning in June 1790. John McKay became master and sailed to Bideford, England, returning on October 30, 1790. She carried news of the continuing impressment of American seamen and that the British fleet was preparing for full-scale operations.[2] Although the Champneys had sold the *Charlotte*, they advertised her as sailing from London in the same issue as her arrival. In all, Captain McKay made four voyages to London before the *Charlotte* was sold in Boston in 1793. After the last arrival, which saw her entering Portsmouth on November 17, 1792, William Scott, at the "Sign of the Spinning Wheel," on Daniel Street, advertised "Fall and Winter Goods" that had come in the *Charlotte*.

Now a bit of a mystery: was this the ship *Charlotte* that was owned by Eliphalet Ladd between 1799 and 1800? The listed tonnages are different, yet a newspaper identified her as being of Portsmouth. Because this "mystery" *Charlotte* was owned in the Port of Portsmouth, what happened to her is of interest. The first printed item was a letter written by her master, William Ladd, and is a commentary on the perils of seafaring in 1800.[3] It said, in part:

> We were boarded off the Caycos' by his Britannic Majesty's sloop of war, the *Tysiphone*, commanded by Captain Davies, who put on board us 12 French passengers, taken from the American brig *Amazon* sent in here on suspicion. — He likewise sent about 20 lb. of beef and pork, and 30 weight of bread for their subsistence. — When we arrived at Port Royal [Jamaica], the ship was stopped and detained for 24 hours on account of said passengers; they not permitting us to go to town, although we had Capt. Davies protection for the passengers. The officer of police then gave us permission in writing, mentioning the Frenchmen as prisoners of war, with direction to turn them over to the Commissary of prisoners, *who*, when we had got to town, would not receive them, but told us not to land *them* on our peril; and would allow us nothing for their subsistence. We then applied to the Governor, and every officer who had anything to do with prisoners or French passengers, but none of them would

take cognizance of the matter, or allow us any satisfaction for their maintenance or the detention of the ship.

At length the Governor wrote us a billet, allowing us a half permission to land them on the condition of their immediately taking passage to America, which we could not guarantee—we of course landed them, but not without some fear of incurring the penalty, which is £200 for each passenger, and 6 months imprisonment for my self. This is a sample of English RECTITUDE!

Available records don't show what happened to this mysterious *Charlotte*, except the following published in 1801:

A Truly Melancholy Affair

Loss of the Ship Charlotte & Crew

....

Extract of a letter from Mr. Barksdale, freighter of the Ship *Charlotte* of this port, owned by Eliphalet Ladd, Esq.

I went on board the *Charlotte* at Cowes [Isle of Wight], bound for Flushing, the wind and the tide would not admit the ship to go in, and I went on shore in the pilot boat that came out for the ship in the evening, that night there came up a gale of wind, which drove the *Charlotte* on the banks, where every person and cargo were lost.

It supposed the gale was about the 10th of November...

The crew of the *Charlotte* were

Tho's Walton, master, of Portsmouth.

Henry Brown,	1st mate,	Kittery
Abraham Pray	2d ditto	
Samuel Ladd,	cook,	Newmarket.
Robert Chisham,	Seaman,	Kittery
John Tobey	do	do
..........Chisham	do	Do
Jesse Cillings,	do	a foreigner.
Levi Rand,	do	Rye
Isaac York	do	Newmarket
William Marden	do	Portsmouth
John Greward	do	do[4]

Whether or not the *Charlotte*, whose fate was given above, is the original Durham vessel is really immaterial. Once again, what is important is to picture maritime life as it was lived in the early 1800s. From the *Charlotte* story, it can be learned what constituted a crew on a ship of that time. The *Charlotte* wasn't huge, but she still needed eight seamen, two mates, a cook and a captain. Also the listing of the lost crew is one of few such examples from that era.

Elizabeth

Specifications: Built in 1792. Burthen, 265 tons. Registered to Thomas Russell. Sold in Charleston, in 1796.

Eliza

Specifications: Built in 1792. Burthen, 274 tons; length, 87.7 feet; beam, 27 feet; depth, 13.5 feet. Owner, August 4, 1792, Edward Jones.

Thomas

Specifications: Built in 1793. Burthen, 215 tons; length, 82.3 feet; beam, 24.6 feet; depth, 12.3 feet. Built for Thomas English of Boston.

Like so many proud new ship owners, Thomas English gave his own first name to his new vessel. Why he went to Durham to get a ship built isn't known, but it may have been that the price was right.

While positive data are lacking, it is possible the ship *Thomas* may have been the one reported in the fall of 1798 as having lost her master, Webster Brown of Portsmouth, and mate, John Vennard, 22, of New Castle. They died of yellow fever two days after leaving St. Barthelemy. They were ill only five days.[5]

Felicity

Specifications: Built in 1794. Burthen, 318 tons; length, 94 feet; beam, 28 feet; depth, 14 feet. Owner, January 27, 1795, Joseph Champney.

Available information indicates that Champney may have played the role of ship broker in the case of the *Felicity*. She sailed out of Portsmouth in February 1795 under a Captain Brown, headed for South Carolina.[6] She never re-entered, having been sold in Boston.

Asia

Specifications: Built in 1794. Burthen, 300 tons; length, 96.3 feet; beam, 27.6 feet; depth, 13.8 feet. Owner, December 17, 1794, Jonathan Chapman.

John

Specifications: Built in 1794. Burthen 316 tons; length, 95.9 feet; beam, 27.5 feet; depth, 13.8 feet. Owner, November 21, 1794, Jacob Sheafe.

Four Sisters

Specifications: Built in 1795 by Stephen Paul. Burthen, 340 tons; length, 98.8 feet; beam, 28.1 feet; depth, 14.05 feet. Owner, March 3, 1796, Joseph Champney.

Customs records indicate the *Four Sisters* left Portsmouth April 23, 1796, for New York. She was apparently lost not long after that. When the ship *Strafford* came in 1797, it was reported:

> Captain Thomas Brown and crew of the ship *Four Sisters*, of this port, came passengers with Captain Balch; the ship *Four Sisters* having been lost off the port of St. Ubes in a heavy gale.

Charles

Specifications: Built in 1796. Burthen, 348 tons; length, 100.6 feet; beam, 28.1 feet; depth, 14.05 feet. Owner, Joseph Champney.

It isn't known how long Joseph Champney owned the *Charles*. One of the Blunt family took her to sea in July 1796, sailing for Virginia, perhaps on the first leg of the trading triangle. There is no notice of the date of her return. Joseph Perkins was in command on January 19, 1798, when she came in from St. Ubes.[7] It is quite probable Champney sold her early on as he did with other vessels.

Mermaid

Specifications: Built in 1796. Burthen, 192 tons; length, 75.6 feet; beam, 24.5 feet; depth, 12.25 feet. Owner, April 11, 1796, William Boyd.

After giving his ship the name *Mermaid*, the question arises as to whether William Boyd's imagination extended to having a mermaid figurehead carved for her? The records don't say.

John Tilton of Portsmouth was the only master the *Mermaid* had during the five years William Boyd owned her. Tilton brought her in from Martinique on April 7, 1796, and Boyd registered her four days later. In November 1796, the *Mermaid* headed for London, via the Caribbean where she loaded with sugar, coffee and cotton. On her passage to London, she was stopped by a French privateer, *L'Eclair*, 18 guns. The privateer let her go, after dumping 20 English Prisoners of War on her. The *Mermaid*'s next voyage was to Martinique from which she returned on September 18, 1798. In May 1799, she arrived in New York in 25 days from Martinique.[8] In September 1801, Boyd sold her in Boston.

Pallas

Specifications: Built in 1798 for Martin Parry of Portsmouth. No further information.

It is fair to speculate that Martin Parry named his ship for Pallas Athene, another name for the Roman goddess of wisdom, Minerva.[9]

Nancies

Specifications: Built in 1799. Burthen, 295 tons; length, 82.3 feet; beam, 24 feet; depth, 12.2 feet. Owner, January 1, 1800, Martin Parry.

The last ship built in Durham in the eighteenth century, the *Nancies* was the first full-rigged ship commanded by Thomas Lunt of Portsmoth. He took the *Nancies* to Liverpool and returned on June 12. Out again, he came home a second time from Liverpool on November 14, 1800. Two transatlantic crossings in less than a year was remarkable sailing. Henry Moore brought the *Nancies* home from Madeira in January 1802, but Parry had sold out in 1800 while Lunt was making his crossings. Nothing more is known of the *Nancies*.

Anglesey

Specifications: Built in 1800 by Robert Lapish. Burthen, 290 tons. Owner, January 1, 1801, Edward Parry.

Little is known about the *Anglesey*. For Robert Lapish, she was the first of four ships built between 1800 and 1808, and the *Anglesey* was the smallest. Her name was derived from the Welsh nativity of her owner, Edward Parry, Anglesey being an island on the Welsh coast across the Menai Strait from Bangor. Parry owned the *Anglesey* for less than a year, selling her abroad in 1802. It is possible she was one of the many vessels sold in England after completing a passage from the United States. Her captain would come home as a passenger on another vessel. The French wars, with the heavy demands for craftsmen, kept England from producing merchant vessels, and the Americans built good ones.

Horace

Specifications: Built in 1800 by James Hackett. Burthen, 382 tons. Owner, William Gray of Salem, Massachusetts.

The first Durham-built *Horace* was the first commercial vessel built by the famed naval contractor James Hackett after the Revolution. Hackett was busy with naval vessels through the 1790s, during which time he added to the training of Master Shipwright William Badger. His reputation as a builder brought William Gray to Great Bay for a ship. Gray sent the *Horace* to Calcutta in 1802...under a Captain Parker.[10] Hackett built one other commercial vessel. In 1811, at Dover, he launched a brig, the *Cocheco*, 196 tons.

Commerce

Specifications: Built by Benjamin Remick in 1801. Square stern, billet head. Burthen, 200 tons; length, 79.1 feet; beam, 24.3 feet; depth, 12.15 feet. Owners, December 19, 1801, James Leavitt of Lee, William Ballard, Durham, and Martin Parry.

Four months after his death in August 1802, Martin Parry's interest in the *Commerce* was sold to Robert Blunt, who had made a voyage in her to Demerara, returning March 10, 1802. On her next voyage, Parry sent the *Commerce* to Russia under George Wiggin. He returned in October 1802, and the partners sold the *Commerce* in New York early the next year.

Argo

Specifications: Built in 1803 by Robert Lapish. Square stern, billet head. Burthen, 325 tons; length, 95.6 feet; beam, 20 feet; depth, 14 feet. Owner, Joseph Winn of Salem.

The *Argo* was named for the vessel in which Jason sought the golden fleece, but her chief distinction was her unusual dimensions. In a period when most builders were fabricating floating bath tubs, Robert Lapish's second ship was almost rakish in appearance. If the Customs figures are correct, the *Argo* was 4.78 times the beam in length, and her depth of hold was better than a foot more than the average.

It can be conjectured that her design was given to Lapish by Joseph Winn. More than 30 years later, when Frederick W. Fernald built the ship *Thomas Perkins* in Portsmouth, she had a ratio with a length of five times breadth. The *Portsmouth Journal* described the *Thomas*

Perkins as the narrowest ship ever built on the river. Even the famed clipper *Sea Serpent* was only 5.02 times length to beam.

Charles

Specifications: Built in 1804 by Robert Lapish. Burthen, 326 tons; length, 99.4 feet; beam, 27.3 feet; depth, 13.65 feet. Owners, Samuel Chauncey, Henry Ladd and George F. Smith.

The second *Charles* was the third and largest of the four ships built by Robert Lapish. It is of interest to note how sharply the *Charles's* measurements differed from those of the *Argo*, built the year before. Lapish had reverted to the bath-tub format.

All but one of the *Charles'* original share holders sold their interests to John F. and William Parrott in April 1809. They promptly put brother Enoch in command, and he brought her in from Liverpool on August 24, 1809, ending a triangular voyage. John F. Parrott took out an advertisement to announce the arrival of "Coarse Liverpool salt," by the *Charles*.[11] A Captain Elwell came in from Lisbon on August 30, 1811. Then the *Charles* disappears from the records, except for a terse note, "Captured by the English," with no date.[12]

It is possible, however, that she was the *Charles*, Captain Walden (William or Nathan), that cleared Portland in May 1815 for Buenos Aires. She was under charter to Langley Boardman of Portsmouth and was loaded with furniture. A newspaper report later in the year reported the *Charles* had been lost near Buenos Aires, "Crew saved."[13]

Henry & Francis

Specifications: Built in 1804 by Ebenezer Thompson. Square stern, billet head. Burthen, 218 tons; length, 81.3 feet; beam, 25 feet; depth, 12.5 feet. Owners, Henry Barnard and Matthew Folger of Nantucket.

The *Henry & Francis* ws the only square-rigged, three-masted vessel built by Ebenezer Thompson in his home town. He didn't build another vessel until the ship *Potomac* in 1810 in Portsmouth. His first vessel was the brig *Rio*, built in Durham in 1801. All of which poses an unanswerable question: Why did knowledgeable men from Nantucket have an untried builder make a ship for them? Perhaps the price was right.

Concordia

Specifications: Built in 1804 by Samuel Cottle. Square stern, billet head. Burthen, 256 tons; length 89.1 feet; beam, 25.7 feet; depth, 12.85 feet. Owner, March 18, 1805, Thomas Sheafe.

Samuel Cottle of Eliot apparently went to whatever yard was available when he had a vessel to build. He built a ship in Berwick in 1800, another in Newmarket in 1802, and the *Concordia* in Durham. Seven years later, he built a brig in Portsmouth. At times, he was closely associated with his brother, Thomas Cottle.

Andrew W. Bell was the *Concordia*'s first master. Bell made his home on State Street in Portsmouth. He brought the *Concordia* from St. Petersburg on January 8, 1806. In April 1806, Thomas Sheafe took on his partner, Charles Coffin, as a part owner of the *Concordia*, but what she did in the next four years isn't known. Probably the Embargo Act took its toll. In May 1810, however, William Rindge arrived from Gothenburg with iron, hemp and duck for the owners.[14] Then, for a five-year period, she either lay idle, waiting out the War of 1812, or sailed from other ports. In 1815, she was reported as being at Liverpool, ready to sail for Portsmouth.[15] A few weeks later, Edmund Coffin brought her in from England. The *Concordia* made the triangular voyage twice more under Captain Coffin, arriving in May 1817 and in 1818. William Martin took over, returning to his home port on December 10, 1818, in 42 days from Liverpool, with salt and coal for the owners. The *Concordia* once crossed from Liverpool in 33 days, her fastest passage.

In July 1819, Samuel Muir, master of the *Concordia*, arrived at Hampton Roads from Savannah. Going out of Savannah, past Tybee Light, her mizzen top mast and head were carried away in a squall. Muir had sailed to Savannah in April, but finding no cargo available, beat his way up the coast to try the James River ports. A news item records the entrance of the *Concordia*, on July 3, 1820, in 44 days from Liverpool.[16] Back down the first leg of the triangle she went—to Savannah. While there, the mate, William Shaw, 21, died. In February 1822, bound from Portsmouth to Havana, the *Concordia* foundered. The crew was taken off the wreck after five days by the ship *Henry* of Boston.

Leonidas

Specifications: Built by Andrew Simpson in 1804. Square stern, billet head. Burthen, 317 tons; length, 99.6 feet; beam, 26.9 feet; depth, 13.4 feet. Built for Ronald McKenzie of New York.

Nothing is known in the Port of Portsmouth records about the *Leonidas*, except that her name honors the Spartan hero who unsuccessfully defended the Pass of Thermopylae against invading Persian hordes.

Horace

Specifications: Built in 1805 by Stephen Paul. Square stern, billet head. Burthen, 328 tons; length, 99.1 feet; beam, 27.5 feet; depth, 13.75 feet. Owners, January 1, 1806, Nathaniel and John Haven and Peter Turner.

There seems to be no record of the early career of the second Durham-built *Horace*. She was either tied up by the Embargo Act or worked out of other ports until 1810. Peter Turner came in from Cadiz on April 18th with salt, then turned command over to William Appleton, a connection of the Haven family. Appleton came in from Bonavista on March 24, 1811, loaded with salt.[17] The Havens were part owners when the *Horace* was wrecked in 1813.

Mars

Specifications: Built in 1807 by Andrew Simpson. Square stern, billet head. Burthen, 305 tons; length, 95.3 feet; beam, 27.1 feet; depth, 13.44 feet. Owners, April 24, 1809, Simpson and John Flagg.

The builder and part owner of the *Mars*, Andrew Simpson, was the son-in-law of Robert Lapish; so the *Mars* was presumably built in the yard below Oyster River Falls, where Lapish would build his last ship the next year.

John Flagg, the other part owner, brought the *Mars* in from Greenock, Scotland, on September 25, 1809, a passage of 51 days. In October 1810, the *Mars* went into New York from Copenhagen with 28 passengers. Most of these were American seamen released from condemned vessels. Denmark was then playing the game of taking American shipping and condemning it. The *Mars* was then commanded by Benjamin Balch, who had had the *Strafford* stolen from him by a mutinous crew.[18] The *Mars* herself had been taken by the Danes, and Balch ransomed her for $600 and court costs.

Augusta

Specifications: Built in 1808 by Robert Lapish. Burthen, 324 tons; length, 98.1 feet; beam, 27.5 feet; depth, 13.75. Owners, April 11, 1809, Samuel Chauncey and Henry and Alexander Ladd.

A glance at the figures shows that Robert Lapish continued his reversion to the lumpish design then prevalent. When he put his last ship, the *Augusta*, in the water, she slid from the same ways used for the *Mars*. Lapish was then 70, but he had energy enough left to build a 200-ton brig, the *Hannah*, in 1810. Lapish died in 1815, at 77. Customs records indicate that Chauncey and the Ladds bought the *Augusta* for the sole purpose of selling her in Virginia.

Elizabeth Wilson

Specifications: Built by Joseph Swazey of Exeter in 1810. Square stern, Billet head. Burthen, 333 tons; beam, 27.2 feet; depth, 12.2 feet. Owners, November 12, 1810, Benjamin Brierley and Samuel Ham.

Two items of note mark the story of the *Elizabeth Wilson*. First, she was the only one of Joseph Swazey's ships not built in Exeter. Secondly, she was the first command of the famed Ichabod Goodwin. He became her master when he was only 25. Before that, he had served on her as supercargo, second mate and first mate.[19]

The *Elizabeth Wilson*'s first master was Richard Phillips, who took her to Virginia on November 17, 1810.[20] He returned in August 1811 with salt in 35 days from the Isle of May. An entry in 1813 shows that the owners had her at sea at least once during the War of 1812. She came in from Cadiz with salt.[21] Samuel Hobart was her first post-war master, clearing out in December 1815 for Havana. Along with the *Thomas Wilson* and the *Islington*, in March 1815, the *Elizabeth Wilson* was put up for auction to settle the estate of Samuel Ham. Exactly what happened at the auction isn't clear. The *Islington* was sold but the records fail to mention the *Elizabeth Wilson*. But in 1818, Samuel and John Lord became the owners, and there is a note to the effect that Samuel Ham's share was sold in 1818.

Samuel Hobart was succeeded in the captaincy by a man named Grinelle, Gridley or Girdler—the records show all three names. When the Lords took over, Ichabod Goodwin became master. Goodwin made three triangular voyages in her. One report has the *Elizabeth Wilson* arriving at Savannah in January 1819 in 70 days from London in ballast.[22] In September 1819, she arrived in Portsmouth in 48 days from Liverpool with salt, iron and coal for the Lords. In 1821, she was purchased by Henry Ladd, who quickly resold her to a Philadelphia firm. With that, the *Elizabeth Wilson* fades from Portsmouth-oriented records, except for a marine item in December 1813 stating that while running down the Savannah River, she ran afoul of the Portsmouth-built *Triton*. Both suffered severe damage.[23]

Alexander

Specifications: Built by James Paul in 1811. Square stern, billet head. Burthen, 318 tons; length, 100.3 feet; beam, 26.8 feet; depth, 12.2 feet. Owners, March 9, 1812, Henry, Alexander and William Ladd, and Samuel Chauncey.

Available records point strongly, by their very paucity, to the probability that the *Alexander*, like so many other vessels, was laid up during the War of 1812. In June 1815, with the peace well established, the Ladds bought full control of the *Alexander*, which, obviously, had been named for the second oldest of the three brothers. They sent her to Charleston in the summer, and she cleared out in September for Cowes, England, "and a market."[24] This appears to have been James Kennard's first voyage as master of a ship, but he had been following the sea for many years, having been born in 1780. Later he commanded other Port of Portsmouth ships, among them the *Maria Tufton* and the *Ann Parry*. James Kennard died in 1856. He had been retired from the sea for years to follow mercantile interests. His obituary read, in part:

> In his business relations he was uniformly upright and honorable. As a citizen he was faithful and generous, ready to contribute his means and his influence for whatever public good demanded...[25]

In April 1817, under the command of Captain Kennard, the *Alexander* came home, via New York, from Malaga, Spain, with wine and fruit for the Ladds. Captain A. Daniels was at Liverpool with her in the summer of 1819, and she came into Portsmouth with a cargo of Liverpool salt. Three years later, Captain Daniels was with her at St. Ubes. On the return passage, which took 50 days, she was blown so far off course that she had to put into Charleston to repair damages to her foremast.

In the fall of 1822, Captain Daniels took her into the River Platte, Argentina, and she went ashore on Point India, having lost her rudder, rigging and so on, in a storm. The crew was rescued and the ship salvaged.

Charlotte

Specifications: Built in 1811 by Stephen Paul. Square stern, billet head. Burthen, 347 tons; length, 104.3 feet; beam, 27.4 feet; depth, 13.7 feet. Owners, Nathaniel A. and John Haven and William Appleton.

The *Charlotte* is another case in which a ship was idle during the War of 1812. She wasn't registered until May 12, 1815, after the peace became known. She sailed for London on August 30.[26] She was gone a bit over a year, returning, under Captain Appleton, from England and entering New York. Five days later she came to Portsmouth. In December, the *Charlotte* went to New Orleans and from there Appleton took her to Liverpool. She was lying in that port in October 1817 with an uncertain sailing date.[27] She sailed from Liverpool about November 10.[28] On another voyage under Appleton, she went to Havana, returning on Janaury 28, 1819, bringing hides and molasses in a passage of 22 days. Again in July 1822, she came in from Liverpool with salt and coal. Appleton's last voyage in her started in November 1822, and, while en route to Savannah, the *Charlotte* rescued the crew of the ship *Emulation*, which had foundered.

George Simes, Jr., of Portsmouth became master, and took her to the West Indies, returning October 1, 1823. Captain Simes then went to Savannah to load cotton. He took that cargo to Havre, arriving there in April. From there, his orders sent him to Bordeaux to load for New York. The passage to New York was without incident, and Simes sailed to Hampton Roads to load for Bremen, Germany. The *Charlotte* sailed on December 31, 1824. On February 3, 1825, she was smashed on the Texel, one of the Western Frisian Islands. She had been caught in one of the most ferocious gales that have ever plagued North Sea shipping. A letter to the *Gazette* of April 12 said it was probable she had gone on shore because a round house had been found with the name *Charlotte* on it. Later a compass box drifted ashore at Terschelling with that name on it. It was somberly reported on April:

> Of those on board the *Charlotte* belonging to this town were Captain George Simes, Jr., Mr. Charles C. Hardy, son of Mr. Charles Hardy, second mate, and Mr. Charles A. Conner, seaman.

Islington

Specifications: Built in 1812 by Andrew Simpson. Square stern, billet head. Burthen, 330 tons; length, 102.3 feet; beam, 27 feet; depth, 12 feet. Owners, February 15, 1812, Samuel Ham, Benjamin Brierley and Thomas Haven.

The *Islington* undoubtedly was named to honor the Islington section of London. Despite their problems with Old England, the people of New England never lost their affection for things English.

The *Islington* went on at least one trading voyage during the War of 1812, going to Cadiz, and returning, under Joseph Swett on April 19, 1813. Quite probably, she was idle during the rest of the war years. Often such idleness was forced on the owners by the inability to get the men needed to man vessels. Service in privateers held out promise of quick riches, a far brighter prospect than life in a merchantman.

In March 1815, the *Islington* was auctioned, along with the *Elizabeth Wilson* and the *Thomas Wilson*, to settle the estate of Samuel Ham. The advertisement said of the three ships:

> . . . The above ships are well found, were built on Piscataqua River of the best materials, under the inspection of the late Mr. Samuel Ham, for his own use. . .[29]

The *Islington's* registration didn't change, however, until after yet another auction on May 18th. In the advertisement for that auction, there is evidence that the voyage under Captain Swett was the only one yet undertaken by the *Islington*. The advertisement reads, in part:

> . . . She is very well found. . . was built on Durham River. . . sails remarkably and stows a large cargo; has made but one voyage, when she carried 4,500 barrels of flour.

Edmund Roberts, John Shackford and Thomas Haven were the registered owners on June 24, 1815. Shackford went to Martinique and came back in September 1815 with 300 hogsheads of molasses for the owners. Shackford's next voyage took him to Yucatan, and, in June 1816, the *Islington* was at Portsmouth, England. The *Islington* came to New York from Yucatan in May 1817 in 38 days with logwood, indigo, cochineal and pimento. On the passage, she rescued the crew and passengers of a brig that had been stranded on Cat Island in the Bahamas.

In March 1818, instead of coming home, the *Islington* went directly to New Orleans from Liverpool. Her passage took 54 days, and by the time she arrived, the crew was mutinous. A news account reported:

> . . . a mutiny broke out on board, on the 10th ult. [March], when the officers lives were attempted, but the mutineers were quelled, after wounding two of the leaders. They had done much injury to various articles of the cargo, and cut and destroyed everything in their way, even the cables fell a sacrifice to the axe.[30]

Whether or not the mutiny prompted her sale isn't clear, but she was sold shortly after the incident.

Maria Tufton

Specifications: Built in 1814 by Stephen Paul. Square stern, billet head. Burthen, 326 tons; length, 98 feet; beam, 27.6 feet; depth, 13.8 feet. Owners, April 30, 1817, Henry and Alexander Ladd.

Few women have been honored by having two different ships named for them, but such was the distinction accorded Maria Tufton (Haven)

Ladd, the wife of Alexander Ladd. Maria Tufton Haven was the daughter of another enterprising Portsmouth merchant, Nathaniel Haven. Seven years earlier, Alexander had named another ship, the *Maria*, for her.

It is hard to understand why the *Maria Tufton* didn't make any voyages until 1818. Her apparent idleness raises the question as to whether Stephen Paul had her on his hands until she was bought and registered by the Ladds on April 30, 1817. It was almost a year later when James Kennard brought her into Portsmouth from Turk's Island in 17 days with salt for the Ladds. That information is a bit misleading, however, because a news item reported her at Amsterdam on November 4, 1817.[31] That meant she had gone south for cotton, crossed to Europe, and then loaded for Petersburg, Virginia. From there, she went to Turk's Island, thence home. In 1819, Kennard made another triangular voyage, returning to Portsmouth from St. Ubes on November 2, 1819. Here again, a news item adds information, placing her at Portsmouth, England, on November 2nd.[32] She sailed for the Thames River that same day. She had the crew of a British schooner, wrecked in its passage from Newcastle, England, to Newfoundland, for passengers.

Captain Kennard's next venture in the *Maria Tufton* was to Rio de Janeiro. Her outward cargo was lumber and hay. When she returned in early November 1820, 57 days from Rio, she brought in coffee, sugar and hides for the Ladds. The Ladds advertised that they were selling "100 bags 1st quality Green Coffee; 100 bags Muscovado sugar; 700 Rio Grande Ox Hides; 500 do. Horse Hides."[33] Kennard came in from St. Ubes on September 21, 1822, with salt for the owners, of which he was now one. Through 1823, Kennard made another run around the triangle, and then, on January 30, 1824, sailed from Portsmouth on his last voyage in the *Maria Tufton*. He went to New Orleans, returning in mid-July via Norfolk.

William Briard was the next master of the *Maria Tufton*. He started out on the traditional triangle, sailing August 10, 1824, for Savannah, taking cotton to Europe. After discharging in Liverpool, he went to St. Ubes for salt. Here he broke the usual pattern by hauling his salt to Montevideo. He was reported there on January 18, 1825.[34] In June, he was at Charleston, loading for Liverpool a cargo valued at $150,405, a high figure for that day.[35] He was home from Liverpool on October 13, 1825, with a load of salt for the owners. Captain Briard stayed four months in his home at the corner of Middle and Summer Streets before going to sea again. Briard and the *Maria Tufton* left on February 26, 1826, for South America. While on that passage, the *Maria Tufton* fell in with a wrecked lumber schooner bound for New York. She took off the crew and landed them at Norfolk.[36]

The *Maria Tufton* made her first rounding of Cape Horn early in 1827, and, on May 1, 1827, the *Gazette* reported she had left Valparaiso, Chile, for Callao, Peru. Presumably she went from there to the Chincha Islands to load with guano. Not until December 1827 was she reported back in the United States. She had taken 111 days to come from Peru and was filled with water when she entered Charleston.[37] Six months later, she came into Portsmouth, in ballast. Within two weeks, under a different master, Supply C. Foss, she sailed from Portsmouth for the last time. She went to Germany, and from there to Rio de Janeiro, then around the Horn and back to Rio. Although named for the wife of an owner, sentiment didn't get in the way of profit. In the fall of 1830, she was sold at Rio de Janeiro.

Chauncey

Specifications: Built in 1815 by Andrew Simpson. Burthen, 378 tons; length, 111.25 feet; beam, 27.55 feet; depth, 19.77 feet. Owner, January 1, 1816, Enoch G. Parrott.

The *Chauncey* was undoubtedly named to honor the Chauncey family and specifically Isaac Chauncey who lost his life in 1792 in the Exeter-built ship *Columbia*. The *Chauncey* was the biggest vessel built by Simpson, and it is of note that, as the years passed, most of the builders were fabricating bigger and bigger ships. The figure given for depth of hold, however, seems inconsistent with the general practice of the time and may be a typographical error in compiling the customs' records.

Parrott sent the *Chauncey* to sea under a Captain Greenough, and the *Gazette* described her as an "elegant, fast-sailing new ship."[38] That was the only glimpse ship fanciers in the Port of Portsmouth had of her. A little later, Parrott sold her in New York.

Henry

Specifications: Built in 1818 by Joseph Coe. Square stern, billet head. Burthen, 333 tons; length, 101.3 feet; beam, 27.3 feet; depth, 13.65 feet. Owners, March 24, 1818, Titus and Henry Salter and James Shapley.

If the ship *Henry* had only one credential for entering the ship-building hall of fame, it would be that she was the first three-masted, square-rigged vessel built and launched by Joseph Coe, the prodigious Durham shipwright. In all, Joseph Coe fabricated 19 craft in a span of nine years. Seventeen of them were built below the falls on the Oyster River, the other two in Newmarket, and close timing of the launches suggests Coe didn't have enough room in Durham for his work.

As soon as the *Henry* had been taken down river to Portsmouth for masting and rigging, as was the general practice at the time, Henry Salter sailed her to the West Indies. In 1820, she went into the triangular trade. Later that year, an advertisement reported her at Portsmouth Pier, at the foot of State Street, loaded with St. Ubes salt. Among her masters were John S. Davis, M.B. Vennard, Joseph Leach and J.E. Salter. In 1828, the *Henry* was sold in Sag Harbor, New York, for whaling. One of her whaling cruises is on record. She was in the South Atlantic from July 5, 1843 to May 14, 1845, and brought in a catch worth $32,712.[39]

Triton

Specifications: Built in 1819 by Stephen Paul. Burthen, 313 tons; length, 100.8 feet; beam, 26.5 feet; depth, 13.25 feet. Owners, February 14, 1820, Enoch G. Parrott and Jacob Cutter.

In mythology, Triton was a son of Neptune and is represented as a fish with a human head.[40] The career of the Durham-built *Triton* was well worthy of the name. She was the first whaling ship ever to enter Portsmouth Harbor, although not originally intended for that business. In March 1834, the *Triton*'s arrival was reported with word she had brought in 1,900 barrels of whale oil and 400 barrels of choice sperm oil. She had been gone about a year and the report said:

> We believe this to be the first whaler that ever arrived at this port—her arrival at the wharf was greeted with the discharge of guns, and a merry peal from most of the bells in town.[41]

The enthusiasm in the news report was backed up by an editorial on the same day:

> We are happy to greet the arrival of a Whale ship in this place. We understand the voyage will be attended with profit to the enterprising owner. The *fact* of profit is the only one we need, to shew [sic] the effects of a business, requiring so much labor, on the prosperity of the Town...

The editor carefully outlined all the profitable consequences of such a trade. Unfortunately, the Port of Portsmouth never developed a real whaling industry. Moreover, there is far more to the *Triton*'s story than a recital of her whaling activities, an industry for which she wasn't originally intended. One misadventure, for example, had taken place on her way home in February when she collided with the schooner *Mary Frances*, Captain Kirwan, "three days from Virginia, for Antigua; while alongside the mate and one seaman came on board. Capt. F[landers] wore ship, and lay till light, then went aboard to render assistance. Capt. Kirwan was so badly bruised that he must have died in a few hours—John Ripley was knocked overboard and drowned—both vessels were slightly injured."[42]

The *Triton's* first return to Portsmouth was on August 16, 1820, when, under Captain F. Toscan, she came in with salt, coal and crates (usually of earthenware) for Enoch G. Parrott. Captain F. Toscan was master for several years but only in 1822 and 1824 did his voyages terminate in Portsmouth. The *Triton* worked out of various southern ports, hauling cotton to Liverpool. In 1825, Captain B. Toscan became master, and the *Triton* came into Portsmouth from Liverpool on November 11th with salt. In January, she sailed to New Orleans and didn't return home until 1827, coming in 32 days from Liverpool with salt and coal. Captain Toscan brought English papers later than any others to the *Gazette* office.[43] In November, she sailed again for New Orleans and arrived there on Christmas Eve. The *Triton* loaded, went to Europe and returned to New Orleans; from there, she went to Turk's Island for salt, and then home. She sailed for Savannah in December. And, until January 1833, that was her way of life. That all changed with the publishing of an advertisement seeking "20 enterprising Young Men for ship TRITON on a WHALING VOYAGE, to whom good encouragement will be given."[44] The ownership had passed to Charles Cushing, and Richard Flanders was master. She sailed in February for the Indian Ocean. In the course of the next year, reports of her successes trickled back home. One such report of the *Triton* was published in the *Journal* on September 28, 1833:

> The ship *Triton*, Flanders, of this port, was at St. Helena July 28, with 410 barrels of oil on board, and expected to sail the same day. It appears from letters received by C. Cushing, Esq, of this town, that she put in on account of landing the officers and crew of the French Whaling Ship *La Commerce de Paris*, of Havre De Grace, Capt. F. Dufour, lost on the West Coast of Africa, in June last, by striking a reef of rocks. The vessel and cargo were totally lost,—Crew saved. 33 American Whalemen had put into that place for supplies and refreshment, from the first of the present year to the 1st of Aug...

After the triumphal return from her first whaling voyage, the *Triton* went out again under a Captain Ritchie. She sailed in January 1835, and in March 1836, she was reported as having taken four right whales and three sperm. Another report had Captain Ritchie as sick on shore at Mozambique. When the *Triton* came home, he was no longer master. Cushing sold the *Triton* in Boston in 1838, and she wound up in

New Bedford. A chart on a wall in the Smithsonian's Marine section in Washington, D.C., has Isaac Howland, Jr., as her owner. In 1848, the *Triton* had her last great adventure. The *New Bedford Mercury* published a letter telling what happened:

> AMERICAN SHIP SEIZED BY SAVAGES.—A letter from Capt. Potter, of ship *Mechanic* of Newport, dated Feb. 12, lat. 4 10 N. long. 1 61 E., states that the ship *Triton*, Spencer, of this port, had been taken possession of on the 6th of January, Seydenham's Island, one of the King's Mill Groupe, by the natives, instigated by a Spaniard living among them. The Captain went on shore to purchase a fluke chain, where he was detained. The natives had possession of the ship about 20 hours and murdered the second mate and several of the crew.—The mate was wounded in the conflict with the Spaniard, who was killed. While they were pillaging the ship, she drifted from the Island, and the natives left her. The ships *United States* and *Alabama*, of Nantucket, touched at the Island afterwards, and rescued Capt. Spencer and his boat's crew. They would proceed to Guam in hopes of finding the *Triton*.[45]

However, like an obituary published before the honoree's death, the *Triton* survived that experience. Late in 1848, the *New Bedford Mercury* published more details, which were reported in the *Portsmouth Journal*. It was datelined Papeete in the Society Islands (Tahiti) on March 28, 1828:

> The ship Triton, Capt. Mills, late Spencer, of New Bedford, arrived here a few weeks since in distress. on the 8th and 9th of January, 1828, at the King's Mills Islands, Capt. Spencer went on shore to purchase the chains and anchors of the ship *Columbia*, wrecked there 18 months since, which were offered him by a Spaniard from one of the islands.
>
> The weather being rough, Capt. Spencer resolved to stay on shore all night. The next morning the Spaniard came on board and told the mate that Capt. Spencer wanted some casks to bring off some chains. The weather continued rough and could not land them. The Spaniard with 11 natives remaining on board. At 10 o'clock P.M., in the 2d mate's watch, the Spaniard managed to arm himself with two pistols from the cabin, and to arm the natives with cutting spades [for whale blubber]. He then told the 2d mate to go below, or he would be a dead man. The 2d mate then went below and awoke the mate, Mr. Mills, who rushed on deck with a sword, and in a struggle with the Spaniard he was knocked down with his own sword. He got up and went into the forecastle, but badly hurt. The 3d killed the Spaniard and two natives and sprang into the forecastle. The 2d mate with some of the crew lowered a boat and left the ship.

The natives now being in possession of her, placed a native boy, one of the crew, at the wheel, and tried to get her aground; the wind and tide being against them, and they not knowing how to tack ship, the boy succeeded in working her off 15 miles in 24 hours.

The natives then left her, taking with them the chronometer, two boats and many other things. Mr. Mills then picked up the 2d mate and boat and came here with only 10 men able to work. He has shipped another crew for a cruise on the N.W. Coast, and will be ready in a few days.

In 1923, on April 2nd, the *Portsmouth Herald* reported still another version of the *Triton* story. It was an Associated Press item from New Bedford and told of the final end of a noted New Bedford whaling firm, J. and R.W. Wing, and mentioned the *Triton* as one of their vessels:

> ...The bark *Triton*, a veteran of exciting experiences before the Wings bought her, was in the whaling business for a hundred years before the Arctic ice finally caught her. In 1846 she was attacked by the natives of a South Sea Island at which she had touched. The crew rallied to the defense with whaling guns, harpoons and lances, but five of their number were killed and seven wounded before two Nantucket ships came up and rescued them.

First, it might be ventured that a 100 years seems quite a long life for the *Triton*. She was built in 1819, and that means she was crushed in the Arctic about the time of World War I. As to the Associated Press' version of her troubles in the Society Islands, it may be a matter of deciding which version has the most appeal to the reader.

Franklin

Specifications: Built in 1819 by Stephen Paul. Square stern, billet head. Burthen, 310 tons; length, 99.4 feet; beam, 26.6 feet; depth, 13.3 feet. Owners, December 1, 1819, Theodore Chase and John Riley, Jr.

In her early years, the *Franklin* was commanded by one of the owners, John Riley, Jr., of Dover. In all, he made six voyages in her. He began her maiden voyage on December 3, 1819, and returned from Liverpool on June 12, 1820, with salt and coal to the owners. In September 1821, he had completed the triangle again, coming home from Liverpool. Two months later, the *Franklin* was at Norfolk, where her mate, William Amazeen, son of Ephraim Amazeen of New Castle, died in the Marine Hospital. The *Franklin* came home in April 1822. On his last voyage in the *Franklin*, before moving to the *Samuel Wright*, Riley brought in on

June 1, 1824, a typical cargo: salt for the owners, paint and sheet lead for the firm of Pickering & Sherburne.[46]

George Dame was the *Franklin*'s next master, and, on July 16, 1825, brought in more than the usual freight. He had on board seven steerage passengers, all Welsh, who had boarded at Liverpool. They included John and Elizabeth Evans and their three children. Evans was described as a laborer.[47] Also on the list were Owen Hughes, 66, a laborer, and Catharine Hughes, 24, single.

In August 1829, came the news report:

> *Loss of the ship Franklin of Portsmouth*—The *Franklin*, Capt. [Samuel] Harding, sailed from Liverpool, 16th June. On 21st July, at 10 A.M., wind W.S.W. and the weather thick and foggy, discovered the water suddenly become discolored: put the helm down immediately, but before the vessel would come to head to the wind, she struck and remained hard and fast. The tide had begun to ebb, and was running 3½ knots over the reef. Got the boats out, and left the vessel. At half past 5 P.M. the fog cleared up, and discovered the ship was ashore about 15 miles from the east end of Sable Island—came to anchor about half mile from the ship and remained during the night. The next morning got under weigh, and pulled for the vessel, but no part of her hull was to be seen, she had bilged, fell over, and her lower yards in the water. At 7 P.M. landed at the east end of the Island, and was very kindly treated by the resident agent in that place. Capt. Harding and the mate took passage on board a schooner loading at the Island, for Halifax, thence arrived in this town.—Merch. Hall Books.[48]

As was so often the case, "the crew saved nothing but what they stood in." Of course, Taylor & Waldron and E.F. Sise lost whatever they might have had in uninsured investments.

Albert

Specifications: Built by Joseph Coe in 1820. Square stern, billet head. Burthen, 322 tons; length, 102.4 feet; beam, 26.6 feet; depth, 13.3 feet. Owners, December 27, 1820, Thomas Haven, John and Benjamin Salter.

To the *Albert* goes the sad distinction of being lost before she was a year old. Before being registered, she was advertised as wanting freight or passengers.[49] Those interested were to apply to Thomas Haven, No. 12 Merchant's Row [east side of Market Street]. Captain John Salter was then 32 years old and living in his father's old house on Washington Street, Portsmouth. He sired nine children, not one of whom married, and the last of whom, Augusta, died in the homestead in 1914.

That the *Albert* was headed for Charleston indicates she was starting a triangular voyage. She probably returned to Portsmouth in the late summer of 1821. Captain Salter took her south again. A news report said she was believed lost on Long Island in the Bahamas. The last notice of her was to the effect she had been lost on Long Island in a gale.[50]

Washington

Specifications: Built in 1821 by Stephen Paul. Square stern, billet head. Burthen, 340 tons; length, 102.3 feet; beam, 27.4 feet; depth, 13.7 feet. Owners, January 14, 1822, Nathaniel Smith and Joseph Coe.

The *Washington* went to work immediately. A news account said she was "new and elegant" as she sailed for Charleston on January 16, 1822, under Nathaniel Smith.[51] Captain Smith completed the triangle in September 1822 with the report of her arrival from St. Ubes with salt for Cushing and Stephen Patten, Jr.

A.B. Craig was the master on her next three voyages. In each case, she came from Liverpool carrying salt, coal and merchandise to Cushing. On one of the passages, a Bostonian, William Davis, probably a seaman, died. Tyler Parsons was master when she entered Portsmouth for the last time, November 3, 1827, coming from Liverpool in 50 days with salt and coal for Cushing and crates for Taylor & Waldron.[52] After her next arrival in New Orleans, she was sold, but Captain Parsons continued as master for several years. She sailed around the triangle from Charleston, Savannah or New Orleans for Havre or Liverpool, then back to New York. In 1831, the *Journal* stopped keeping track of her movements, which meant the local man, Captain Parsons, was no longer master.

Edward

Specifications: Built in 1822 by Joseph Coe. Square stern, billet head. Burthen, 339 tons; length, 108.2 feet; beam, 26.45 feet. Owners, December 13, 1822, Thomas and William Haven, John Salter and Benjamin Holmes.

Not until the 1820s did the newspapers pay any real attention to ship-building, and so the following item in the *Journal*, October 5, 1822, was one of the first of its kind:

LAUNCHES

On Tuesday [October 1st] was launched at Durham the elegant ship EDWARD, of 340 tons, owned by Thomas Haven and John Salter, intended for the southern & Liverpool trade; and to be commanded by Captain Salter. She was built by Joseph Coe, and is considered inferior to no ship built in this river.

In keeping with the stated purpose of her construction, the *Edward* went south under John Salter, who had only a short time before lost the ship *Albert* in the Bahamas. On May 14, she returned to Portsmouth with salt for the owners.[53] In September, it was noted that the *Edward* was at Gothenburg discharging her cargo.[54] From there, Captain Salter went to St. Ubes for salt; on the homeward passage, the *Edward* and her master made news. A letter was published from Captain S.H. Martin of the brig *Phoenix* of Boston, who told of being in a savage gale, during which the first mate was lost overboard. Martin and his crew battled to save the brig, but she sprang a leak. They "found the leak fast gaining on us; hove over anchors and cables and ballast until water covered the latter in the hold...we all made for the long boat as she floated off the deck, except Thomas Walden, who was drowned."[55] They were several days in the long boat, "constantly drenched with water, our benumbed limbs and chilled, and we nearly exhausted, were providentially fallen in with by ship *Edward*, Capt. Salter, from St. Ubes for Portsmouth...Some bread and water and a compass was all that was saved." Captain Martin was so grateful that he published:

A CARD

> Capt. S.H. Martin and surviving crew, late of brig *Phoenix* of Boston, offer—the thanks of grateful hearts, to Capt. J. Salter, of ship *Edward*, for his generosity and kind attention to them when taken on board his ship, in a feeble and nearly exhausted condition. All that could be done to relieve their distresses and mitigate their sufferings was generously done by this worthy man.

Many people live out their lives without hearing themselves hailed so eulogistically. John Salter spent little time enjoying the praise; he cleared out on another triangle, returning in June 1824, a really quick trip. Salter turned the *Edward* over to A.J. Comerais, who took her to New Orleans on another run around the triangle. Salter took command of another Coe-built ship, the *Eliza Grant*.

Under Captain Comerais, the *Edward* was gone from the Port of Portsmouth for nearly four years. One listing in that period has her, on December 1827, at New Orleans, loading for London. During that passage to London the *Edward* was chased for 24 hours by a Caribbean pirate but outsailed the marauder. It was one of the few examples on record of pursuit by pirates after a three-master. An extract from a letter by Captain Comerais to the owners affords another glimpse into the career of the *Edward;* it was dated while at sea, March 3, 1829:

> We left Liverpool on the 15th December and were 12 days in clearing the land. On the 29th Jan., long. 61, in a very severe gale, lost our rudder, head and sails. We shipped a temporary rudder as soon as possible, but the gale raged with such fury, it was soon washed from the ship, breaking all the guys and a new 6-inch hawser. We shipped a second rudder which did not stand long—the ship drifting to the eastward very fast, we could not wear around to the southward, and cut away the mizzen mast. On the 23rd Feb. we had a third rudder shipped, made of spars all solid, with chain guys. After beating for 27 days, endeavoring to gain our port or the Bermudas, I bore away for Fayal—provisions and water getting short.[56]

The *Edward* was sold in 1830 to become a whaler. Her new owners were in Hudson, New York. On her first cruise, she was highly successful with a catch of 3,720 barrels of whale oil, worth $28,720, and 1,349 barrels of sperm, without any figures for whalebone.[57] She made three more voyages to the Pacific. The last was her best: 179 barrels of sperm; 2,050, whale; 7,400 pounds of bone—total value $34,235.

James

Specifications: Built in 1823 by Joseph Coe. Square stern, billet head. Burthen, 345 tons; length, 106.2 feet; beam, 27 feet; depth, 12 feet. Owners, February 10, 1824, James Shapley, Titus and Henry Salter, and Joseph Coe.

Henry Salter was master when the ship *James* dropped down the Piscataqua on February 17, 1824, on a passage to the Chesapeake, a run of seven days. Henry Salter was another of the many captains generated in that family of mariners. Born in Portsmouth, September 10, 1780, he died in Portsmouth in 1857. He lived long enough to know that his eldest son, Charles Henry Salter, born in 1824, was the master of the clipper *Typhoon*, which, in 1851, set a record between Portsmouth and Liverpool (see the author's *Clippers of the Port of Portsmouth*).

Henry Salter took the *James* on her maiden voyage to Liverpool. From there, the *James* came home in 47 days with bagged and coarse salt for Titus Salter and James Shapley. Salter made another voyage in the *James* before turning her over to John H. Sise, who was master on three triangular voyages. Samuel Shackford was master from 1818 to 1829. In that period, a passage from London to New York took her 94 days, more than 13 weeks. A news account said:

> The ship *Ann Maria*, Hobron, arrived at New London, spoke April 8th...ship *James*, Shackford, of Portsmouth, 85

days from London for N. York, with the loss of nearly all her sails, very short of provisions and water, having only 90 biscuits, and no kind of meat—crew in a famishing condition and almost in a state of mutiny. Supplied them with pork, bread, flour, molasses, tea, oil, water and a spare mizzen topsail.[58]

The *James* limped into New York a few days later with the timely assistance of the *Ann Maria*, a home-bound whaler. The misfortunes of one voyage, however, rarely deterred another. Late in May, the *James* sailed for Trieste, Italy, coming home on November 28, 1829, in 62 days from Trapani via Portland. A fourth part-interest in the *James* was sold while she was lying at Portsmouth Pier discharging cargo. The hard-luck shipowner Langley Boardman joined the syndicate along with John Lake. The *James* continued in the triangle trade, sailing from Portsmouth in January 1830 for New Orleans. She was gone two years before returning home in September 1832 from Norfolk in ballast. Out again in early December, she made regular crossings, coming home in the summer of 1834. She cleared out again in October for the last time, arriving at Charleston on November 6th. On April 7, 1836, she was lost at sea. For Langley Boardman, it meant another lost vessel. He had lost all but two of his investments, four of them being wrecked within a year, two after two years, and the *James* in six years.

Laconia

Specifications: Built in 1823 by Dudley Chase. Square stern, billet head. Burthen, 336 tons; length, 100.8 feet; beam, 27.5 feet; depth, 13.75 feet. Owners, February 6, 1824, Henry and Alexander Ladd.

The *Laconia* went into the cotton trade, arriving in Liverpool for the first time from Savannah on June 15, 1824.[59] In January 1825, she was at Havre, heading for St. Ubes. Wherever she took that cargo of salt, it wasn't to Portsmouth, because she didn't arrive home until August 1827 with salt for the owners and hardware for Sherburne & Blunt and Harris & Pickering.

On December 12, 1827, Captain A. Daniels sailed to Charleston for a load of cotton. The next notice of the Durham-built *Laconia* was a news report to the effect she had been lost off the Hook of Holland while en route to Hamburg, Germany. One of the dreaded North Sea gales drove her ashore. "The master, mate, cook, boy and four of the crew were washed overboard and drowned."[60]

PJ, May 16, 1829

Eliza Grant

Specifications: Built in 1824 by Joseph Coe. Square stern, billet head. Burthen, 353 tons; length, 110.2 feet; beam, 26.7 feet; depth, 13.35 feet. Owners, January 10, 1825, John, Benjamin, and William F. Salter and Joseph Coe.

The Salter family was heavily involved in the *Eliza Grant* from her beginnings. Yet nothing in the Salter genealogy makes mention of the ship by name. John Salter took her on her first voyage to the south and then for the return from Liverpool. Joseph Coe sold his interest in October 1825, and it is possible that he was part of the ownership while the Salters were paying for the ship. William C. Tibbetts, John Salter's cousin and brother-in-law, commanded the *Eliza Grant* after the maiden voyage. She was gone from Portsmouth for four years, returning in April 1829 under John McManus. That was a rough passage from Liverpool, taking 53 days, and she brought coal and salt to John Salter. On April 14, 1829, the *Gazette* reported that the *Eliza Grant* had supplied the ship *Pacific* with provisions, and it was also learned that the *Pacific* had supplied the ship *Edward*, 106 days out of Liverpool, with provisions. John Salter advertised the *Eliza Grant*'s cargo as being 1,500 hogsheads of Liverpool salt and "25 chaldrons coal." In the same ad, Salter was seeking 50 tons of "screwed hay," often an article shipped to southern ports.

Although the *Eliza Grant* was sold in 1829, Captain Tibbetts resumed command, and, on May 6th, with the *Sarah Parker*, arrived at Charleston from Portsmouth. The *Eliza Grant* came into New York on September 9, 1830, with 120 passengers.[61] In December 1831, she was again pressed into packet service for the transport of immigrants to the United States. At that time, she brought into New York 136 unfortunates who had steerage accommodations. Again in 1833, she was in that service.[62] She sailed from Liverpool on May 26 for New York but put into Boston, en route to renew her provisions. In April 1834, the *Eliza Grant* entered her former home port under Captain Tibbetts with salt for Lewis Barnes and Ichabod Goodwin. The passage from Liverpool was rough; the ship lost bulwarks, stanchions and boats. Nevertheless, she sailed on April 19 for New Orleans, then crossed the ocean, and was in Savannah on November 2, 1834.[63] Tibbetts took her back and forth across the Atlantic until 1837. She went into Charleston in July, having been severely battered by a summer storm. She went from there to Savannah. While there, Captain Tibbetts was fatally stricken. Captain John Salter went south to get the ship, and, on her passage north, she was wrecked on the treacherous shoals of Cape Hatteras.

Eliza

Specifications: Built in 1824 by Joseph Coe. Square stern, female figurehead. Burthen, 355 tons; length, 109.4 feet; beam, 26.9 feet; depth, 13.45 feet. Owners, December 25, 1824, Thomas Haven, John Winkley and Joseph Coe.

Once again, it would seem that Joseph Coe retained a share in one of his ships until the other owners made enough out of a voyage to pay what was owed on the vessel. That her owners registered the *Eliza* on Christmas Day occasions no surprise when it is remembered that Christmas wasn't yet a big holiday in New England. The *Eliza* went to sea under John Winkley on January 3, 1825, headed for Charleston and a crossing to Europe.[64] She came back to a southern port with passengers from Belfast.

A moment of maritime fame came for the *Eliza* in 1831, while Daniel Wise of Portsmouth was master. She had been sold to Baltimore interests in 1828, although the news items of 1831 describe her as "of Portsmouth." It was reported in January that the *Eliza* had been badly damaged on November 29 and that she had lost her rudder and had had part of her stern stove in.[65] She had sailed from the Downs on November 18, 1830, and was nearly wrecked in a gale but beat her way into Plymouth, England, thanks to the ingenuity of Captain Wise, who told his insurors in Boston about it in a letter written from Plymouth:

Dear Sir.—I take this opportunity to inform you of the serious disaster which befell this ship on 28th November...in a most dreadful gale while lying too, (the helm nearly amidships and two men tending the wheel) a most tremendous cross sea broke on her quarter and under the counter at 5 o'clock in the morning, which carried away all three of the lower pintles of the rudder, broke and tore off the rudder brace from the stem under the counter, and snapped the tiller into two pieces near the middle, and before we could break the iron bands and braces that secure the tiller to the rudder head to let the rudder go, it beat in all the rudder case, tore off many of the stern planks, arch board, several planks off the counter, and the whole stern and large part of the counter exposed to every sea, and in the most iminent danger of being foundered, the cabin all open, and free communications for the water through the counter timbers to the hold...[66]

With painstaking detail, Captain Wise outlined the steps he took to make the ship as watertight as possible, using tarpaulins and boards. It was, of course, no small boost to the spirits of the *Eliza*'s crew to have two other ships standing by as they labored. One of the accompanying ships tried to tow the *Eliza* when the weather eased, but it didn't work. Finally, the two ships had to leave the stricken vessel to her fate. Captain Wise wrote, "Necessity being the mother of invention, I then set my wits at work to plan a temporary rudder."[67] His explanation of what he did was printed in full but would be beyond the comprehension of twentieth century landlubbers. His jury rig did so well that he was able to steer clear of the rocky Scilly Isles and work his way around to Plymouth. He took great pride in reporting:

> The great naval characters from the King's Dock Yard, have visited my ship to see this rudder, and how it would work, and were astonished at it, and how easy it worked, and the simplicity of it, and thought we deserved great credit; and I have received a flattering letter from Lloyd's, London...I have had to discharge a great part of my cargo, go into Dry Dock, to look at the lower rudder braces and bottom; I have taken all on board again...

When the weather calmed, Wise sailed again for his home port, Philadelphia, making the passage without difficulty. He was hailed by the insurors for his feat. So grateful were they that they presented Wise with a silver service. On an urn was engraved:

Presented to
Capt. Daniel Wise, Jr.
of the
SHIP ELIZA
by the President & Directors, in behalf
of the
Stockholders of the Pennsylvania, Union
Atlantic, Phoenix and United States
Insurance Offices of Philadelphia

It isn't known what eventually happened to the *Eliza*. She had been sold out of the Portsmouth District and wouldn't have been reported again if it hadn't been for Captain Wise's adventure.

Superior

Specifications: Built in 1825 by Joseph Coe. Square stern, billet head. Burthen, 348 tons; length, 104.4 feet; beam, 27.4 feet; depth, 13.7 feet. Owners, February 22, 1826, Charles Cushing, Stephen Patten and Joseph Coe.

From the very outset, the *Superior* was employed in the cotton trade with William Thompson as her first master. She completed her maiden triangular voyage on September 6, 1826, coming into Portsmouth from Liverpool with salt for Charles Cushing. Her run was 34 days. Thompson took her out again the week before Christmas, 1826, heading for Charleston. In November 1828, the *Superior* was reported ashore south of Wellfleet, Cape Cod, at 4 a.m. on the 6th.[68] She was en route home from St. Ubes with salt and sat on the sands for four days before floating off. Later, it was reported that she had suffered little damage, although 300 tons of her cargo had been thrown off. She sailed from Boston on the 30th, heading for Savannah, and made it in 18 days.

The *Superior* visited her native river once again in September 1830. With Thompson still in command, she came from Liverpool with salt and coal for Cushing, and merchandise for William Goddard and Richard Jenness. It was also reported that the *Superior* had sailed for Savannah, but she was in Charleston 30 days later. Late in October 1831, she returned to Portsmouth with a cargo of Liverpool salt. She made the same circuit in 1832.

Joshua Bailey, who made his home at what then was 40 Court Street, took the *Superior* to Charleston in November. An 1833 news report said:

> The *Charleston Courier* of the 11th ult says: A very violent storm of rain, accompanied by much thunder and lightning, occurred yesterday between 12 and one o'clock. The ship *Superior*, Bailey (of Portsmouth), bound to Havre, lying in the Roads, was struck during the squall. The lightning entered the main mast royal head, and ran down the top-gallant mast, shivering them to pieces, it passed from thence to the sheave hole of the topmast, tearing off a large piece, continued down the topsail tye on to the main sheets, and when it reached the deck, it tore off the pump coat, went below; and came out about 5 feet abaft the mast, tearing up a deck plank with it. The Cook was knocked down, but received no material injury...

Repairs were made, and the *Superior* sailed to Havre, returning to New York in August. On her passage, the ship gave aid to a brig that was foundering. The *Superior* was sold in New York in 1834, but Bailey continued as master, constantly plying the Atlantic triangle. She ventured to Palermo, Italy, and she was at Apalachicola loading cotton in 1857. What ended her service isn't known.

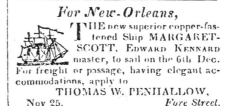

PJ, November 25, 1826

Margaret Scott

Specifications: Built in 1826 by Joseph Coe. Square stern, female figurehead. Burthen, 307 tons; length, 101.4 feet; beam, 26.1 feet; depth, 13.05 feet. Owners, December 5, 1826, Thomas W. and Oliver W. Penhallow and Joseph Coe.

Thirty-five years after her launching, the *Margaret Scott* suffered an unusual ending to her useful career. With one other Piscataqua-built ship, the *Lewis*, she became part of the "Stone Fleet," a little-known phase of the Civil War. There was no thought of things like that, however, when the Penhallows advertised her in November 1826:

For New Orleans

The new superior copper-fastened ship MARGARET SCOTT,
Edward Kennard, master, to
sail on 6th Dec. For freight
or passage, having elegant accommodations, apply to
THOMAS W. PENHALLOW
Fore Street

The *Margaret Scott* didn't sail until December 11th but in the days of wind power that was practically on schedule. Kennard didn't bring her home until June 1828, coming from New York, where she had landed her cargo. Her next voyage was to Turk's Island for salt, then out again in February 1829. It was more than a year before the *Margaret Scott* re-entered Portsmouth, having dropped off 130 passengers in New York. She went to New Orleans on March 5, 1831, and was in London in time to be chartered January 15, 1832, as the immigrant packet to New York, where she arrived in April. From New York, she was sent to City Point, Virginia, from there to Europe, and, ultimately to the Isle de Sal in the Cape Verde Islands. It was reported in October 1832, that the *Margaret Scott* had gone ashore on Little Boar's Head, North Hampton, New Hampshire, but managed to get off without serious damage, coming up the Piscataqua on October 4th.[71] Her next voyage, under Thomas Lunt, was around the triangle: New Orleans, Liverpool and Portsmouth, where she arrived on August 3, 1834. Lunt had her in October 1836, when she came in with salt for T.W. Penhallow and William Jones (the latter had bought an interest in 1830). While making that entrance, she went up on the mud on the southeast tip of New Castle Island in a gale but again escaped without injury. She sailed for New Orleans in December 1836, then to Liverpool, and from there to Cadiz for salt. At the end of what was to be his last voyage, Captain Lunt brought the *Margaret Scott* into the Port of Portsmouth from Spain. Lunt was then 69 and decided to quit the sea. He died a year later. Lunt's first command had been a 90-ton schooner, the *Dispatch*, in 1795. The first three-master he skippered was the *Howard* in 1802.

John Amazeen, a member of the long-established New Castle family, took the *Margaret Scott* on a quick voyage to Bonaire for salt. Then she was taken by Pearce W. Penhallow, master on two salt runs. Captain Penhallow went on to become one of the most respected master mariners of his time, as related in the author's *Clippers of the Port of Portsmouth*. But time was running out on the *Margaret Scott*'s Portsmouth service:

> FOR SALE, if applied for soon, the Copper-fastened and Coppered Ship MARGARET-SCOTT, built in Durham, N.H., in 1826, of white oak and salted on the stocks—is a good carrier and sails well...She has been examined the present year by Marine Inspectors, Boston and their certificate may be seen...[72]

It should be explained that "salting" was quite often done in the construction of vessels. It was a process whereby every nook and cranny in a vessel's hull and ribbing was treated with salt brine, thus adding "seasoning" to the wood. An allied technique, used especially in dealing with really green timbers, was to soak them for six months or so in a salt pond. Only a few years ago, the Portsmouth Naval Shipyard had timbers for the *U.S.S. Constitution* soaking in a salt pond.[73]

S.A.W. Ingalls, an owner and operator of New Bedford whalers, bought the *Margaret Scott* and put her under a Captain Smith. She made four whaling cruises between 1841 and 1855, earning $135,569. Rerigged as a bark in 1855, she made two more whaling voyages. From the first of these, her catch was worth $66,332. No figures are available for her second cruise as a bark. Shortly after her return, she was sold to an unscrupulous syndicate of Yankee entrepreneurs that had plans for her far different than whaling. She was being equipped for a slaving voyage to Africa when seized by the Federal authorities. With the Civil War in full spa, the federal government realized the necessity of trying to blockade all Confederate ports.

This realization developed into a concept that became the "Stone

Fleet." The attention of the United States Navy to the problem and the many technical details involved have been well reported in an article by Commodore Arthur Gordon, entitled *Union Stone Fleets of the Civil War*, so a lengthy discussion isn't necessary here.[74] In brief, the naval strategists envisioned assembling fleets of old vessels, loading them with stone, and sinking them in the major channels of southern ports. The Navy ordered the first purchases for the Stone Fleet on October 17, 1861. The *Margaret Scott* wasn't bought at that time, although the ship *Lewis* was. A second contingent of worn-out whalers was acquired, and the *Margaret Scott* was one of them. As noted earlier, she had been condemned because of the efforts to use her as a slaver. At a public auction, the Navy put in a bid for $4,000. The first flotilla of stone-filled whalers went to Savannah, but the *Margaret Scott* and her sisters had their date with destiny in Charleston. The *Margaret Scott* was sunk in Maffitt Channel, January 25–26, 1862, with 12 others. Her last master was Henry F. Tobey, and the second Stone Fleet was commanded by Arthur Gordon, a commodore. While the plan seemed workable on paper, it failed after execution. So much so, that it became part of seafaring legend in a couplet:

A Failure, and complete
Was your Old Stone Fleet[75]

Montgomery

Specifications: Built in 1826 by Joseph Coe. Square stern, male figurehead. Burthen, 399.9 tons; length, 112.8 feet; beam, 28 feet; depth, 14 feet. Owners, February 6, 1826, James Shapley and Henry and Henry P. Salter.

It's a bit puzzling as to why Joseph Coe simply didn't assign 400 tons burthen to the *Montgomery*. Among the ships he built, she was second in size only to the 403-ton *Nile* he had constructed at Newmarket the year before. Who could have argued if he had given his ship a tenth of a ton (200 pounds) more?

The pragmatic Salters wasted no time in pondering trivia like the above. They put the second *Montgomery* into the triangle trade immediately. It was reported a week after her registration that the "new and elegant ship *Montgomery*" had sailed for New Orleans on the 11th.[76] It was at Savannah, however, that she loaded her first cargo for Liverpool. No doubt, the master, Henry Salter, had the option of putting into cotton ports as he sailed and found a cargo in Savannah. With the slowness of communications, captains were given great leeway in such matters. Henry Salter, son of Captain John Salter, lived at what was then 20 Court Street. Henry Salter died in 1837.

Under Captain Salter, the *Montgomery* completed her first triangle on July 23, 1827, coming from Liverpool with salt for the owners, hardware for Sherburne & Blunt and J.F. Pickering, and crates for Edward F. Sise. But the pattern of employment for the *Montgomery* was one that would become increasingly familiar in the Portsmouth District in the years ahead: the *Montgomery* rarely came back to Portsmouth. Instead, she sailed a triangle based on New York. Not until 1833 did she come home with John Sise as master. Captain Samuel Shackford made a similar voyage in 1835. The *Montgomery* made one more entrance into Portsmouth. That was under Joseph Grace in 1837; on September 4th, she came in ballast from Turk's Island where she had gone for salt. Captain Grace reported salt prices very high—17 cents a bushel, which may have been why he returned without a cargo.[77]

The *Montgomery* sailed from Portsmouth, under Captain Grace, on November 1, 1837, her last departure. She headed for Mobile and took the month of November to get there. From Mobile, she went to Liverpool, and then back to New Orleans, finally arriving in New York, on September 29, 1839, with salt from St. Ubes.[78] In December, she went south to Mobile and loaded for Havre. On January 31, 1840, after rounding the treacherous Florida Keys, she grounded on Carys Fort Reef. The *Montgomery* was badly damaged by the pounding, but, after a day of work, wreckers got her off and took her into Key West. News reports coming out of Key West were far from encouraging: the *Montgomery* was "perceptibly hogged" (arched in the center like a hog's back), and fears were general that she couldn't be repaired.[79] Progress was slow; there were court actions. Finally, to settle the claims of the wreckers, she was sold. Captain Victor Constant of Boston bought her for $4,500, and she disappeared from Portsmouth annals.

John Hale

Specifications: Built in 1827 by William Hanscom of Eliot. Square stern, male figurehead. Burthen, 368 tons; length, 108.9 feet; beam, 27.5 feet; depth, 13.75 feet. Owners, December 31, 1827, Samuel Sheafe, Mark W. Peirce and Ebenezer Thompson, Jr.

The *John Hale* was the first of two ships built in Durham by the peripatetic shipwright William Hanscom. From whence came the name for the ship can only be speculated. It might have been to honor a prominent Rochester lawyer, John Parker Hale, who had died in 1819. He was the father of one of New Hampshire's leading politicians in the mid-nineteenth century, also John Parker Hale.

The *John Hale* sailed from Portsmouth on December 11, 1827, more than three weeks before her registration date. Ebenezer Thompson, Jr., was master, and she made a decent run to Savannah. News accounts reported:

> The ship *John-Hale*, of and from this port. arrived at Savannah Dec. 24th in 13 days. On the night of the 23d December, being dark and blowing fresh from N.N.E. steering S.W., 1/2 S. came in contact with the ship *Eliza-and-Abby*, of Providence, bound to Savannah. The jib boom of the *John-Hale* caught in the spanker of the *Eliza & Abby*, and she fell alongside to the leeward, there being a considerable sea. The *Eliza-&-Abby* received considerable damage, losing all her spars but the foremast and fore-yard; the main and mizzen masts being carried away near the deck, and nearly all their sails were lost. The John-Hale had the cutwater started off, trail boards broke, jib-boom carried away, jib torn; the larboard [port] anchor hooked in the rail of the other ship; the cable was cut to get clear... The scene for about 20 minutes was dreadful, it being so dark, it could not be seen what held the ships together. At first all the crew but two jumped on board the *John-Hale* but as soon as clear, returned on board their own ship.— The *John-Hale* stood off and on by her until daylight... Another Providence ship being close to the Eliza-&-Abby took her in tow and got safe up to Savannah...

The accident was probably unavoidable. The *John Hale* limped into Savannah on the 27th, was soon repaired, and went to Havre, although she grounded on her way out. She arrived in Boston on September 21st, taking 47 days from France.[80] She ended her voyage by coming into Portsmouth in mid-October. Back she went to Savannah, sailing from there to Liverpool and arriving on February 8, 1829, then back to the United States, a classic example of Portsmouth ships in the triangular trade.

It was on a voyage from Portsmouth in November 1830 that a report concerning the *John Hale* brought great delight to the offices of the *Portsmouth Journal*, a newspaper dedicated to the cause of temperance. It came in a letter in which it was said that Captain Thompson and the entire crew of the *John Hale* bound for New Orleans and Europe had *no ardent spirits* on board of any variety. The officers and men had willingly signed articles to that effect. A few misguided souls may have quaffed deeply in ports like New Orleans and Liverpool, but it also could be that Thompson had recruited only temperance men, as the movement was quite strong at that time.

The *John Hale* followed the triangle through the years. One of her most exciting arrivals in Portsmouth was on October 13, 1832, when she came in with 88 Swiss immigrants.[81] Five children died on the passage, all of them under the age of 4. Two of them were members of the Haist family, 25 of whom were on the *John Hale*. Then there were Francis T. Klump, 42, a baker, and Anna, 30, his wife, and eight little Klumps. The Klumps had lost a son. Johanns Mast, 50, a laborer, lost his 30-year-old-wife, Regina. There was a Morle family; and Mathias Mosback and wife, with three children, plus Grandpa Mosback, 79.

Later, the *John Hale* was commanded by Samuel Crowell, who, on July 3, 1835, brought 150 steerage passengers into New York. The passage had taken six weeks from Greenock, Scotland. The *John Hale* was back in Portsmouth in December 1837, when Samuel Sheafe advertised 1,400 hogsheads of Cadiz salt, which was being landed on Rindge's Wharf in the North End.[82] Less than a year later, Sheafe was advertising 150 tons of "No. 1 Scotch PIG IRON, received per ship *John Hale* from Greenock."[83]

While there were occasional diversions, the cotton trade was the *John Hale*'s life. For example, in 1841, a Captain Perkins had her at Hamburg, Germany, after a passage from Matanzas. She was at Hamburg to load railroad iron for Portsmouth.[84] However, she actually loaded the rails at Cardiff, Wales. They were used in the construction of the Eastern Railroad between Boston and Portsmouth.[85]

Time ran out on the *John Hale*. She had been at Havana and was chartered to go to the Dry Tortugas, presumably for salt, which was intended for Europe. The *John Hale* was lost in June 1843 on Eleuthera, the Bahamas. Some materials were salvaged, and the hulk was sold in Nassau for $1,100.[86]

Mary & Harriet

Specifications: Built in 1827 by Joseph Coe. Square stern, billet head. Burthen, 397 tons; length, 112.9 feet; beam, 28 feet; depth, 14 feet. Owners, John Salter and Samuel Cushman of Portsmouth; W.F. and B. Salter and W.C. Barstow, all of New York.

The *Mary & Harriet* was named for one of the daughters of Benjamin Franklin Salter of New York. Mary lived to be 78, dying in Apalachicola in 1902, where her husband had been in business for many years. Harriet was the given name of her mother, Harriet Chase Tibbetts, who died in New York in 1872 at 77.[87]

As indicated in the ownership, the *Mary & Harriet* was almost entirely a Salter enterprise. The New York Salters were cousins of the Portsmouth family. W.C. Barstow was master on the *Mary & Harriet*'s maiden voyage but, after that, Hall Jackson Tibbetts, another Salter relative, was master. With him as mate on the voyage went John Lake Salter who had married the captain's sister, Elizabeth. John Lake

Salter later left seafaring so far behind as to take up farming in Illinois.[88]

The *Mary & Harriet* was wrecked near Anglesey, Wales, in December 1836 and apparently sold in the spring after being floated off the rocks.

Ann

Specifications: Built by William Hanscom in 1828. Square stern, female figurehead. Burthen, 334 tons; length, 109.5 feet; beam, 26 feet; depth, 13 feet. Owners, January 28, 1829, Thomas Haven and Thomas Goddard.

During the two decades the *Ann* had Portsmouth for a hailing port, she was a faithful and profitable performer in the triangular cotton trade. She left the Port of Portsmouth on February 6, 1829, for Savannah under the veteran shipmaster John S. Place. In the first years, she plied back and forth across the Atlantic, returning often to Philadelphia and New York. In December 1831, the *Ann* arrived in New Orleans, via Philadelphia, with 381 steerage passengers. It is beyond modern grasp to realize the hardships of a steerage passage 150 years ago.

Captain Place left the *Ann* before she was sold at auction in 1834. An advertisement by McClintock & Adams, auctioneers, described her as in "A-1" condition and that she had been "salted on the stocks."[89] The *Ann* was sold to Charles Ladd and William Briard. They promptly sent her to sea under J.P. Penhallow, who took her to New Orleans for cotton, thence to Liverpool. The *Ann*'s first master, John S. Place, became master of the Portsmouth-owned ship *Emerald*. Although not locally built, the *Emerald* did yeoman service for her owners. In 1837, the *Emerald* was lost in the Gulf Stream despite Place's heroic efforts to save her. Captain Place and 11 men managed to reach Jekyll Island on the Georgia coast. A news item reported:

> Capt. Place arrived at Brunswick, Georgia, Sept. 25th, after great exposure, having encountered all the troubles incident to looking after a wreck on a coast unknown to himself and his crew... In those arduous exertions he was obliged to sleep on the beach, whereby a vigorous constitution was undermined. He took passage on the ship *Gov. Cass*, which arrived here [New York] on Sunday from Savannah... in a few hours after his arrival was removed to Holt's Hotel where he breathed his last soon after a physician was called in.[90]

Getting back to the *Ann*, J.P. Penhallow was master until 1841, when Nathan Godfrey took her out of Portsmouth on November 6th. It was the intent to load at Charleston, but no cargo was available, so Godfrey took her around the Florida Keys to Apalachicola. There was no cargo there either, so the *Ann* sailed along the Gulf Coast to Mobile, Alabama, where she loaded cotton for the mills of New York, arriving in that port on May 15, 1842. Her cargo discharged, she came to Portsmouth on June 13th, and was tied up until October 29th. That gave Captain Godfrey a chance to spend time with his wife and family on old Vaughan Street.

The *Ann*'s next orders took her to Mobile, where, in January 1843, she loaded for Ghent in Belgium, arriving there in March.[91] As far as can be determined from the Customs records, the *Ann* was away from Portsmouth for several years. One of her frequent ports of call was New Orleans, going from there to Havre. On one passage in 1846, she put into Key West to load with materials salvaged by wreckers on the Florida Reef. Throughout her service on the East Coast, she never suffered serious damage, even with an occasional boisterous passage. Several different masters strode her quarter deck, among them Nathaniel S. Rogers and men named Curtis and Henderson.

Captain Curtis had the *Ann* on one of her worst passages when she sprang a leak off Sand Key on January 23, 1849.[92] An easterly storm opened her up to such an extent that the pumps were going 650 strokes to the hour—exhausting work. Other adventures awaited her. The *Ann* had made her last trip to the Piscataqua the year before, when she loaded with hay for the United States Army at Vera Cruz, Mexico. Federal charters of this kind went to several Portsmouth-built vessels during the Mexican War.

Gold had been discovered in California, and gold fever was raging virulently on the East Coast. Any vessel that could stay afloat while rounding Cape Horn was being pressed into service by the gold seekers. The *Ann* was sold at Boston and sailed June 30, 1849, for San Francisco. She never returned.

Mersey

Specifications: Built in 1829 by Joseph Coe. Square stern, billet head. Burthen, 372 tons; length, 111.3 feet; beam, 27.3 feet; depth, 13.65 feet. Owner, William Bowne of Westchester, N.Y.

The *Mersey*, named to honor the river of cotton mills in England, was not only Coe's last ship, she was also the last three-masted, square-rigged vessel built in Durham. Other smaller craft were built, but the shipbuilding era in Durham was over.

VI *Exeter*

NHG, November 10, 1801

LIKE THE REST OF THE PORTS on the upper Piscataqua, Exeter's shipbuilding bent spanned four centuries. Founded in 1638, there can be little doubt that the early Exeter settlers put many vessels on the water in the seventeenth century and that activity didn't cease until 1902. Charles H. Bell notes:

> As early as 1651 Edward Gilman, Jr., had upon the stocks a vessel of about 50 tons burden. In the returns of the custom-house in Portsmouth for three months in the year 1692, two clearances from Exeter for Boston are found; one of the sloop "Endeavour" of Exeter, 20 tons burden, *plantation-built* [Emphasis added], having on board six thousand of pipe staves, and 400 feet of pine planks; the other the sloop "Elizabeth" of Exeter, of 20 tons, Francis Lyford, commander, plantation-built...[1]

No one knows the name of that 50-ton vessel on the ways in 1651, but many are familiar with the name of the last, the schooner *Merrill*, built by Stewart Russell in 1902. Between the two events, countless vessels were built in Exeter. However, the purpose of this study is to tell the stories of three-masted, square-rigged vessels built between the end of the Revolution and 1829. Exeter's shipyards made solid contributions, although all the major building ways are now buried beneath the beautiful Swazey Parkway, which is indeed appropriately named.

First the statistics: Exeter's yards saw the building of no fewer than 23 ships, for a total tonnage of 6,378, an average of 277.3 tons. And it must be emphasized that this was done in less than two decades. Exeter's last ship was launched in 1807, although Exeter's shipyards in the first 30 years of the republic also produced 14 brigs, with a total tonnage of 2,080; one bark, 187 tons; one snow, 152 tons, plus six schooners and six sloops.[2]

The greater part of the story of Exeter shipbuilding centers on two men: Eliphalet Ladd and Joseph Swazey. Whether Ladd personally ever touched a tool to the vessels credited to him is open to speculation. The feeling comes through strongly that he was more the organizer, manager and owner than shipwright wielding a chisel. Again it is guess work, but probably Ladd's successes as a privateersman established him both financially and as a leader of men. The family genealogy is insistent on this point, although the family-serving interest of a genealogy is always suspect.[3] Exactly who the craftsmen were that Ladd employed in Exeter isn't known; perhaps Joseph Swazey may have been one of them. There is no question, however, that ships, either fully or partly owned by him, slid down the ways frequently in Exeter. He continued to have ships built there after he had moved to Portsmouth. In fact, his masterpiece, the *Archelaus*, was built after his removal.

Joseph Swazey, on the other hand, was completely the master shipbuilder. Unlike Joseph Coe in Durham, Swazey wasn't involved in the ownership of his vessels. He built them and let others own and sail them. Swazey, given the title of captain in the family genealogy, was born in Exeter in 1743, lived there all his life, dying at the ripe old age of 86.[4] Because the first United States Customs' records don't list the builders, it is impossible to know when he became a master builder. The first vessel credited to him was a brig, the *Planter*, built in 1800, when he was 57. He was in his mid-60s when he built his last Exeter ship, the *Maria*, in 1807. With the dawn of 1800, it becomes possible also to learn the names of a few other Exeter builders. Among them were Thomas Savage, Daniel Conner, Benjamin Smith, Eliphalet Giddings and John Page, but only Ladd and Swazey left heavy imprints on Exeter shipbuilding.

Betsy

Specifications: Built in 1788. Burthen 191 tons. Owner, January 3, 1788, John Salter of Portsmouth.

Customs records indicate more than a dozen arrivals in the Port of Portsmouth by the *Betsy* between 1790 and 1801. Throughout the period, John Salter was the owner. Captain Salter first entrusted command to Thomas Thompson, whose home at present-day 179 Pleasant Street is an outstanding example of early federal architecture. Under Thompson, the *Betsy* came in from England. Four months later, she arrived from Tobago under Richard Salter. who was obviously related to Titus Salter and was the next master of the *Betsy*, holding the command from 1791 to 1793. John Salter took her himself to England in 1793, returning in May 1794. Except for the customs entries, not much is known about her voyages. Three other men also served as master: William Edwards, Mark Blunt and yet another Salter, Joseph. The *Betsy* was condemned and broken up in 1804.[5]

Arethusa

Specifications: Built in 1789. Burthen, 140 tons. Owner, Gilbert Horney of Portsmouth.

The *Arethusa* was small, even by the standards of her day. Gilbert Horney doubled as both merchant and captain. He had a shop on Court Street across from the Pitt Tavern. In the 1780s, he made several voyages to England, but the *Arethusa* was sold out of the district shortly thereafter.

Cleopatra

Specifications: Built in 1790 by Eliphalet Ladd. Square stern, billet head. Burthen, 301 tons. Owners, James McClure and Eliphalet Ladd.

Little or nothing is known about the Exeter-built *Cleopatra*. Eliphalet Ladd apparently sold his interest to McClure shortly after she was launched. There is one customs record that notes her arrival in Portsmouth from Boston on August 16, 1799.

Rainbow

Specifications: Built in 1790. Burthen, 198 tons. Owners, September 25, 1790, Richard Salter and James Sheafe.

Richard Salter made two voyages in the *Rainbow*, arriving from London on August 29, 1791, and from Amsterdam on October 3, 1792. Captain Salter was then 44 years of age. During the Revolution, he had continued to be active in merchandising, and his sloop, the *Friends Adventure*, was captured by an American privateer. Salter had duplicate papers, one set for the British, the other for the Americans. The courts held Salter's vessel was British and he lost her.[6] Tobias Lear, also of Portsmouth, suffered the same kind of loss a year before in 1776. Later in the Revolution, Salter commanded a letter-of-marque, the *Swan*, owned by John Langdon. Captain Salter died in 1812 at 66. His son Richard, born in 1773, advertised in 1816 that he would teach navigation to those interested.[7]

There is no information as to the ultimate fate of the *Rainbow*. Several possibilities exist: (1) She could have been wrecked; (2) she could have been sold; (3) she could have been taken by a French privateer during the Quasi War.

Columbia

Specifications: Built in 1791 by Eliphalet Ladd. Burthen, 286 tons. Owner, June 27, 1791, Eliphalet Ladd.

The story of the *Columbia* is both brief and tragic: she never finished her first voyage. Isaac Chauncey of Portsmouth, one of the town's promising young shipmasters, took the *Columbia* to Kennebunk on June 30, 1791, to load lumber for Liverpool. The outward passage was successful, but disaster ended the return. The news report in March 1792 said:

> Saturday evening the 10th inst., a ship from Liverpool, Capt. Isaac Chauncy, belong to Col. Ephalet Ladd, of Exeter, was bilged on a ledge of rocks off Duxbury Beach [Five miles noth of Plymouth, Massachusetts]. The master and 13 other persons were drowned — two only of the hands were taken off the wreck alive by a boat from Plymouth lighthouse. Among the dead were two young gentlemen from Birmingham [England], who intended to settle in this town, and had large property on board. It is said that the Captain was confined to his cabin by sickness, and the Mate, trusting rather to his own judgment than the Captain's directions, kept the ship too far to the westward; and when the mistake was discovered it was too late to rectify it. Capt. Chauncy met death with much composure, and gave his pocketbook, containing his most valuable papers, to his cabin boy who happily was one of the survivors.. — The corpse was brought hither on Wednesday last, and deposited in the family tomb with the remains of his worthy grandfather the late Rev. Dr. Chauncy.

The Mate, the passengers, and some of the seamen were washed ashore at Marshfield and decently interred.

The shore for several miles round were covered with pieces of the wreck and goods which the *Columbia* was laden with.[8]

Archelaus

Specifications: Built in 1793 by Eliphalet Ladd. Square stern, billet head. Burthen, 498 tons; length, 112.3 feet; beam, 31.3 feet. Owner, February 4, 1793, Eliphalet Ladd.

What prompted Eliphalet Ladd to create the largest merchant vessel yet launched in the Port of Portsmouth will never be known. Was he obsessed with the loss of his 20-gun fighting ship, the *Hercules*, during the Revolution? At two tons short of 500, the *Archelaus* must have been near the *Hercules* in size. The *Archelaus* wouldn't be surpassed by any Piscataqua merchant ship until 1833 when George Raynes built the *Rockingham*, 513 tons. Historian Bell wrote:

> The ship-building interest gradually decreased in the town, after the coming of the present century [nineteenth], though the manufacture of sail-cloth and twine and many blacksmith's shops are remembered by our oldest citizens. One who recently deceased [c. 1888], used to describe a large vessel of probably 500 tons that he saw on the stocks, the bowsprit of which projected beyond the fronts of adjacent buildings, into Water Street, between Spring and Centre Streets. A vessel of that size had so great a draft of water that it had to be buoyed up by empty hogsheads in order to pass down the river at ordinary tide.[9]

Unfortunately, not much is known about Eliphalet Ladd's gigantic creation, except that, besides her three masts, she was one of the first ships to have three decks. Bell's observation as to how large vessels went to sea from Exeter is the best clue as to why the town's shipwrights stopped building large vessels when they did.

As for the *Archelaus*, the Exeter leviathan, the customs records have little to offer. They do say, however, that she was sold in Boston and later wrecked on Cape Cod.[10]

Fame

Specifications: Built in 1793. Burthen, 240 tons; length, 87.5 feet; beam, 25.1 feet; depth, 12.55 feet. Owner, June 11, 1793, Eliphalet Ladd.

His ownership of the Exeter-built *Fame* indicates Eliphalet Ladd probably was her builder. Certainly she was launched during the time he was active in ship construction in Exeter, although he already moved to Portsmouth. Robert Blunt was the *Fame*'s first master. He later suffered misfortune with the *Eudora*. The next master was John McClintock, son of the Bunker Hill chaplain, the Rev. Samuel McClintock of

Greenland, New Hampshire. McClintock took her on two voyages to the West Indies.

Joseph Brown was the last master of the *Fame*. He had her when she was captured by a French privateer in 1796, at a time the Quasi War was smoldering. The *Fame* was taken to Curacao by her captor, the *LePandoor*, and there condemned, becoming part of the long-dragged-out French Spoliation litigation. When finally settled in the 1900s, the heirs of Elijah Hall, her last owner, received what little was allowed for the *Fame*.

Randolph

Specifications: Built in 1795. Burthen, 264 tons; length, 89.9 feet; beam, 26 feet; depth, 13 feet. Owner, February 14, 1795, John McClintock.

Perhaps the *Randolph* was named for the Virginia statesman, Edmund Randolph, who played an important role as United States attorney general in the early days of the republic. John McClintock sent the *Randolph* to St. Ubes twice for salt, with George Greenough as master. When she came in from her second voyage, McClintock sold her to Elijah Hall, but still took her to Jamaica himself, returning on March 9, 1798. John Hilton took her to Demerara after that, and then Robert Oran was master on a voyage to St. Ubes in 1799. She was lost later that year.

Eliza

Specifications: Built in 1795 by Eliphalet Ladd. Square stern, female figure-head. Burthen, 285 tons; length, 91.7 feet; beam, 26.8 feet. Owners, June 6, 1796, Samuel Chauncey and Eliphalet Ladd.

In her first four voyages, the Exeter-built Eliza was a salt ship, making runs to St. Ubes as fast as sailing and turn-around times permitted. Those voyages were made under the command of one of the owners, Captain Chauncey. His last voyage ended in the Port of Portsmouth on February 9, 1799. Ebenezer Ricker then made two voyages to Demerara before turning the *Eliza* over to William Ladd in 1802.

That gave the *Eliza* the distinction of having been commanded by a son of Eliphalet Ladd and also his son-in-law, Samuel Chauncey. William Ladd was only 24 when he became master of the Eliza, his first command. His first voyage with the *Eliza* was one that made a bit of national history. What was a bare-faced attempt by William Ladd to smuggle a new cable into the port, led, in its final outcome, to the first impeachment and conviction of a federal judge. The story has been told more fully in the author's book, *A Tale of Two Documents*. However, a letter written by the port collector, Joseph Whipple, to Treasury Secretary Albert Gallatin on November 15, 1802, puts the matter succinctly:

> ... This ship [the *Eliza*] arrived at Boston from Bonavista in the month of September, the cargo consisted of the following articles, 189 moys of salt...2 boxes to William Ladd the master, 180 goat skins, 4 pcs of canvas, 1 second hand cable consigned to William Ladd the master as stated by the manifest... On her arrival here the consignee of the salt, Eliphalet Ladd, made entry of it and secured the duty. There now remained on board 4 pcs of canvas and one second hand cable on which the duties were to be secured...[11]

Collector Whipple then told Gallatin that several days went by and nothing happened. Finally, an informant told Whipple that two cables had been loaded at Bonavista, one of them new, which William Ladd bought for his own account. When Whipple's agents went in search of it, they found Ladd had already smuggled it on shore. And let there be no doubt, smuggling was as rampant as it is today. Americans have ever been reluctant to pay customs duties. Legal notice of the libel served on the Ladds was published in October 1802 and set forth Whipple's allegations against the *Eliza*. Specifically he charged:

> ...that sundry goods and merchandize—viz Two Cables, and 100 pieces of Check'd linen, of foreign growth and manufacture, and of the value of $400, were imported in said ship, and unladen & delivered in said district.

The legal notice was authorized by U.S. District Court Judge John Pickering, who set a hearing for November 11, 1802, "at three o'clock in the afternoon." At the hearing, it was observed that Judge Pickering was drunk, and it was confirmed when he accepted a motion to adjourn, saying, "Adjourn. I shall be sober tomorrow morning. I am now damned drunk." To sum up, Pickering threw the case out of court, without justification, which is where political infighting began. Judge Pickering was a Federalist, appointed by George Washington. Collector Whipple and the U.S. district attorney, John Sherburne, were Jeffersonian Democrats. Politics change but little; the removal of Pickering would create a judgeship for President Jefferson to hand out. The United States House impeached the alcoholic justice; the United States Senate, on a party-line vote, convicted him. Rewards were distributed by the triumphant Jeffersonians: Sherburne became the United States District

Judge John Pickering, NHHS.

Court justice; one of the key witnesses against Pickering became the United States district attorney.

As for the ship *Eliza*, she was lost at sea shortly thereafter.

John

Specifications: Built in 1796. Burthen, 289 tons; length, 92.6 feet; beam, 26.8 feet; depth, 13.4 feet. Owner, June 6, 1797, Benjamin Boardman.

The Exeter-built *John* made one voyage under Samuel Boardman, coming in from St. Ubes on May 21, 1799. Then she was sold in Boston. Samuel Boardman was listed as a resident of Exeter and was probably connected to the Portsmouth family.

Charlotte

Specifications: Built in 1798. Burthen, 285 tons; length, 90.6 feet; beam, 27 feet. Owner, June 18, 1799, Eliphalet Ladd.

The year after Ladd registered the *Charlotte*, Samuel Chauncey brought her in from the West Indies, June 28, 1800. Later she was listed as lost at sea.[12]

New York

Specifications: Built in 1799. Burthen, 291 tons; length, 93 feet; beam, 26.85 feet; depth, 13.4 feet. Owner, May 7, 1799, Levi Coit of New York.

Tom

Specifications: Built in 1800 by Joseph Swazey. Square stern, billet head. Burthen, 288 tons; length, 92.5 feet; beam, 26.8 feet; depth, 13.4 feet. Owner, February 12, 1801, Nathaniel Haven.

It is hard to believe that a pragmatic shipowner like Nathaniel Haven waited four years to put the *Tom* into operation, despite problems with French privateers. The probability is that she sailed out of other ports. That belief is supported by a news item in November 1801 to the effect that Peter Turner had command of her on a passage from Hamburg to Philadelphia.[13] Wherever she was over the unaccountable four years, Captain Turner was master on April 4, 1805, when the *Tom* came into Portsmouth from Martinique. In June 1805, Turner became a part owner. John Seaward, however, was master in 1807, arriving from Copenhagen on October 4, 1807.

Samuel and William Ham bought the *Tom* in 1809 and sent her to Europe under Job W. Hall. She returned September 7, 1809.[14] The next public notice of her was that she was "repairing at Liverpool" in 1811.[15] Was she caught at Liverpool by the War of 1812 and interned? Or did she get home and sit out the war tied to a dock? Samuel Ham was listed as owner when she was reported lost in 1817.[16]

It is worthy of note that the *Tom* was the first ship credited to Joseph Swazey, who would be Exeter's master builder for the next seven years.

Hampshire

Specifications: Built in 1801 by Joseph Swazey. Square stern, billet head. Burthen, 243 tons; length, 87 feet; beam, 25.5 feet; depth, 12.75 feet. Owners, December 31, 1801, Gilman Leavitt, Daniel Conner and J.T. Gilman.

Perhaps the name of the *Hampshire* was given as a bit of an honor to Governor John T. Gilman of Exeter, who was then chief executive of the state. But that made little difference. The *Hampshire* was sold in Boston in 1803, after making a voyage to Barbados under a Captain Chamberlain in 1802.

Orozimbo

Specifications: Built in 1803 by Joseph Swazey. Square stern, billet head. Burthen, 264 tons; length, 89.4 feet; beam, 26.1 feet; depth, 13.05 feet. Owner, August 17, 1802, William Boyd.

John Tilton was master of the *Orozimbo* when she came into the Port of Portsmouth from the Isle of Wight, one of her two entries. It took Captain Tilton 57 days to make the passage. For passengers, he had the owner and his family. In September 1804, she cleared for New York under a Captain Brewster. A customs note says she was cast away; no date given.[17]

Monticello

Specifications: Built in 1803 by Joseph Swazey. Square stern, billet head. Burthen, 211 tons; length, 79.2 feet; beam, 25 feet; depth, 12.5 feet. Owners, September 2, 1803, John McClintock and Robert Treadwell.

The only Portsmouth entry for the *Monticello* had her coming in from the Isle of May, off Scotland, on March 20, 1805, under Henry McClintock. Treadwell sold his interest to John McClintock on May 6, 1805. Later that year, she was sold to Walter Folger of Nantucket.

It is probable that the *Monticello* was named to honor the residence of the incumbent president, Thomas Jefferson, because the owners might have been Republican-Democrats, as the Jeffersonians were called. It is fair speculation to wonder if the *Monticello* would have been so named had the hard-headed ship captains of Portsmouth foreseen Jefferson's Embargo Act and its dire consequences.

Frances

Specifications: Built in 1803 by Daniel Conner. Square stern, billet head. Burthen, 259 tons. Owners, Nicholas Gilman and others of Boston.

Exeter

Specifications: Built in 1804 by Joseph Swazey. Square stern, billet head. Burthen, 291 tons; length, 92.2 feet; beam, 27 feet; depth, 13.5 feet. Owner, Thomas Osgood of Salem, Massachusetts.

Samaritan

Specifications: Built in 1804 by Benjamin Smith. Square stern, billet head. Burthen, 212 tons; length, 82.7 feet; beam, 27 feet; depth, 13 feet. Owners, Daniel and Thomas Farley of Newburyport.

General Eaton

Specifications: Built in 1805 by Eliphalet Geddings. Square stern, billet head. Burthen, 294 tons; length, 82.7 feet; beam, 27 feet; depth, 13 feet. Owners, February 8, 1806, Isaac Waldron, et al.

When the *General Eaton* was built, the entire country was in the convulsions of hero worship. William Eaton, a graduate of Dartmouth College and a soldier with a flair for derring-do, had recruited a band of Arab and Greek mercenaries in Egypt. Backed by a hard-bitten cadre of seven United States Marines, Eaton had marched across the Libyan Desert to capture by storm the Bey of Tripoli's port of Derna. Eaton's success gave birth to the line in the Marine hymn, "To the shores of Tripoli..." When the details of his exploit, promoted by himself, reached the United States, Eaton became an instant hero, as fast as early nineteenth century communications allowed.

The *General Eaton* was sold in Boston in 1807, but there were subsequent news reports of her. One had her in a German port, late in 1807, getting ready to sail for Philadelphia. In 1811, it was reported that she had been captured by the French and was being held at Calais. Thomas Brown was then master.

Doris

Specifications: Built in 1807 by Joseph Swazey. Square stern, billet head. Burthen, 287 tons; length, 92.2 feet; beam, 26.8 feet; depth, 13.4 feet. Owners, Henry and Alexander Ladd and Samuel Chamberlain of Exeter.

The sixth of the seven ships built by Swazey, the *Doris* was the smallest. In 1808, Gideon Lamson sold her to Salem parties.

Roxana

Specifications: Built in 1806 by John Page. Square stern, billet head. Burthen, 331 tons; length, 98.6 feet; beam, 27.7 feet; depth, 13.85 feet. Owners, June 18, 1808, Daniel Conner and Nicholas and Nathaniel Gilman.

Maria

Specifications: Built in 1807 by Joseph Swazey. Square stern, billet head. Burthen, 287 tons; length, 92.2 feet; beam, 26.8 feet; depth 13.4 feet. Owners, Henry and Alexander Ladd and Samuel Chamberlain of Exeter.

The *Maria* was Joseph Swazey's last Exeter ship. He built the *Elizabeth Wilson* in Durham in 1810, as related in Chapter V. In 1816, Swazey crafted his last vessel, a 32-ton sloop, the *Nymph*. Perhaps it was a way of keeping his hand in, despite advancing age.

The *Maria* also was named for Maria Tufton Haven, who became Alexander Ladd's wife on December 29, 1807. When it came to making a dollar by the sale of a ship, however, sentiment held no sway. The *Maria* was sold in Norfolk in 1809.

VII *Kittery*

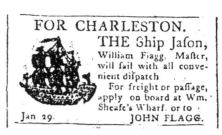

NHG, January 29, 1811

THROUGH THE CENTURIES, since the first coming of English settlers to the Piscataqua Valley, thousands of tons of shipping have been launched on the Maine side of the river within the bounds of Kittery. This unofficial estimate doesn't include any of the warships that have been constructed at the Portsmouth Navy Yard or at its predecessor, Langdon's shipyard, on what is now called Badger's Island.

It isn't clear who the earliest seventeenth century Kittery builders were, but there were Hanscoms in that period, and the family stayed in the trade for generations. In the period of this study, 1783 to 1829, civilian shipbuilding in Kittery is, basically, the story of William Badger, one of the most prolific builders ever known on the Piscataqua. Master Badger's career is described in the author's book, *Clippers of the Port of Portsmouth*, but a bit of review will be helpful. William Badger learned the shipwright trade from the great master builder, William Hackett, and his cousin, James Hackett, who master-minded construction of the Continental warships *Raleigh* and *Ranger*. William Badger later had a leading role in the building of frigates for the early United States navy. Badger worked in the Langdon yard under the Hacketts but, after the Revolution, went back to his native Newfields. When the building of warships resumed during the Quasi War with France in the 1790s, Badger returned to the island that bears his name. By that time, Badger was playing a major part in the projects. Hundreds of receipts for the purchase of ship timber, signed by him, are in the possession of a local family. Badger traveled hither and yon through inland towns like Nottingham, Northwood, Epsom, Deerfield and Deering in constant search for the white oak so vital to Piscataqua-built ships.

When the flurry of federal shipbuilding subsided, Badger again returned to Newfields. It is fair speculation that had the United States Navy bought Langdon's Island for a public shipyard, Badger might have lived out his days on the upper river. However, canny Benjamin Stoddert, first Secretary of the Navy, found the price too high. Instead, he bought Dennett's Island as a site for the first United States Navy Yard. It also meant that a well organized shipyard was available at the upper end of Langdon's Island. Badger bought it, the purchase including three acres spread across the whole tip of the island. From that shipyard, between 1800 and 1829, William Badger launched 53 vessels. Of these, 24 were three-masted, square-rigged ships; eight were two-masted, square-rigged brigs; 19 were schooners; and two were sloops. On his death bed, Master Badger boasted that he had his 100th vessel on the stocks and that he would come back to build 100 more. That 100th vessel was the *Howard*, finished and launched in 1830 by William's nephew, Samuel Badger, who became a prolific builder in his own right.

Master Badger died in his home in 1829 on the island that bears his name. He was buried near his house and a table-top monument, badly deteriorated, marks the spot.

There were, of course, other builders working in Kittery during the Badger era, but many of them also operated out of yards in other Piscataqua towns. One of the first on the list is Joseph Cutts, a member of the long-time Kittery family. He is credited with the brig *Minerva* in 1800. Another was Richard Cutts. One of the busiest for a span of time was Benjamin Remick, who built the brig *Enterprise*, 182 tons, in 1800. Remick built another brig in 1802 and several other vessels. James Paul, Jr., built two ships in Kittery. Other builders were Stephen Paul, Josiah Remick, John Follett, John Weeks, Hugh Paul, Timothy Spinney, Samuel Tetherly, Isaac Staples, Samuel Cottle, Ebenezer Thompson, Stephen Story, Rufus Remick, Thomas Cottle, and Alfred Libbey.

The first two ships on record in Kittery have the intriguing names of *Nine Sons* and *Eleven Sons*.

Nine Sons

Specifications: Built in 1786. Burthen, 110 tons. Owner, December 30, 1786, Neil McIntire of Portsmouth.

If nothing else, the *Nine Sons* has the distinction of being one of the smallest ships built after the Revolution. Her name is suggestive that the owner was the proud father of nine sons.

Four different masters commanded the *Nine Sons*, the first being

Samuel Briard, who came in from the West Indies, November 16, 1787. A Captain Parker went to the West Indies in 1788 and was followed by a Captain Parsons. The last master in the customs records was William McIntire, who might have been one of the nine sons. He came in from Port au Prince, Haiti, on June 28, 1790. As to what happened to her, it can only be speculated that she was sold. In an indirect way, the story of the ship next in line seems to confirm that conjecture.

Eleven Sons

Specifications: Built in 1786. Burthen, 178 tons. Owner, July 21, 1790, Neil McIntire.

Analysis of the data available concerning the two ships *Nine Sons* and *Eleven Sons* leads to the conclusion that the construction date for the latter is in error. The date comes from the customs records. The correct date for the *Eleven Sons* is more apt to be 1790. Why would Neil McIntire wait four years to register the *Eleven Sons*? He was a successful merchant, but he wasn't wealthy enough to let a ship lie idle for four years. The day after the *Eleven Sons* was registered, she cleared for Hispaniola.[1] She returned from Cape Francis on October 23rd. Captain McIntire cleared for the West Indies again in December 1790. He was back home on October 10, 1791. She was sold in New York in 1794.

One more point can be raised in arguing for the date of 1790 for the *Eleven Sons*: it gives Mrs. McIntire four years in which to produce two more sons.

Reunion

Specifications: Built in 1791. Burthen, 210 tons. Built for France.

Lydia

Specifications: Built in 1792. Burthen, 239 tons; length, 87.1 feet; beam, 25.1 feet; depth, 12.55 feet. Owner, October 13, 1792, Richard Salter Tibbetts.

Richard Salter Tibbetts took the *Lydia* to the West Indies right after registering her.[3] There is no customs record showing a return entry, and she was listed as sold in New York, July 9, 1792.

Superb

Specifications: Built in 1793. Burthen, 282 tons; length, 91.5 feet; beam, 26.7 feet; depth, 13.35 feet. Owners, March 6, 1793, Richard and Joseph Champney.

Nathaniel Sherburne took the *Superb* on her maiden voyage, clearing for Cork, Ireland, in March 1793.[4] She returned from Dublin in September, taking 40 days for the passage and in company with several other vessels.[5] After discharging cargo, Captain Sherburne again went to Dublin, returning home July 8, 1794. Later in the month, the *Superb* was cleared for Virginia to start the first leg of a triangular voyage. Tragedy struck. On August 26, 1794, the death of Captain Sherburne was reported. The *Gazette* gave his age as 31 and that he left a widow, son, mother and brothers. William Appleton was sent to the James River to take command. Appleton brought her in from St. Ubes in March 1795 in 76 days. Later that year, she was sold in Boston.

Margaret

Specifications: Built in 1793 for Thomas Thompson. Burthen, 221 tons; length, 84.4 feet; beam, 24.6 feet; depth, 12.3 feet. Registered on December 29, 1793. Sold in Philadelphia.

Amity

Specifications: Built in 1794 for Thomas Thompson. Burthen, 300 tons; length, 93.6 feet; beam, 27 feet; depth, 13.3 feet. Registered on October 17, 1797.

Thomas Thompson's rapid disposal of both the ship *Amity* and the *Margaret* hint strongly that he was doing a bit of ship brokering. And the same thing happened with the next ship.

Criterion

Specifications: Built in 1796 for Thomas Thompson. Burthen, 285 tons; length, 92 feet; beam, 26.7 feet; depth, 13.35 feet. Registered, April 6, 1796.

The *HOWARD* for fale.

TO BE SOLD
AT AUCTION
On Wednefday *the* 10th *day of*
November next,

 THAT excellent, faft
failing, and burthen-
fome SHIP, the
HOWARD,
now lying at Capt. Shapley's wharf,
together with her Cargo, confifting of
SWEDISH and RUSSIA IRON,
HEMP, GLASS, &c. juft ar-
rived from Hamburg, being property
of the late MARTIN PARRY, deceafed.
To thofe acquainted with this vaiua-
ble Ship, a particular detail of her
good qualities is unneceffary—Suffice
it to fay, that fhe was built the laft
feafon under the infpection of the late
owner, of the beft materials, and by
the moft approved workmen : fhe is
293 tons burthen, completely found.
The higheft character is given her as
a faft failer and good fea boat The
conditions will be liberal, and may be
known by applying to the fubfcribers
at the ftore of MARK SIMES in Bow-
ftreet.   MARK SIMES,
              SAM'L SPARHAWK,
Adminiftrators on M Parry's eftate.
Portfmouth. Oct. 26, 1802.

NHG, October 26, 1802

Howard

*Specifications: Built in 1801 by James Paul, Jr. Square stern, billet head.
Burthen, 290 tons; length, 94.6 feet; beam, 26.5 feet; depth, 13.25 feet. Owner,
April 21, 1801, Martin Parry.*

Like other mortals, Martin Parry little dreamed that he wouldn't live to
see the *Howard*'s first return cargo unloaded. She came home the week
of October 26, 1802, and on that date, the *Gazette* published an advertisement for the sale of the *Howard* "on Wednesday the 10th day of
November next, that excellent, fast sailing, and burthensome ship, the
Howard, now lying at Capt. Shapley's wharf, together with her Cargo,
consisting of Swedish and Russia Iron, Hemp, Glass, &c. just arrived
from Hamburg, being property of the late Martin Parry, deceased. To
those acquainted with this valuable Ship, a particular detail of her good
qualities is unnecessary—Suffice to say, that she was built the last

season under the inspection of the late owner, of the best materials, and by the most approved workmen; she is 293 tons burthen, completely found. The highest character is given her as a fast sailer and good sea boat..."

The sponsors of the advertisement were Mark Simes and Samuel Sparhawk, who described themselves as "Administrators on M. Parry's estate." The *Howard* was bought by the Salem merchant prince, William Gray, and on her next voyage went to Calcutta from Lisbon, via the Cape Verde Islands. The *Gazette* stopped listing her voyages, but on March 10, 1807, it reported:

> The ship *Howard*, belonging to Wm. Gray, Esq. of Salem, commanded by Capt. Benjamin Bray, of Marblehead, was wrecked on Eastern Point, near Gloucester, and bilged immediately; the captain, second mate (Mr. Isaiah Leeds) and two seamen... were drowned. The ship was from Calcutta, with a valuable cargo; she had on board 200 bales of cotton, besides sugars, &c. and will be nearly a total loss.

Bristol Packet

Specifications: Built in 1801 by William Badger. Square stern, billet head. Burthen, 249 tons; length, 87.1 feet; beam, 25.7 feet; depth, 12.85 feet. Owner, December 7, 1801, Abel Harris.

To the *Bristol Packet* goes the distinction of being the first merchant ship constructed by William Badger on Badger's Island. Badger built a pair of schooners in his yard in 1798. Late in 1801, he launched the *Bristol Packet*. On December 8th, the *Gazette* reported that the *Bristol Packet* had cleared for Bristol, England, under a Captain Orr. Less than six months later, Abel Harris sold the *Bristol Packet* in Boston.

Orb

Specifications: Built by William Badger in 1803. Square stern, billet head. Burthen, 278 tons; length, 90.7 feet; beam, 26.6 feet; depth, 11.8 feet. Owners, Samuel Swett and Ebenezer Farley of Boston.

Farmer

Specifications: Built in 1804 by Timothy Spinney. Square stern, billet head. Burthen, 216 tons; length, 84.7 feet; beam 24.2 feet; depth, 12.1 feet. Owner, December 26, 1804, Daniel Goodwin of Berwick.

The ship Thomas Wilson, *built in Kittery by William Badger in 1809, was "sold foreign," in 1829. MM.*

One of Ichabod Goodwin's favorite ships might have been the Sarah Parker, *named for his wife. Built in Kittery in 1827, the ship's portrait hangs in the Goodwin Mansion at Strawbery Banke.*

Durham, New Hampshire waterfront at the Falls, circa 1822, a painting completed in 1954 by Durham artist John Hatch. The original painting is eight feet long and to show it to best advantage it is necessary to reproduce it in two parts. Above is the left half of the painting showing two schooners under construction by Joseph Coe, a builder who leased the town-owned shipyards. Further left, adjacent to the falls of the Oyster River, are a grist mill, saw mill and the Ffrost family stores. The buildings on the hill behind the schooners are homes and various buildings associated with shipbuilding such as a blacksmith shop, Coe's workshop and, at right, a mast shop.

Built in Kittery in 1801, the Howard was home ported in Salem, Massachusetts, and flew the house flag of William Gray. PM.

The ship Horace, *built in Durham, also was owned by William Gray of Salem. PA.*

The Mary and Harriot, *built by Joseph Coe in Durham in 1827, sailed out of New York. PM.*

The *Farmer* was familiarly known in what is now the Town of Eliot as the "Farmer Goodwin." Spinney's yard was in the upper part of Kittery that became Eliot.

Several days before Daniel Goodwin registered the *Farmer*, she had been advertised in the *Gazette* as bound for New York under Thomas Goodwin. For Captain Goodwin, going to sea was a chance to get away from personal grief: his 22-year-old bride of four months had died not long before. A news item indicates she caught a cold and died from the complications. From New York, Goodwin took the *Farmer* to Charleston, thence to the West Indies. Thomas Goodwin must have been born under an evil star. On April 29, 1806, the *Gazette* reported:

> April 28,— Arrived ship *Farmer* at this port, Capt. Goodwin, master of the ship, having, by the bursting of a gun, lost part of his left hand, had taken the long boat on Tuesday, 11th March, manned by his mate and three seamen, gone over to Laguira, Venezuela, to have his hand dressed, with the intention of sending back the boat with the mate and hands next day to carry the vessel home,— the captain, mate and seamen being detained at Laguira, the ship came out in consequence of an alarm from the Spaniards, thro' fear of being captured, and arrived here in safety.

The *Gazette* item doesn't say where the *Farmer* was when Captain Goodwin suffered his injury. It does, however, emphasize the danger that lurked everywhere in Caribbean waters. Yet, for those who lived, the profits were great. Captain Goodwin didn't realize these profits, as the *Gazette* reported in an obituary of May 6th:

> At Laguira, Capt. Thomas Goodwin, late commander of the ship *Farmer*, of Kittery. His death was occasioned by a wound he received from the bursting of a gun— Thus from an unfortunate accident, the friends of this estimable citizen mourn the untimely loss of a son, who was an honor to his aged parents...

In 1806, Thomas Lunt took the *Farmer* to sea, traveling the triangle. He was in Russia on July 10, 1807.[6] Presumably, the *Farmer* brought back hemp and iron, but there's no record of an entry into Portsmouth. In September 1809, she was at Greenock, Scotland, discharging cargo.[7] From that time until 1816, there's no information about her. In those years, there was the Embargo Act, the Non-Intercourse Act and the War of 1812, which kept a lot of ships in port. In January 1816, William Walden brought the *Farmer* home in 26 days from Martinique with rum and molasses for the owner, Abraham Shaw. That same issue of the *Gazette*, January 23rd, also advertised the auctioning of the *Farmer*'s cargo at Abraham Shaw's wharf. Shaw's wharf has long since been buried in land-fill, but Shaw's warehouse still stands in Prescott Park. The new owners of record became Jacob Cutter, Joseph M. Salter, James Shapley and Andrew W. Bell.

Joseph M. Salter took her to the Caribbean in November 1817.[8] Salter returned to Boston in November 1818 after a 77-day passage from Havre, entering Portsmouth Harbor on December 6th.[9] James Shapley offered his quarter share, but there were no takers.[10] William Martin sailed the *Farmer* to Europe and then on a voyage to Havana in 1821.

Under Captain Walden, the *Farmer* had one of the most miserable passages in her career. It was reported by the *Oracle*, on May 17, 1821, that she had been in bad straits off Sandy Hook, New Jersey. A revenue cutter attempted to help by attaching a cable but the cable snapped, so the *Farmer* headed south. On May 9th, however, the *Farmer* arrived in New York, after taking 153 days to come from Cadiz with salt. In the course of the passage, five different ships supplied her with provisions. She was sold in New York, September 12, 1821.

Resolution

Specifications: Built in 1804 by William Badger. Square stern, billet head. Burthen, 304 tons; length, 94 feet; beam, 27.3 feet; depth, 13.65 feet. Owners, February 25, 1805, Thomas and Elihu Brown.

Little information is available about the *Resolution*, the first ship of the name built by William Badger. The Browns chose a bad time to get into the shipping business. If they did send her to sea, it must have been out of ports other than Portsmouth. She was reported sold in 1812.[11]

Erin

Specifications: Built by William Badger in 1805. Square stern, billet head. Burthen, 282 tons; length, 90.8 feet; beam, 26.8 feet; depth, 13.4 feet. Owner, Ebenezer Breed of Boston.

Liverpool Packet

Specifications: Built in 1805 by William Badger. Square stern, billet head. Burthen, 277 tons; length, 90.4 feet; beam, 26.6 feet; depth, 13.3 feet. Owners, November 21, 1805, Ebenezer Thompson and Alexander Ladd.

James Place was the first master of the *Liverpool Packet*. He brought her in from Liverpool on October 7, 1806, with salt for the owners.

Thompson advertised in the *Gazette* on October 21 that he had for sale, "400 hhds. Liverpool Salt; 20 Chaldrons Coals [A dry measure equal to 36 bushels); 48 crates Crockery Ware, containing a general assortment, among which are some very elegant gold and white, and blue and gold Tea Setts, complete, gold and white Coffee pots, ditto Fruit Dishes, ditto Pitchers of different sizes, blue printed Tea Setts, ditto Coffee Pots, ditto Bowls and Saucers."

Henry Ladd bought an interest in the *Liverpool Packet* in 1807 and still held it when the ship was sold. James Kennard was the next master of the ship, and he bought an interest in 1809, which he sold in 1816. Captain Kennard came into Portsmouth from Bonavista on July 10, 1810, after a voyage of 43 days with salt for the owners.[12] No records about her are available during the War of 1812. Not only are the customs records uninformative, but the usually reliable *New Hampshire Gazette* didn't publish shipping news.

Normalcy returned after the Treaty of Ghent. A Captain Tibbetts brought the *Liverpool Packet* into Baltimore from Belfast, loaded with salt and passengers.[13] She was 77 days on the passage and came to Portsmouth from Baltimore on November 9th. Captain Tibbetts took her out December 19th bound for Savannah and a crossing to Europe. The *Gazette* reported September 1, 1818, that the ship had arrived August 10th from Liverpool after 44 days with salt and coal for the Ladds. Almost a year is missing from her record, but she came home again in August 1819 in 10 days from New York. A year later, Elijah Ricker was the master, and an advertisement in the *Portsmouth Oracle*, in December 1820, offered "freight or passage" to New Orleans. The *Liverpool Packet* was apparently away for the next three years, but in 1823, she appeared to be working out of Portsmouth again. These triangular voyages continued until 1827 when the highly dependable *Liverpool Packet* was "sold foreign."[15]

Two Brothers

Specifications: Built in 1805 by John Follet. Square stern, billet head. Burthen, 209 tons; length, 80.6 feet; beam, 24.1 feet; depth, 12.05 feet. Owners, November 19, 1805, Robert and John Follet.

The ship *Two Brothers* was appropriately named, owned as she was by the Follet brothers. John Follet was only 28 when he built the *Two Brothers*. He spent 31 years following the sea, dying in 1820 at 53.[16] It isn't known where the *Two Brothers* was between the time of registration and her first listed entrance into the Port of Portsmouth. Again, it has to be emphasized that the Embargo Act, which took effect in 1807, brought shipping almost to a standstill. When the embargo was eased in 1809, William Dennett took the *Two Brothers* to Lisbon for salt, the commodity so vital to local fishermen. That was on March 4, 1809. It is possible that she was the ship *Two Brothers* reported by the *Gazette* on January 13, 1807, as having arrived in Boston in 66 days from Liverpool.

Captain Dennett turned her over to a Captain Greenough, who cleared for Jamaica in May 1810.[17] On her return, she was auctioned off to Thomas Haven and G.F. Smith, along with John and Nathaniel Haven. The partners sold her in Boston in 1811.

Ceres

Specifications: Built by William Badger in 1806. Square stern, female figurehead. Burthen, 287 tons; length, 92 feet; beam, 26.8 feet; depth, 13.4 feet. Owners, Thomas Elihu Brown.

The *Ceres* took her name from the Roman goddess, but who first owned her isn't that clear. She arrived in Portsmouth in July 1806 with Elihu Brown, master.[18] But the Browns didn't become owners of record until July 9, 1809.[19] The Brown brothers sold out to Theodore Chase and Matthew S. Marsh in 1812, about the time the United States declared war on England. The sale could have coincided with the arrival of the *Ceres* under Richard Salter Tibbetts from Orinoco, South America, on April 19th. John Winkley, a well known privateer captain, was master in 1815. The last heard of her is a customs notation to the effect she had been sold in Charleston on March 13, 1818.

Agenoria

Specifications: Built by Isaac Staples in 1806. Square stern, billet head. Burthen, 190 tons; length, 74.4 feet; beam, 24.1 feet; depth, 12.05 feet. Owner, January 13, 1807, William Rice.

William Rice, himself, took the *Agenoria* to Cadiz for salt in 1809, reentering the Port of Portsmouth on November 2nd. Rice had kept the *Agenoria* tied up during the life of the Embargo Act and then sold her after his voyage to Spain.

Prince Madoc

Specifications: Built in 1808 by Isaac Staples. Square stern, billet head. Burthen, 285 tons; length, 94 feet; beam, 27.1 feet; depth, 12 feet. Owners, September 1, 1809, Edward Parry and Joseph Cutts.

Isaac Staples' timing for building the *Prince Madoc* wasn't of the best with the Embargo Act in full force. She went to sea in 1809 under a Captain Moore, taking 10 days to get to Norfolk on September 10th. Samuel Woodman took her to London later in 1810 and came home on April 13, 1811, 67 days, in ballast.[20] The ship sailed for London again on May 29th under Benjamin Balch of the ship *Strafford* fame. She triangled by the way of Virginia, sailing on August 4th.[21]

Edward Parry sold his interest in 1811. There's little reason to doubt that the *Prince Madoc* name was given her by Edward Parry, a man who loved Wales. Prince Madog was a legendary Welsh prince, Madog ab Owain Gwynedd, who died in 1169. According to tradition, he sailed to America "and established a colony on the southern branches of the Missouri. About the same time, the Aztecs forsook Aztlan…and founded the empire called Mexico, in honor of Mexitli, their tutelary god. [Robert] Southey's poem, *Madoc* (1805) harmonizes these two events…;;[22]

Not long after Edward Parry sold his interest, Joseph Cutts sold his to a Norfolk syndicate.

Thomas Wilson

Specifications: Built in 1809 by William Badger. Square stern, billet head. Burthen, 287 tons; length, 91.1 feet; beam, 26.8 feet; depth, 13.4 feet. Owners, August 3, 1809, Samuel and William Ham, Benjamin Brierley and John L. Thompson.

The *Thomas Wilson* went to work with the repeal of the Embargo Act. On April 28, 1810, under Emanuel Morris, she sailed for Norfolk and the second leg of the triangle.[23] Captain Morris returned to Portsmouth from Liverpool with salt on April 14, 1811. In June, Morris headed for London. The timing, as reported by the *Gazette*, seems a bit awry, but in August, after being captured by an English warship, the *Thomas Wilson* was on trial in Halifax. She had been en route from Europe to Philadelphia. On September 24th, however, the *Gazette* reported the *Thomas Wilson* arriving in Portsmouth from Portugal on the 22nd, bringing no fresh news.[24] Captain Morris also brought her in from Spain, April 29, 1813, and that was her last entry until 1815 when the war was over. In March of that year, the *Thomas Wilson* was sold, along with the *Islington* and the *Elizabeth Wilson*. In December 1815, under John Thompson, she left Portsmouth on the 18th, headed for Norfolk, a passage that took five days.[25] Her triangle took nearly eight months, ending when she arrived in Portsmouth on August 16, 1816, from Gothenburg in 57 days with iron and steel for Brierley and the Havens. Thompson took her out again on May 4, 1817, heading for Savannah.[26] On July 28th, *Thomas Wilson* was in Dublin, Ireland, having come from New Orleans. The *Gazette* reported on May 30, 1818, that the *Thomas Wilson* was in from Liverpool, in 54 days, with salt and coal for Brierly and the Havens.

In and out went the dependable *Thomas Wilson*. The *Oracle* reported on July 29, 1820, that a half interest in her was for sale at the New Hampshire Fire and Marine insurance office. John McClintock bought it and kept it until 1825. Through the 1820s, she made entrances under five different captains into the Port of Portsmouth. In August 1828, she came in from Bahia, South America and was "sold foreign" in 1829.[27]

Jason

Specifications: Built in 1810 by William Badger. Square stern, alligator figurehead. Burthen, 334 tons; length, 97.9 feet; beam, 28 feet; depth, 12 feet. Owners, March 4, 1811, John and William Flagg.

Like her namesake, Jason of the Golden Fleece, the *Jason* went through many trials and tribulations in her career. The Flaggs put her to work immediately, advertising her as available for freight or passage to the south—those interested could apply at William Sheafe's Wharf.[28] William Flagg brought the *Jason* into the Port of Portsmouth from Lisbon on October 8, 1811, completing her first triangular voyage. Flagg made an almost identical voyage in 1812 but coming from Liverpool and docking on July 12, 1812, only a month after the declaration of war.

Available records fail to show her doing anything during the war years, but on October 31, 1815, the *Gazette* reported her arrival in Salem on the 22nd. She had come from Fayal in 37 days loaded with wines, oils and tallow. She also had on board the cargo of a British ship which had been captured by the Salem privateer *America*.

Shortly after her arrival, the *Jason* was sold. John Flagg, one of her owners, had died, and the *Jason* was sold to settle his estate. The *Jason* was lying at Waldron's Wharf. The executor, John P. Flagg, probably a son, also advertised the sale of Flagg's residence in Lee on December 27th, "along with '16 full blooded Merino sheep.' "[29] James Orne, her master, John P. Flagg, Charles Blunt, and James Shapley bought Flagg's half interest. The Merino sheep were probably part of a lot that had been brought in from Lisbon on the *Jason*'s maiden voyage.[30]

Captain Orne sailed the *Jason* to New York on September 3, 1816, where customs records note she had been sold to the Campbells. Orne, a veteran master mariner, died five years later in Genoa, Italy, at 63. The *Gazette* said of him, February 21, 1821:

Capt. Orn, for a great length of time, sailed from this port and was considered one of our most able navigators. In his integrity, perfect confidence was reposed, and his nautical skill and great experience rendered him valuable as a ship-master, and highly useful as an instructor of young seamen.

Resolution

Specifications: Built in 1810 by William Badger. Square stern, billet head. Burthen, 332 tons; length, 101.6 feet; beam, 27.2 feet; depth, 12 feet. Owner, September 14, 1810, Thomas Brown.

That a second ship with the name, *Resolution*, was launched from the same yard within six years of the first is strongly supportive of the belief that the first had been wrecked or sold abroad. If the second *Resolution* was active before the War of 1812, it was out of ports other than Portsmouth. Brown had lost interest in her because she was advertised as for sale at Sheafe's Wharf.[31] It isn't clear who bought her at the December 31 auction. Her next registered owners were John McClintock, Theodore F. Jewett and William Badger. That was on May 10, 1815, and she went to sea that week under Captain Jewett. Brown may have sold her to raise money for financing a privateer, very possibly the *Fox*, which was commanded by his brother Elihu. There is no record of the *Resolution*'s return to Portsmouth until 1819, but Jewett did bring her into Alexandria, Virginia, in early November 1817.[32] She was 45 days from Havre with French plaster and burrstones (grindstones). In 1819, McClintock sold out to John Rice, and on February 19, 1819, she sailed, under Jewett, for the south but was forced to put back for a day or two by contrary winds. Jewett brought her home from Rotterdam on October 28th in ballast.[33] He made a similar voyage in 1820, coming into Portsmouth on August 20th with salt, iron and coal for William Badger, Rice and the master.[34] Jewett was master through 1822, docking the *Resolution* after a 42-day passage from Liverpool "with salt, coal & crates. to Rice and the master."[35]

Edward Kennard was the *Resolution*'s next master and followed the usual pattern of sailing south for cotton and then to England. She came home on August 11th, reporting she had left the ship *Frederick*, owned by Jacob Cutter, off the Skerries with loss of cable and anchors. Passengers in the *Resolution* were Mr. and Mrs. Staniford and Mr. and Mrs. Clark and four youngsters.[36] In 1824, Kennard went the triangle but returned to New York. His last two voyages saw the ship returning home from Liverpool.

Under a Captain Craig, the *Resolution* left on her last triangular voyage, sailing on January 29, 1827, for New Orleans.[37] The next news of her was in the *Gazette* on May 22, 1827. While en route from New Orleans for Liverpool, the *Resolution* was abandoned while sinking. She had struck on Orange Cay, west of Andros Island on April 29th. The captain and crew were taken off by the schooner *Mary* and went into Charleston.

Alfred

Specifications: Built in 1810 by James Paul. Square stern, billet head. Burthen, 314 tons; length, 100.3 feet; beam, 26.6 feet; depth, 12.2 feet. Owners, March 6, 1811, Nathaniel A. and John Haven.

A month after they registered the *Alfred*, the Havens sent her to Russia for hemp and iron.[38] In the summer, she was reported at Cronstadt with no sailing plans. In the *Gazette*, January 7, 1812, there appeared:

> The ship *Alfred*, Greenough, from St. Petersburg[Leningrad] for Boston, was driven on shore at Halibut Point (Cape Ann) on Friday morning at 4 o'clock, vessel bilged, and very little of her cargo is expected to be saved—none able to do duty on board except the captain, mate and boy—one man was lost overboard—another had previously fallen from the mast head, and bruised himself severely, and another man was sick with the scurvy—It was reported by the man who came for the doctor, that the man who had fallen from the mast head had lived in that condition 46 days—the ship had been out about 70 days—the above ship is new, owned at Portsmouth, N.H. and very valuable—Considerable insurance has been effected in this town on her—between 20 and 30 people were employed in saving her cargo, by last accounts.

An unverified note suggests the *Alfred*, or what remained of her, was sold in Gloucester, which was logical considering the proximity to that town.

Potomac

Specifications: Built in 1810 by Ebenezer Thompson. Square stern, scroll figurehead. Burthen, 342 tons; length, 104.2 feet; beam, 27.2 feet; depth, 12.2 feet. Owner, Charles Bradford of Alexandria.

The *Potomac* was the only ship Ebenezer Thompson built on the Maine side of the river. Customs records are contradictory, having her built in both Portsmouth and Kittery, but the latter seems more logical. Thompson's previous construction had been in Durham, and he probably took the first available yard when he moved down the river. In 1814, he built a schooner in Kittery.

Charles Bradford sailed for Alexandria on March 21, 1811. Considering Alexandria's location on the Potomac, the ship's name was fitting.

Harmony

Specifications: Built in 1818 by William Badger. Square stern, billet head. Burthen, 318 tons; length, 99.2 feet; beam, 27 feet; depth, 13.5 feet. Owners, November 25, 1818, Samuel Sheafe, Robert Rice and Mark W. Pierce.

The disastrous effects of the War of 1812 on the shipbuilding industry in the Port of Portsmouth is clearly evidenced by the launching of the *Harmony* in 1818. She was the first ship built in Kittery in a span of eight years; only four were built anywhere else on the Piscataqua during the trying war years. In 1818, with the war well behind them, the Port of Portsmouth shipwrights built three: one in Dover, one in Durham and the *Harmony* in Kittery.

To the *Harmony* goes the dubious distinction of being wrecked on the treacherous ledge at the Portsmouth Harbor entrance, known as the Whale's Back. That mishap will be described later. When the *Harmony* was fully fitted and rigged, she went into the Liverpool trade. She entered Portsmouth Harbor for the first time on June 8, 1819, under Edwin L. Coffin, having taken 45 days on her passage with salt. Coffin took her to Norfolk late in the summer on the first leg of another triangle. On October 12th, the *Oracle* reported in its obituary column:

> On Board ship *Harmony*, lying Hampton Roads, 2d inst. Captain Edwin L. Coffin, of this town, and master of said ship, aged 31.

The young master was succeeded by Samuel Woodward, who brought her in from Liverpool on February 3, 1820. Woodward made a fast turnaround and was able to enter Portsmouth again in July from Liverpool. In March 1822, the *Harmony*, under Woodward, along with three other ships, was forced to put back into Portsmouth, after being at sea several days. After she beat her way out, she went to Liverpool, re-entering Portsmouth on May 8th in the remarkably fast time of 23 days from Liverpool. She brought salt, coal, iron and crates to Samuel Sheafe.[39] In March 1823, she was back in port again from St. Ubes with salt.

Shadrach H. Sise became master, sailing for Charleston in mid-July 1825.[40] The *Harmony* made it all the way around the triangle and then disaster came in her home waters. Christmas night, 1825, 46 days out of Liverpool, she struck on the Whale's Back, then an unmarked ledge, at the entrance to Portsmouth Harbor. Part of her cargo of salt was saved, the rest added to the salinity of the harbor. On January 3, 1826, the *Gazette* reported the *Harmony* had floated off the day after Christmas, then went aground on Wood Island. "She had been previously sold for $166, stripped of sails, rigging and spars, etc. She will probably be got into port without much difficulty."

There the story could have come to rest. But 76 years later, on April 4, 1901, the *Portsmouth Herald* reported:

> James Malone, an insurance man of Dover, made a decidedly interesting find while strolling along the shore of the Bellamy River, near Pinkham's Grove [About opposite the Spaulding Turnpike toll station.] a few days ago. The find was a large package of bills and documents belonging to the ship *Harmony*...
>
> Among the contents of the package is a letter which shows that the vessel sailed from Charleston, S.C., bound for Liverpool, Eng., in the month of August, 1825, and was wrecked during the passage. She was commanded by Capt. Shadrach Hodgdon Sise; Samuel Ware, mate; Samuel McFarland, second mate, and Samuel Perkins, Levi Noah, John Morgan, Samuel Jordan, John Chase, Samuel Elea and Joseph Freeman, seamen; William Green, cook; Hiram Nutter, ordinary and Charles Fernald, boy.
>
> The bills give a full account of the cargo carried by the ill-fated vessel...
>
> All the documents and deeds are in excellent condition, but how they came to be lying on the shores of the Bellamy is a mystery. Mr. Malone will hold on to the package and investigate as to the value of its contents.

As far as can be determined, the mystery of the *Harmony* papers continues three-quarters of a century later. Robert A. Whitehouse of Dover, who has made the maritime history of the upper river a hobby for half a century, knows of no repository that has the *Harmony* papers.

Arethusa

Specifications: Built in 1819 by William Badger. Square stern, billet head. Burthen, 319 tons; length, 100 feet; beam, 26.9 feet; depth, 13.45 feet. Owners, October 28, 1819, Thomas Sheafe and Charles Coffin.

Under a Captain Merrill, the *Arethusa* started in what was a customary pattern. She went south for cotton, crossed to Liverpool, and returned to Portsmouth on May 8, 1820. Captain Merrill took her next on a voyage to Russia, from which she returned on September 17, 1821. In July 1823, she went to New Orleans and then Rotterdam. From there, in late September, she went to St. Ubes, arriving home on December 5,

1823. She sailed for Charleston in January 1824, and the *Gazette* reported on February 10 that the *Arethusa* was in Savannah and that, on the passage, she had been struck by lightning, "which shivered the fore and main masts, and carried away every spar above the caps." She went to Baltimore and from there she sailed to Rio de Janeiro. When she returned to Baltimore, she was sold on February 25, 1826.

Lewis

Specifications: Built in 1820 by William Badger. Square stern, billet head. Burthen, 280 tons; length, 94.3 feet; beam, 26 feet; depth, 12.8 feet. Owner, October 18,1820, Lewis Barnes.

Unlike the first ship with the name *Lewis* built by Wiliam Badger, the second was constructed on Badger's Island, and she was owned in Portsmouth for 12 years. It was her ending that brought fame of a sort to the *Lewis*: she became part of the "Stone Fleet." Before arriving at that climax in her career, she had many other adventures. With her owner, Lewis Barnes, as master, she was employed in various trading ventures, some of them involving the cotton routes. It is reasonable to believe that Barnes put his ship into service as soon as he registered her. The first entry recorded by the customs office, however, was on October 1, 1823, when she came in from Liverpool with salt consigned to the master. The *Portsmouth Journal* published an advertisement on October 4th in which Barnes offered for sale "Coarse Liverpool salt, 200 sacks fine do. Iron Hollow Ware, a small invoice of dry goods, consisting of Bombazetts, Bombazines, Norwich Crapes, Ginghams, Flannels, Cambricks and Cambrick Handkerchiefs." It is obvious that Captain Barnes served as his own buyer but that doesn't answer the inevitable question: Who was minding the store when he was away so much? Perhaps Mrs. Barnes?

The *Lewis* cleared for New Orleans in January 1824, arriving there on February 21st. She loaded a cargo of cotton for the Lancashire mills and then returned to New York. When she came home from there, she was carrying an unusual cargo: powder and shot for the Portsmouth Navy Yard. The *Lewis* made a triangular voyage in 1826 and suffered a mishap outside of Liverpool when she collided with the *Arethusa*, also of Portsmouth.[41] Captain Barnes took her to Italy in 1827, and she arrived home on September 5th in 42 days from Gibraltar.[42]

The next year, Barnes turned his ship over to Oliver Cromwell Blunt, who took her south to Exuma for salt. She came in from Rum Cay on October 1st and sailed for New Orleans on November 23rd. Jeremiah Pike was the next master; he brought her in from Cadiz in

September 1830 with salt for Barnes. On the passage, Captain Pike spoke the *Margaret Scott*, on passage from Liverpool to New York with 122 passengers. Pike supplied her with bread. The *Margaret Scott* was the other Piscataqua vessel that became part of the Stone Fleet.

After she came in from Exuma, Barnes put the *Lewis* up for sale, along with the cargo of salt she brought for his store at No. 5, Portsmouth Pier. In an advertisement, he described the *Lewis* as being "in good order, and can be sent to sea at small expense. She is well calculated for a whaling ship."[43] At that point, there were apparently no buyers, and the *Lewis* continued as a merchantman. She went to New Orleans in October 1830, reaching Liverpool on February 23, 1831. She returned to New Orleans and was at Antwerp and Shields, England, in 1832. In the fall, she came back to Portsmouth for the last time and then went to Gloucester on November 10th for conversion into a whaler.[44]

With a Captain Seaward as master, the *Lewis* became part of the Gloucester whaling fleet. As soon as she was outfitted, she went to the Indian Ocean. The *Lewis* returned from that cruise on December 13, 1834, with 480 barrels of sperm valued at $5,443, the only item listed.[45] Assuming a 55-gallon barrel, it results in 21 cents a gallon, perhaps a bit cheap for sperm. The next owner of the *Lewis* was based in Boston, who sent her to the South Seas where she earned $25,830, which, in terms of present-day dollars, would have been worth half a million. The *Lewis* became part of the New Bedford whaling fleet, making four cruises out of that port between 1841 and 1857 and earning a total of $144,692.

The pace of the whaling business slackened in the years immediately before the Civil War. So the *Lewis* was lying idle when the South Carolinians opened fire on Fort Sumter in Charleston Harbor in April 1861. As previously discussed in the case of the *Margaret Scott*, the federal authorities recognized, at an early date, that they had to cut off supplies to the Confederate States. Therefore, ports like Charleston were early put under blockade. So the Stone Fleet concept became reality. The *Lewis* was one of the vessels purchased; the United States paid $3,250 for her, and a total of $160,205 for the 60 in the *Lewis*'s part of the fleet. Stone, sold to the Navy by shrewd Yankee contractors, went into the vessels. The *Lewis* and her rock-filled fellows went south under the command of a commodore. But *Lewis* was not one of those scuttled. Under a Captain Walker, the *Lewis* was wrecked before she could be put to better use.

Mary Beach

Specifications: Built in 1821 by William Badger. Square stern, billet head. Burthen, 312 tons; length, 99 feet; beam, 26.6 feet; depth, 13.3 feet. Owners, November 12, 1821, Thomas W. Penhallow, James Shapley and John Allen.

The *Mary Beach* honored the wife of one of the owners, Thomas W. Penhallow. Perhaps Mrs. Penhallow was rowed across the river to Badger's Island so she could witness the launching. Such affairs have always been exciting in the Port of Portsmouth. Mary Beach Penhallow died on June 16, 1843, at 56. The seagoing *Mary Beach* was sold in New York in 1829.

The ship soon established a reputation for fast sailing. While owned in the Port of Portsmouth, she was commanded by only two men: John Allen and B.S. Allen. On her first voyage, the *Mary Beach* left Portsmouth on February 5, 1824, for the Chesapeake under John Allen. The *Gazette* reported on July 13, 1824, that "the fast-sailing *Mary Beach*" had arrived from Lisbon in 32 days with salt for Penhallow. What made the feat notable was that the *Mary Beach* had sailed from the Chesapeake to Rotterdam, thence to Lisbon, and then home in an at-sea time of three months and 10 days. A year later, under B.S. Allen, she was 27 days from London to Portsmouth; at that, she had been hung up off Cape Ann for five of those days by contrary winds. A passenger on that occasion was Dr. Charles Chauncey of Portsmouth. But it wasn't always smooth sailing for the *Mary Beach*. The *Gazette* reported on April 14, 1829:

> Havre, Feb. 23.—The *Siroc* of this port, on 23d Jan.... fell in with the ship *Mary Beach*, Allen, from New York for Cowes, out 7 days—had experienced a heavy gale, shifted her cargo, and sprung a leak. Capt. A. hoisted a light at the mast head, and requested the *Siroc* not to lose sight of him, as he was in great danger, but the weather being very rough, the vessels separated and lost sight of each other in the night.

The *Mary Beach* had been sold in New York before she left on that passage to Bremen, Germany. After weathering the storm, the *Mary Beach* put into Harwich, England, for repairs.[46] In May, the *Journal* reported her as being at Bremen, and in December, her arrival in New York, her new hailing port, was noted. With that, the *Mary Beach* disappears from Portsmouth record keeping.[47]

NHG, July 23, 1823

Fame

Specifications: Built in 1822 by William Badger. Square stern, billet head. Burthen, 288 tons; length, 96.8 feet; beam, 26 feet; depth, 13 feet. Owners, December 6, 1822, Nathaniel Folsom, Theodore and William Chase and C.S. Toppan.

On Saturday, October 26, 1822, the *Portsmouth Journal* published one of the first real launching stories ever seen in a Portsmouth newspaper. It wasn't lengthy, but it showed shipbuilding on the Piscataqua was undergoing a revival:

LAUNCH

It is with much pleasure we state that the important art of Shipbuilding is renewed with vigor on our River. During the present season some specimens of naval architecture have been exhibited by our shipbuilders which will not suffer in comparison with any in the United States. Within a few weeks no less than four ships, each being between 300 and 400 tons, have been added to our navigation. On Saturday last the elegant ship *Fame*, owned by Theodore Chase, was launched at the yard of Mr. Badger. It was pleasant to notice the interest which so beautiful a sight created; a large concourse of spectators, among them many Ladies, were present to witness her majestic descent into the water. The *Fame* is intended for the European trade and will be commanded by Nathaniel Folsom.

The *Fame* went immediately into the transatlantic service, returning to Portsmouth on July 5, 1823, from Antwerp, via St. Ubes, with salt for the Chases. Back and forth she went. She arrived in New York in December 1826 in 55 days from Liverpool with passengers. By that time, she was no longer owned in Portsmouth, having been sold in Savannah in 1825. Her ultimate fate isn't known, but she was still in the triangular trading pattern in 1831.[48]

Perseverance

Specifications: Built in 1823 by William Badger. Square stern, billet head.
Burthen, 319 tons; length, 100.4 feet; beam, 26.8 feet; depth, 13.4 feet. Owners,
December 31, 1823, John Rice, Samuel E. Coues and Theodore F. Jewett.

The life of the *Perseverance* was short, but her story will be a bit long in
the telling simply because it is such a graphic portrayal of the perils of
life at sea. The *Perserverance* met disaster on her maiden voyage,
killing 15 of the 16 people on board. She sailed from Portsmouth on
January 8, 1824. On March 20, the *Journal* reported:

> The tidings of the last week have cast a gloom over the
> town that will not soon be dissipated.—it is our painful duty to
> publish the particulars, so far as they are known. On Saturday
> afternoon, the 30th of January, the Ship *Perseverance* and the
> brig *Hector* of this port, the ship *Marathon* of N. York, and
> another ship laden with lumber whose name is not known, were
> at anchor under the Great Isaac, on the Bahama Banks. Towards
> sunset a gale commenced, and in a short time the *Hector* and the
> *Perseverance* were dashed to pieces on the rocks, and the
> unknown Ship was lost, and every soul on board perished.
> Of the 16 persons on board the *Perseverance*, one only was
> saved; and four out of ten on the *Hector*. The *Marathon* rode out
> the gale, and the next morning took the five survivors from the
> rocks and carried them to New Orleans. So entire was the
> destruction of the three vessels, that nothing of them was visible
> the next day but several shattered fragments thrown over the
> island, and seen hanging from high rocks. Capt. Barnes in the
> Ship *Lewis* of this port, passed the Hole-in-the-Wall on Friday in
> company with the *Perseverance*, but, intending to cross the
> Bank, he laid to during the night. The next morning, finding the
> wind unfavorable, he followed the *Perseverance*, and came in
> sight of her at sunset; but unable to reach the anchoring ground,
> he put about as the gale commenced, and with great difficulty
> escaped.

Then the *Journal*, in an unusual service to its readers, published a
complete list of the persons on board the two vessels. The listing tells
much about the makeup of a ship's company:

The Perseverance

William Rice	Commander	Portsmouth
Oliver Osgood	Mate	Salisbury
Thomas Clark	2d mate	Portsmouth (Saved)
James Adams	Boatswain	

William Clark	Mariner	
P. Hendrick	"	Residence not
C. Kain	"	known
L. Malony	"	
Joseph Oliver	"	
Wm. Christopher	"	Portsmouth
Thomas Simes	Young men learning	"
Daniel Vaughan	navigation	"
Joseph Gilman	Boy	"
William M'Comb	Carpenter	Foreigner
B. Howard (Colored)	Cook	Portsmouth
Eliphalet Porter	Passenger	"

The Hector

John B. Trickey	Commander	Portsmouth
Oliver B. Simes	Mate	"
Thomas A. Harris	Passenger	"

William Avery, the 2d Mate, and three Seamen whose names we have not been able to ascertain, were saved.

In the *Journal* of April 3rd, a letter writer offered eulogistic sketches for some of the men lost in the wrecks. Of Captain Rice, son of Alexander Rice of Kittery, he wrote:

> ... A young man of no common promise... skilful in his profession... In 1813 he entered as a Midshipman in the Navy of the United States, in 1821 he passed the examination which entitled him to promotion, and obtained a furlough for the purpose of availing himself of the many advantages and opportunities for improvement offered by the merchant service,—but he perished in his first command....

The writer had kind words for Eliphalet Porter, the son of the Reverend Mr. Porter of Rye:

> ... A young man of amiable disposition and gentle deportment... Unfortunate in business here, he determined with laudable enterprise, to push his fortune in other climes, but his fortune is now sealed forever...

There was also lament for Captain John B. Trickey, who apparently had suffered many of the misfortunes of a mariner's life:

> ... A Sailor from his youth, he had passed through all the grades and felt the hardships of each; but the checkered course of his life had not the effect to corrupt the heart or deprave his manners; he was no less valued for his skills as a mariner than esteemed for his sterling integrity.

Comments about Thomas Harris were made in the chapter on Portsmouth merchants, and the writer ended his letter as follows:

Among the other individuals composing the company of these ill-starred vessels were several young men of promise; two of them, Mr. Oliver B. Simes, chief mate of the brig, and Mr. Thomas Simes of the ship, were cousins...

Samuel Wright

Specifications: Built in 1824 by William Badger. Square stern, billet head. Burthen, 372 tons; length, 110 feet; beam, 27.5 feet; depth, 13.75 feet. Owners, December 15, 1824, Theodore Chase and John Riley.

Her owners immediately put the *Samuel Wright* into the lucrative cotton trade under John Riley. She sailed for Savannah after registration, arrived there January 4th, and was loaded for Liverpool. Her return from Liverpool to Portsmouth took 35 days, and she came in on May 12, 1825, with salt and freight for the owners and C.S. Toppan and James and Olive Sheafe.

Isaac Gage was master on her second voyage and went through a stormy ordeal with her off Cape Hatteras as he was heading for Savannah. The violence of the gale flipped the *Samuel Wright* onto her beam ends, shifting her ballast. When another heavy sea struck her, the ballast shifted back to its original position, but she had been on her beam ends for 20 hours. As soon as the *Samuel Wright* was repaired, she loaded cotton and went to Liverpool. Captain Gage completed the triangle on December 12, 1825, arriving home in 26 days with salt and coal for the owners, crates for Taylor & Waldron and hardware for Sherburne & Blunt.

The *Samuel Wright* was sold in New York in 1829 but continued in the cotton trade until the mid-1830s, operating between the cotton ports and Liverpool and New York. It isn't known when she went to Salem for service as a whaler, but she arrived in the Witch City on August 30, 1836, under Captain Pitman with 2,000 barrels of whale oil taken in the Pacific. She went out again on November 24, 1836, and was gone until March 1, 1839. Her catch was worth $23,562. A Customs note says she was cast away in 1840.

Shaw

Specifications: Built in 1825 by William Badger. Square stern, billet head. Burthen, 343 tons; length, 102.7 feet; beam, 27.5 feet; depth, 13.75 feet. Owner, January 4, 1825, Abraham Shaw.

With Abraham Shaw as owner and Thomas M. Shaw as master, the ship *Shaw* was truly a Shaw family affair. The *Shaw* was put into the cotton trade, her first southern port of call being Savannah. Captain Shaw brought her in from Liverpool twice before turning her over to John S. Shaw, who commanded her on five triangular voyages between American ports, north and south, and Europe.

William Shaw, Abraham's son, became owner in 1818. He put his interest on the auction block in January 1829.[49] The advertisement said she would be sold on January 22nd, and the *Shaw* was "now in complete order and can be got ready for sea in a few hours." William Stavers, along with Samuel Hale, Ichabod Rollins and John S. Davis, bought William Shaw's two-thirds interest. John Davis became master and kept his share while in command. One of the treasures in the Counting House, headquarters of the Old Berwick Historical Society, is a log book of the *Shaw* kept by Captain Davis on his first voyage in her.

The *Shaw*'s log is, unfortunately, like so many other other volumes of its kind—mostly a daily journal giving weather and position reports. The *Shaw* sailed from Portsmouth on January 31, 1829, a few days after the sale. The log opens with the dropping off of the pilot at 4 p.m. on that day and notes that at 6 p.m., the "Isles of Sholes light" was off to port, and by 8 p.m., she had the Cape Ann light in sight. On Thursday, February 5th, Cape Hatteras' light was seen. Five days after that, she was tied up at a wharf in Charleston and had discharged 64 bundles of hay. A seaman named Gould was arrested and jailed by the sheriff. Masters usually had personnel problems when in port, so Captain Davis didn't waste much ink on Gould. On February 12th, he noted that he had unloaded the last of the hay, 105 bundles, plus dumping 91 tubs of ballast. Six days later, he was still getting rid of ballast. On the 19th, he recorded "lazy weather," that the ship had been receiving rice all day, and "cleared out all the between decks and got ready for stowing cotton." By the 26th, 14,000 bundles of rice had been stowed on the *Shaw*, and the captain noted she was drawing 13 feet, 7 inches aft; 13 feet forward. The next day, it was recorded that "James Dixon, Andrew Flaggenson, Leonard Rymes and John French deserted the ship without any grievance whatever." On the 28th, the *Shaw* was drawing 14 feet, nine inches, aft; 14 feet, three inches forward. On board were 19,620 bushels of rice and 281 bales of cotton. More cargo was loaded, and the next week the *Shaw* was drawing 15 feet, nine inches after; 15 feet, 3 inches forward. She was ready for sea. A John Parsons reported for duty, and Davis was able to hire three more seamen. The heavily laden *Shaw* went over the Charleston Bar on March 18th. By April 21st, she was off the Scilly Isles and picked up her pilot in the Downs, off Deal, on the 28th. James Shuttle, the pilot, shuttled the *Shaw* up through Margate into the Surrey Dock in London. The *Shaw* had completed two legs of the triangle. While the cargo was being discharged, John Parsons deserted the ship. The American consul, however, sent two men, George Fowles and Lewis Wilson, on board. Her cargo out, ballast in, she was under weigh for St. Ubes on May 22nd. By June 6th, she was ready to load salt and over the next few days took on 716 "moys" of salt—a moy being an ancient unit of dry measure. She went out on the 26th and headed for Portsmouth. The Portsmouth leg must have been recorded in a different log, or pages are missing, because the next entry is for October 26th, as she headed once again for Charleston.

The *Shaw* made at least one voyage to India under Charles Chase. That was in 1839, and her time was far from good. She sailed from Saugor, India, on April 2nd and was 112 days getting to St. Helena, finally limping into Boston on September 19th, a passage of 170 days.[150] She came home on October 18th for refitting and sailed in December for Charleston. Not finding a cargo there, she went on to Mobile, loaded and went to Liverpool. The *Journal* reported on March 7, 1840, that the *Shaw* and the ship *Ann Mary Ann*, also of Portsmouth, had been chartered to go to Cardiff, Wales, to load railroad iron (rails) for the Eastern Railroad in New Hampshire, a line running between Newburyport and Portsmouth. The *Shaw* was sold in Boston, October 31, 1840. Two versions are available as to the end of the *Shaw*: One is in the customs records and has her sunk because she mistook Seguin light for Pemaquid light.[51] The other was in the *Journal*, February 2, 1850, and said the *Shaw*, "formerly of this port, about 24 years old, has been sold for $8,000 to go into the California trade."

Ann Parry

Specifications: Built in 1825 by William Badger. Square stern, billet head. Burthen, 348 tons; length, 107 feet. Owners, November 11, 1825, William Jones, Jr., Samuel E. Coues, James Kennard.

Few vessels built in the Port of Portsmouth gave longer or better service than did the rugged, dependable *Ann Parry*. Her life span exceeded 35 years, a remarkable feat for a wooden vessel that sailed on all the seven seas.

James Kennard took the *Ann Parry* on her maiden voyage, a venture into the cotton trade. She sailed on December 5, 1825, for Savannah where she loaded for Liverpool. Not until September 1827 did she come home, arriving from Liverpool. Kennard sailed her to New Orleans in 1828. After loading, she went to Europe, unloaded, and then went to Cadiz for salt. She sailed for Portsmouth on February 4, 1829, and had a rough winter passage. She lost two of her hands from the rigging while entering Holmes Hole, Massachusetts, after 60 days at sea. When she arrived in Portsmouth, she had been 67 days on the way. In 1830, after discharging cotton at Liverpool, she brought 180 passengers to Baltimore from Belfast. Thomas Jones was then master, and he was succeeded by Thomas Lunt, both of them Portsmouth shipmasters.

The *Ann Parry* continued in the freighting business until late in 1832, when she was bought by the Portsmouth Pier Company for conversion into a whaler. Portsmouth entrepreneurs were becoming aware of the importance of whaling and wanted to get in on the action. The *Ann Parry* wasn't the first Portsmouth ship to hunt whales. The *Triton* was the first whaling vessel to enter Portsmouth, and another Portsmouth-owned ship, the *Pocahontas*, was already employed by the Portsmouth Whaling Company, of which Ichabod Goodwin was president. Reuben Ray, Jr., was master on the *Ann Parry*'s first whaling voyage. She sailed for the Pacific in January 1833.[52] Portsmouth next heard about her in August, when her owners had a letter reporting that she was at Talcahuano, Chile, after a 140-day passage from Portsmouth and hadn't killed any whales. A year later, she was at Oahu, Hawaii, with 500 barrels. A letter in November reported that the whaler *Pocahontas*, the *Ann Parry* and the *Arabella* of Sag Harbor, New York, were all at Mowee (Maui), in the Sandwich Islands (Hawaii). The *Ann Parry* came home on September 8, 1836, with more than 2,200 barrels. Little time was wasted in getting her ready for another cruise, and her success made it easy to recruit a crew. Charles Swain was master, and on June 9, 1838, the *Journal* reported that the *Ann Parry* was at Ile de France, "all well," with no date given; 1,700 barrels of oil stowed.

It was April 9, 1839, however, before the *Ann Parry* appeared off Whale's Back Light in 91 days from Madagascar in the Indian Ocean. She had 500 barrels of sperm and 1,250 barrels of whale oil on board. James Kennard, her agent, also advertised 11,000 pounds of whale bone.[53] She had been gone 27 months and had lost two men. One was John Burdy, 37, the cook, who had died April 19, 1837, of apoplexy. The second was Samuel Baltz, who drowned October 24, 1838, when a whale upset a boat, one of the most hazardous aspects of the whaling trade.

The *Ann Parry* was put up for auction on June 1, 1839.[54] In his advertisement, Kennard said, "she is considered a fine vessel for the whaling business." Kennard asked newspapers in Boston, New Bedford and Salem to copy the advertisement in the *Journal* and send their bills to that paper. In the first week of July, another advertisement appeared in the *Journal*, seeking "20 smart enterprising Young Men, as Whalemen on board the ship *Ann Parry*, bound on a whaling voyage to the Indian Ocean." The new owners included Henry and Alexander Ladd, Mark W. Peirce and Samuel Sheafe. The advertisement sounded their confidence in the *Ann Parry*:

> Any young Man who will do his duty well, and prove himself a *smart fellow* will be certain of rapid promotion; in proof of which, the present Officers, from the Captain downwards, have been promoted to their present stations since they sailed in the *Ann Parry*—that *Lucky Ship*, which has never had an accident happen to herself or crew.

That sweeping statement apparently ignored what had happened to poor Sam Baltz, but perhaps his fate was deemed as part of the cost of doing business. By February 14, 1840, the ship was in the Indian Ocean under James Youngs. In June, the owners had a letter from Captain Youngs, dated January 15th. She was then between New Holland and Dieman Land, latitude 43° south in the Indian Ocean. The *Ann Parry* had already harvested 1,400 barrels, 300 of which were sperm. One mishap had temporarily blighted the cruise. A Charles W. Bodge, 17, of Portsmouth had fallen from the top gallant head on the mizzen, landing on the capstan; he died two hours later. But Captain Youngs cheerfully reported that the ship was "in good order" and the crew in good health. Youngs added that he had provisions for 17 more months and, at the end of that time, expected to have the hold filled with oil.

It was June 1, 1842, when the *Ann Parry* came home, having come from St. Augustine's Bay, Madagascar, in 84 days with a brief watering stop at lonely Ascension Island. She brought in 2,300 barrels of whale oil, 470 of sperm, and 15,000 pounds of bone. Leonard Cotton, an enterprising merchant in the Portsmouth Puddle Dock area, was the first into print with an advertisement offering 90 barrels of crude oil, 22 barrels of sperm and a thousand pounds of bone for sale.[54]

After the *Ann Parry* discharged her cargo, she was converted into a bark. Her mizzen mast was changed from square rig to the fore-and-aft type of schooner. Many of Portsmouth's full-rigged ships, including clippers, underwent the change. The reason was quite pragmatic: it took fewer hands to man the fore-and-aft rig, and fewer men meant more profit to the owners. Having just wed, Captain Youngs decided to stay ashore for a bit, a fatal mistake. James Dennett took the bark *Ann Parry* to sea in October 1842. In June 1843, she was in Madagascar with 700 barrels already stored and the crew all well.[55]

But all was not well with her former master, James Youngs. With a companion, John Owen of Pickering Street, Youngs left Portsmouth Pier in a whaleboat for a fishing trip outside the harbor. At 2 p.m., one of the squalls dreaded by every Portsmouth fisherman blew up. Youngs' boat was about three miles beyond Whale's Back Light when it capsized, and Youngs was drowned—an ironical death for a man who had sailed the seas of the world in the risky whaling trade, only to die a few miles from his own doorstep while fishing for cod. Owen clung to the over-turned whaleboat and was picked up by a passing schooner. Youngs, 35, "has left a wife to mourn his departure."[56]

All the while, the *Ann Parry* continued on her cruise. On May 31, 1845, "by an Arrival," it was learned that she had 1,800 barrels of sperm on board, a report that kept whaling gossips clacking in every Water Street grog shop. Yet, on Sunday, July 13, 1845, the *Ann Parry* came home after more than 32 months, and she was actually carrying the huge amount of 1,950 barrels of sperm. She had left St. Helena, the exile home of Napoleon Bonaparte and watering place for ships in the South Atlantic, on May 21st. Thirty-two men and boys were in her crew when she departed from Portsmouth; all but three returned in her. The unfortunates were Ebenezer Moulton of Exeter, 20, killed by a whale in February 1842; George K. King of Salem, about 40, who fell from a ladder in the forecastle and "expired almost immediately, and February last, in the Indian Ocean, William Wentworth, son of John Wentworth of this town, colored, aged 21, who jumped overboard in a fit of insanity and was drowned..."[57]

Once again, Leonard Cotton was busily advertising his share in the *Ann Parry*'s cargo. His portion amounted to 3,900 gallons of sperm, and it could be bought "by the cask, barrel, or single gallon." With three successful voyages behind her, the *Ann Parry* was a lively investment. James Dennett took her to the Indian Ocean in October 1825. Seven months out, she was reported at Johnanna Island, May 26, 1846, with 130 barrels of sperm. In August 1846, she put into Zanzibar with an ailing captain. Leaving him ashore, she cleared out under the former mate, Abiel Perry. She returned home, July 23, 1848, with a disappointing cargo of 650 barrels.

Behind that frustrating, unprofitable voyage is a story that must have been whispered in every waterfront saloon in Portsmouth. But it was more than a century in finding its way into print. David Z. Zink was doing research in 1971 in the Peabody Museum, Salem, and found a manuscript journal compiled by two different men during that cruise of the *Ann Parry*. Zink published an article, "Who Was the *Ann Parry's* Jonah?" in the *American Neptune*, January 1972.[58] For lack of space, only excerpts are used here. These portray a far different picture of whaling life than found in the more romantic versions offered by fiction writers. Ezra Goodnough started the journal before the *Ann Parry* left New England waters, and he maintained it until he took a discharge on the island of Mauritius, rather than continue serving in a vessel he thought was carrying a Jonah. In his first paragraphs, Zink made several observations about the manuscripts:

> The journal he [Goodnough] kept contains a tale of inept leadership, continual disorders among the crew, the usual desertions at exotic islands, the marvel of too much shore liberty even for seamen, ludicrous accidents, sickness, death, and worst of all, few whales...

> Except for its poor fishing, the voyage of the *Ann Parry* was similar in its externals to many another whaling voyage of its day. While the length of the voyage was somewhat shorter than usual, the bark was out of her home port long enough for 12 desertions, one change of command; four discharges (one was the third mate in Mahe); four deaths among the bark's company, and numerous injuries. Most of this was usual enough in the whale fishery, which, for a brief moment in history, brought great wealth to New England but also took its toll of lives.

Zink adds that it was unlikely that a journal such as Goodnough's could be published at the time it was written because "the coarseness of the ordinary seaman's life style would have offended most genteel readers. Certainly its bitter humor would not have found the appreciative audience it would in our own century." Edited by Zink, the journal recounts that voyage of the *Ann Parry*. Apparently all went well until Captain Dennett became ill and had to go ashore at Zanzibar. The United States consul boarded the *Ann Parry* and informed the crew that the first mate, Abiel Perry, would take command, at which the crew refused duty. They couldn't go ashore, however, because one of them had killed a native and the local government wanted to jail him. The crew finally agreed to serve if Captain Perry would go to Mauritius. Trouble continued, and, to compound it, they took only 118 barrels of oil. On February 18, 1847, the *Ann Parry* was becalmed 25 miles off the Island of Agalega, and Goodnough noted that she was "the first whaler that ever touched at this island." The crew learned of the death of Captain Dennett when the bark arrived at a place called Nossi Be. What happened next was probably typical:

> Starboard watch went ashore on liberty in the forenoon. They got kind of loony [drunk], and in the afternoon went over Nigger Hill to see the ladies, and it was great times amongst the women.

In his next entry, Goodnough criticized Captain Perry for taking items out of the ship's inventory to convert to cash for his own shoreside pleasures:

> All hands kept aboard to do nothing. Captain Perry sold 20 fathoms of hemp hawser for 50 dollars and then went ashore to blow it out...

"There is deep pathos when the journalist notes that he has sold a letter ...received from a young lady of Salem and the only one I have received this voyage for two heads of tobacco, it being a very scarce article," meaning the letter. GIs in the South Pacific 40-odd years ago knew the loneliness suffered by the whalers. The *Ann Parry* continued her long string of misadventures, and finally was at Mahe, India, where shore leave meant a round of grog shops and women for both watches. The journalist was relieved when the *Ann Parry* cleared out after 38 days "in blowing it out with the girls. If that does not bring good luck it will not be their fault for they wished us all the luck imaginable. The reason they wished that is they expect us back again in four or five months. Mahe is a merry port for girls and rum, all the sailor wants of it whilst you're young for when you get old you can't."[59]

Another disappointing cruise at sea, and the *Ann Parry* went back to Mahe for another bout of pleasure. Captain Perry was no inspiration to his men:

> At 7 p.m. the old man came on board after playing billiards all day and brought five whores with him and spent the evening. He had 15 or 20 dollars worth of cakes that he had made ashore. What he did not eat he gave to the whores to take ashore with them...

The above excerpts are enough to convince the reader that the *Ann Parry*'s "Jonah" was none other than Captain Abiel Perry, although the second journalist didn't voice that conclusion. He continued the journal when Ezra Goodnough left and quickly became just as bitter about Perry's profligate ways. John Joplin, the second writer, concluded his account on July 22, 1848:

> ... Thus ends a most unsuccessful voyage for both the owners and the crew.

A new career, however, awaited the *Ann Parry*. A substance more valuable than sperm oil had been found in California. Men were scrambling in all directions to find the quickest ways to get out to the gold fields. The *Ann Parry* was a proven vessel, and a group of Salem adventurers bought her for $3,600, and she went around Cape Horn to San Francisco. The tough old vessel did out her days on the West Coast as a timber hauler between San Francisco and the Washington Territory. She was in that trade as late as the Civil War.

Caroline Augusta

Specifications: Built in 1826 by William Badger. Square stern, female figurehead. Burthen, 406 tons; length, 114 feet; beam, 28.2 feet; depth, 14.1 feet. Owners, January 2, 1827, Theodore Chase, Nathaniel W. Merrill and John Riley, Jr.

The *Caroline Augusta* was the first and only ship built by William Badger that topped 400 tons. But it should be noted that Badger, like other shipwrights, was building bigger and bigger ships as the years went by. Although, at that time, the *Caroline Augusta* was larger than almost all the commercial ships built on the Piscataqua or its branches. Therefore, it was a proud moment for Nathaniel W. Merrill to be in command as she left for New Orleans on her maiden voyage and a start in the triangle trade. She suffered one mishap when she put into Hampton Roads. The *Gazette* on February 13, 1827, quoted a Norfolk newspaper as saying the *Caroline Augusta* had been forced ashore by ice near the Point of Shoals; other vessels were damaged by it. Whatever happened, the *Caroline Augusta* loaded there and sailed to Liverpool. She returned to New York on September 30th in 39 days.[60] For the next year or two, that was her employment: cotton or other raw materials to Liverpool, and heavy loads of immigrants on the westward passage. In April 1829, she was reported as 53 days out and short of provisions for 100 passengers. When she finally made it into New York, she had taken 62 days, with three deaths from the measles among her passengers.[61] It must be remembered that in the early days of transatlantic travel, passengers, especially in steerage, provided their own food. No matter how well the immigrants might plan, if the weather brought lengthy delays, there was plenty of suffering from hunger.

By the time of her April 1829 crossing, the *Caroline Augusta* had been sold to New York interests. They continued her service as a transport of immigrants. In the 1840s, she was in the Calcutta trade. Finally, in 1850, she was sold to a California firm and went to the Pacific Coast.[62] There she probably served out her years hauling timber from the Washington Territory to the booming city called San Francisco.

Crescent

Specifications: Built in 1826 by William Badger. Square stern, billet head.
Burthen, 341 tons; beam, 27 feet; depth, 13.5 feet. Owners, November 6, 1826,
John Rice, John B. Haley and Charles Coffin.

Those who love to romanticize life on the bounding wave can spin wild tales about the *Crescent* and her career, which lasted nearly half a century. The early years weren't all that exciting; she did the drudgery work of the cotton trade under John B. Haley. Early on, she ran between New Orleans, Havre and New York, occasionally carrying passengers, as she did when she went to New Orleans from Havre with five in the cabin and 333 unfortunates in steerage. That was late in 1831. John Rogers was master. She quickly loaded and the *Journal* reported on January 28, 1832, that the *Crescent*, on her way from New Orleans for Havre, had gone ashore on Orange Cay. She put into Nassau, New Providence Island, after being hauled off the reef by wreckers. The wreckers were awarded $4,500 for their work, and the *Crescent* went on to Havre with the loss of only 33 bales of cotton. She was back in New Orleans on May 14th, bringing in 134 passengers.[63] In December, she was back in New Orleans with 84 passengers.

In 1837, the *Crescent* was sold in New York, but she continued her yeoman work on the transatlantic runs. In May 1841, the *Crescent* figured in a dramatic incident when she picked up survivors of the ship *William Brown*, which struck an iceberg on passage from Liverpool to Philadelphia. The *Journal* gave its readers a stark account of human cruelty:

> ... It appears when the vessel struck, 33 passengers, the mate, and eight of the crew took to the long boat; the captain, three of the crew and eleven passengers took to the jolly boat; all the rest sunk with the vessel. The boats parted in the night. Some days after, the mate and crew determined (as they say in order to lighten the boat) to throw 17 of the passengers overboard, which they accomplished, and some of the most horrid and revolting scenes took place.
>
> There were two brothers and a sister of one family; the brothers were thrown over, and the sister jumped in after them. One fine boy prayed for a few minutes to say his prayers; they refused and hurled him into the sea at once. Some clung to the sides of the boat, praying for mercy, but their hands were cut off, and they were pushed into the deep.— Fifteen ladies and two men remained in the boat.
>
> One hour after the massacre the *Crescent* fell in with the boat, and saved the survivors of this horrid deed.

The account was supplemented with more news in later issues. In essence, when the *Crescent* arrived at Havre on May 12th, under George T. Ball, the previous report was confirmed in all its gory detail. There was also the story of a quick-witted boy of 12 who was thrown out of the boat but managed to get a hold on the boat under the bow, out of sight of the murderous crew. He lived to tell about it. Although it seems hard to believe, the odds are that the mate and crew were able to argue successfully that dire necessity forced them to the action they took.

A few years later the *Crescent* was sold again; this time for service to the Pacific Coast where gold fever was raging out of control. What happened to her out there is told in an article published in the *Portsmouth Chronicle*, January 6, 1873. It was taken from the *Sacramento Union*:

> ...The old ship *Crescent*, which served as a landing at that city [San Francisco] for more than a score of years, has been removed to be broken up for firewood, and the copper and iron in and about her timbers. The *Crescent* was 341 tons register... In this day she would be regarded as small, but in her day she was a superior vessel. Seven years in the salt trade running to Liverpool; and subsequently two whaling voyages. Early in 1849, she was purchased by the Salem Mechanics Trading and Mining Association, the company numbering about 60 men, who had taken the gold fever, and was loaded with 130,000 feet of lumber, framed and ready for erection into houses, and with the framework of a little steamer, she was sent to California... Besides this there were on board provisions to last 100 men nine months. On September 6, 1849, the *Crescent* left Salem with a full crew and as much freight as she could stagger under.
>
> Not a good traveler at best, the *Crescent* didn't reach San Francisco Bay until May, 1850, and, on her way, had made one stop at the Island of Juan Fernandez for only three days. On arrival she tied up in the immediate location of the present Pacific Iron Works, and was sold, together with her cargo immediately...

Minerva

Specifications: Built in 1827 by William Badger. Square stern, billet head. Burthen, 308 tons; length, 100.5 feet; beam, 26.3 feet; depth, 13.15 feet. Owners, William A. Rice and William Badger.

William A. Rice was master of the *Minerva* throughout her career. He made at least six voyages to Europe in her, probably triangular, and each time she returned with salt for the fishermen of the Port of Portsmouth. The *Minerva* was lost at sea in 1836, and William A. Rice became master of the ship *Isaac Newton*.

Sarah Parker

Specifications: Built in 1827 by William Badger. Square stern, billet head. Burthen, 387 tons; length, 111.9 feet; beam, 27.8 feet; depth, 13.9 feet. Owners, January 23, 1828, Goodwin & Coues and Ferguson & Jewett.

If Ichabod Goodwin, future governor of New Hampshire, ever admitted to having a favorite ship, it would have been, in all probability, the *Sarah Parker*. She bore the name of his wife, and Goodwin was master on her maiden voyage, when she sailed for Savannah to enter the cotton trade.

That first voyage terminated in Philadelphia. When the *Sarah Parker* discharged her cargo, she went to Savannah to begin the cycle over again. She arrived in Liverpool on December 1st. On Saturday, March 28, 1829, the *Sarah Parker* entered Portsmouth with cargo for her owners. Her passage had taken 71 days, and the most troublesome part was in her native waters. Coming into the wharf the day after her arrival, the *Sarah Parker* was caught in the Piscataqua's seven-knot tidal current and grounded on a rock on Noble's Island. By the stalwart efforts of boat crews and her own people, the *Sarah Parker* was freed on the next tide. She was less damaged than feared, but much of her cargo of salt was lost.

The *Sarah Parker* left Portsmouth in April 1829 for Charleston.[64] She didn't come home until June 20, 1831, bringing salt from Liverpool for the owners. It was Ichabod Goodwin's last voyage in her and his last command at sea.

With Robert West as master, the *Sarah Parker* continued in the cotton trade. She came into Portsmouth in May 1832 with salt for Goodwin & Coues, crates for Taylor & Waldron, iron for Sheafe & Lyman and hardware for Richard Jenness and William Goddard.[65] Quickly unloaded, the *Sarah Parker* cleared for Savannah on May 16th, arriving May 27th, put in at Liverpool on July 11th, and was in Portsmouth on September 3rd, for a total time of 100 days in perambulating the triangle. When she arrived in Portsmouth in April 1835, the *Journal* thanked her captain for bringing Liverpool papers dated as late as March 19th.[66] But, as happened to so many of her fellows, the time had come for her to be sold. Even if she was named for an owner's wife, sentiment rarely stood in the way of a bargain. Exactly how she was employed after she was sold isn't clear. There are hints that she went into the East Indies trade. By 1847, she was owned in Nantucket by David Main and sent whaling under Thomas Russell. One 47-month cruise in the Pacific is on record. She returned from it on May 28, 1849, with 59 barrels of sperm, 2,700 barrels of whale oil, and 12 tons of whale bone—a total value of $42,627.[67]

That year the *Sarah Parker* was sold again, the sale price being $9,600. The Gold Rush was in full spate. Once on the Pacific Coast, she went into the lumber business and in 1853 was working out of Puget Sound. The *Chronicle*, September 20, 1880, published what was almost a eulogy for her:

> A writer in *Harper*'s Magazine, a former captain of the celebrated fast ship, *Sophia Walker*, which was once the pride of the port of Boston, thus mentions a former Portsmouth ship:
>
> True, the old "Sarah Parker" was my first love and the proudest day I ever knew was that on which I stood the monarch of her peopled deck, when the pilot descended into the skiff, and we filled away the main yard, bound to the East Indies. But the old girl was far advanced in life, and, when, after five years of faithful companionship, I saw her sold to become a whaler, a few tears of sorrow were speedily dried by the smile of gladness with which I beheld my new bride, and I congratulated myself on the promotion.

The *Chronicle*'s article concluded with the observation that an oil painting of the *Sarah Parker* had been hanging for half a century in Ichabod Goodwin's "Counting Room" on Market Street. Today the *Sarah Parker* hangs in the Governor Goodwin Mansion at Portsmouth's Strawbery Banke.

William Badger

Specifications: Built in 1828 by William Badger. Square stern, billet head. Burthen, 334 tons; length, 106 feet; beam, 26.55 feet; depth, 13.275 feet. Owners, November 4, 1828, Lewis Barnes and Theodore Harris.

Did the old man, Master Badger, sense that this vessel would be his swan song? Or did the owners offer a tribute to a great craftsman? Obviously such questions are beyond answer, but William Badger knew the years were running out on him. A year after this ship was launched, he built a 40-ton schooner, and the ship *Howard* was on the stocks when he died.

As indicated previously, Master Badger was following the trend into building ships that were a bit longer and narrower than the short, beamy vessels of his youth. In the case of the *William Badger*, the ratio of length to width was 4:1. Formerly, most of Badger's ships hovered around a ratio of 3.5:1, length to width.

Theodore J. Harris, one of the owners, took the *William Badger* to sea, sailing for New Orleans on November 21, 1828. She loaded there and sailed for Europe on April 5, 1829.[68] Harris brought salt for the owners on September 21, 1829. The *William Badger* spent the next decade and a half in the triangle trade.

William W. Thompson succeeded Harris, sailing the *William Badger* to New Orleans, from there to Liverpool, and was back in New Orleans, June 14, 1830, loading again for Europe. Not until October 18, 1831, did she return home, with salt for the owners. When she cleared out in February 1832, she didn't return until September. She sailed again and made another entrance into the Port of Portsmouth on June 23, 1833, with cotton for the mills in the Dover area.[69] Harris returned as master and was relieved by John Lake, Jr. It was during Thompson's tenure that the owners advertised against a sailor who had collected his advance pay and then disappeared. Their complaint was brought in court against John T. Beck, seeking attachments against any property he might own in the Portsmouth area. They contended in their advertisement that Beck had signed ship's articles on September 13, 1833, for a voyage to Rio de Janeiro, "as a faithful mariner for the term of 12 months, unless sooner discharged by the termination of said voyage— and in pursuance of said contract... and thereafterwards, on the 8th day of March, A.D., 1834, deserted and ran away from said vessel, whereby he became liable to pay the plaintiffs such damages as they in consequence thereof sustained, which damages the plaintiffs aver, amount to one hundred and ten dollars."

If nothing else, the advertisement gives an inkling as to the wage of an ordinary seaman in the fourth decade of the nineteenth century. It was customary to pay wages in advance, for, oft times, the sailor was leaving behind a family in need of support. When voyages exceeded the time scheduled, there were often arguments over wages due, and when voyages were shorter, contrary arguments took place. In Beck's case, he had carried out his duties between September and March. Therefore, when he deserted, he owed the owners six months' service, which they valued at $110, making his pay a bit less than $20 a month. Above that, of course, he was fed and sheltered, and, on some ships, drew a rum ration. If he wanted tobacco or a bit of clothing, he had to buy it through the ship's stores, one of the little rackets operated by the masters.

The *William Badger* would occasionally be diverted from the triangle trade for passages to ports like Rio or Havana. Masters came and went. Lake was relieved by John Tripe, who came in from Liverpool on June 22, 1840, with salt. Her next master was Woodbury Langdon. On December 27, 1842, the *Journal* reported his death at sea, aged 41. The obituary was unfortunately more a eulogy than a record of the man's life. In four-point type, it ran 27 lines, about 300 words. It is known, however, that he was a son of Judge Woodbury Langdon and a nephew of Governor John Langdon. Joseph L. Whipple replaced Langdon and brought the ship into Portsmouth from Spain on December 22, 1842. Oliver Coffin was master on her last two voyages under Port of Portsmouth ownership. In 1845, the *William Badger* was sold in Boston and became a whaler. Andrew Breed of Lynn was the owner with a Captain Perkins as master. She made two whaling voyages for Breed. On her first, she came in with 900 barrels of sperm and 1,600 of whale oil for a total value of $50,778. On the second, with only the sperm recorded of 1,484 barrels, her cargo was worth $59,970.[70]

The *William Badger* was then sold to B. P. Howard and John Braley of New Bedford. Between 1853 and 1861, she made two whaling voyages. On June 1, 1861, the *Journal* reported:

AN OLD SHIP

Ship Wm. Badger, 334 tons, and ship Roman, 2d, 350 tons, both having lately arrived at New Bedford, have been withdrawn from the whaling business, and sold to parties who will transfer them to the merchant service. Both were towed from New Bedford for New York, and it is stated that they are to be used as store ships...

The ship *William Badger* was built at this port in 1828... Being the 50th vessel built by Master Badger at his yard on Badger's Island, she received the name of the venerable builder, and it has thus been perpetuated and sent over the world for 31 years. Master Badger used to say, that he should "come back" in a 100 years from the time of his death. Perhaps the old ship may yet be his representative until that term expires.

It is no small compliment to our Piscataqua shipbuilders, that their work can stand the storms of a third of a century, and still be sound and still be fit for service.

What better eulogy for an old lady who must have been weary after all the years of tramping the seas? The *William Badger* was the last Kittery ship of the 1783–1829 period, but, even with Master Badger gone to the Great Shipyard, the yards in Kittery would continue to produce great three-masted sailing vessels for over 40 more years.

Many years after the *Journal's* tribute to the *William Badger*, the *Portsmouth Herald*, February 23, 1904, published some of the recollections of a man named Benjamin P. Shillaber, a newspaper reporter, born and brought up in Portsmouth. Among the items was the following:

For a long series of years the largest ships on the river were but of 300 tons, and I remember when the *William Badger* of 600 tons was launched from Badger's Island, the fuss made over it, it seeming audacious to build of such vast proportions. People came from miles around to see her launched, and all sorts of predictions were indulged in regarding results; one, that the ship must strike Portsmouth and carry away large portions of the opposite shore the failure of which was a great disappointment to many. She ran off the ways as light and graceful as a yacht, as I well remember...

Shillaber's reminiscence has one flaw; the *William Badger* was only 334 tons burthen. Not until 1837, when Charles Raynes built the *Columbia*, did a Kittery ship reach 600 tons. Shillaber's account, nevertheless, is valuable to show the excitement that prevailed at launchings. And in his defense, it has to be said he was an old man when he wrote the above.

VIII   *Newmarket*

PJ, May 16, 1829

BEFORE LAUNCHING into a discussion of shipbuilding in New-market, it is necessary to define what is meant by Newmarket. This will mitigate somewhat any civic indignation in the Town of Newfields. No one is really at fault for crediting Newmarket and not Newfields as a shipbuilding center. At the time customs records were started in 1789, Newfields was part of Newmarket. In 1849, 20 years after the end of the shipbuilding period covered in this study, Newfields was set off as a township called South Newmarket. Part of it came from New-market and another portion from Exeter. Exeter's borders once touched Dover's, but other towns were carved from it in the early years.[1] New-fields remained South Newmarket until 1895. Newmarket's early records were destroyed by fire in 1875, but Newfields' sources make the following available:

> To what extent, ship-building was carried on in Newmarket before the Revoltuion it is impossible to tell. No records of the business are available, but it was an important industry both at Lamprey River [Newmarket] and Newfields. At one time seven vessels were on the stocks in the shipyards of Lamprey River, and the "Landing" at Newfields was a very busy spot. So pressing was the work that shipwrights were exempted from military training. In 1778, the privateer *General Sullivan* was overhauled and refitted at Newfields Landing. The Shutes, the Badgers and Gen. James Hill were the principal shipbuilders of the period.

> The ship-building and commercial interests of Newmarket were seriously injured by the War of 1812. After the spring of 1813 our seacoast was blockaded by a British squadron. Three years of blockade practically destroyed ship-building on the

183

Squamscot. Among the last to engage in the industry at Newfields were Zechariah Beals, Dudley Watson, Samuel G. Tarlton and George Hilton. The last vessel built here was the *Nile* in 1827. When we were a ship-building town the launching of a ship was an event of great importance and interest. Men, women and children, all attended, and refreshments were provided for all. The ships were floated to Portsmouth where they were rigged and prepared for sea.[2]

Newmarket launched its first post-Revolutionary ship, the *Hannah*, in 1788. Its last, the *Elizabeth Frith*, came in 1828. Between those dates, the town's shipyards produced 26 square-rigged, three-masted vessels for a total tonnage of 6,948, an average of 267 tons. In addition, the shipyards produced 17 brigs, total of 2,589 tons; 12 schooners, 691 tons; one sloop, 78 tons; one snow, 154 tons. Gross tonnage for the period was 10,460.

The average tonnage of Newmarket ships, however, is a clue in itself as to why the up-river shipyards were largely out of the shipbuilding business by 1830. That average tonnage was about the same in the other up-river towns. For various reasons, the inland yards could not meet the demand for larger and larger ships. It will be remembered that Eliphalet Ladd's giant *Archelaus* had to be floated down river, buoyed on water casks. Similar problems prevailed on the Cocheco. And, in 1820–21, an additional obstacle was put in the way of up-river builders: the Portsmouth Bridge was built across the Piscataqua between Kittery and Portsmouth. There was a draw, but passing was difficult for vessels depending on a bit of sail and the tide. The Newmarket yards, however, built some fine ships for Port of Portsmouth annals, starting with the *Hannah*.

Hannah

Built in 1788. Burthen, 228 tons.

Early customs records are skimpy with information about the *Hannah*. But she was the first ship credited to Newmarket builders after the Revolution. Who knows, perhaps William Badger had a hand in her construction. Naval vessels were no longer being built at Portsmouth, and Badger had returned up river to ply his trade. Aaron Hill of Portsmouth was her first registered owner in 1789. She made two voyages to the West Indies in that year under Peter Turner. In December 1790, she came in from London under Captain Turner and that is the end of the record.

Fanny

Specifications: Built in 1792. Square stern, billet head. Burthen, 228 tons; length, 82.9 feet; beam, 25.3 feet; depth, 12.65 feet.

Reports of the *Fanny*'s early years are missing from the records. It appears her home port was in Newburyport in 1799. At that time, Jonathan Clark and George Conner, Exeter merchants, held shares in her, along with Samuel Ham and Benjamin Conner. Between 1799 and 1801, the *Fanny* made three voyages from Portsmouth under different captains. She went to Tobago under Henry Parsons in 1800; the next year, she came in from the Isle of May under William Walker. Robert Jenkins was the third master. In 1801, she was sold at the Cape of Good Hope, but the records tell none of the circumstances.

Catharine

Specifications: Built in 1792. Burthen, 203 tons; length, 80 feet; beam, 24.7 feet; depth, 12.15 feet. Owner, May 16, 1792, Woodbury Langdon.

Woodbury Langdon is more often thought of as a politician and jurist than as a ship owner. But, in the years right after the Revolution, he owned, at one time or another, four vessels. The *Catharine* was the only ship. Langdon made his home on the site of the present-day condominium complex called the Rockingham on Portsmouth's State Street.

Langdon sent the *Catharine* to St. Eustatius under Samuel Gerrish. She returned to Portsmouth in July 1792.[3] Captain Gerrish took her out again in September 1792, and there is no record noting her return. A note in the Customs records says she was sold in Philadelphia on May 20, 1793.

Apollo

Specifications: Built in 1792. Burthen, 234 tons; length, 86 feet; beam, 25.1 feet; depth, 12.05 feet. Owner, January 9, 1793, James Sheafe.

The *Apollo* went into the European trade. James Sheafe sent her to Liverpool under John Moore, and she returned on October 23, 1793. Samuel Jones was the next master, and he commanded her on three Liverpool voyages. In 1795, Sheafe advertised that he had "Just recieved by the *Nancies* from Bridport [On the Dorset Coast of England], and the *Apollo* from Liverpool... Heavy & light Bridport navy canvas; Twine; Deep Sea Lines; Shoe Thred; cream colr'd. blue and green edg'd Earthenware in crates, assorted."[4] The *Apollo*'s voyages were lucrative for James Sheafe, but in 1798, she was captured by the French and taken into Rochfort on the Bay of Biscay. The Quasi War with France was simmering; ship owners operated at their peril.

Pacific

Specifications: Built in 1793. Burthen, 230 tons; length, 84.5 feet; beam, 25 feet; depth, 12 feet. Owner, December 28, 1793, James Sheafe.

For James Sheafe, trading was a risky business indeed. Not only did he lose the *Apollo* to a French privateer, but on her maiden voyage, the *Pacific* was captured while commanded by Richard Salter. Sheafe was able to ransom her, and the *Pacific* returned in September 1794. Abraham Isaac advertised:

> Begs leave to inform the public and his customers in general, that he has just received a fresh supply of glass ware, by the ship *Pacific*, from Hamburgh, and now ready for sale, at his shop in Buck Street [State Street], consisting of elegant Decanters, Tumblers, Wine Glasses, etc. etc. . . . [5]

Richard Salter was master through three more voyages to Europe. He came from Havre, September 2, 1795, and informed the *Gazette* that provisions "of every kind" were cheap in Havre, that the people were "quiet and don't discuss the war any more than is done in the United States." The *Pacific* came from London on October 24, 1796. After a voyage to Surinam, Salter turned the *Pacific* over to John Bowles. The latter was master when the *Pacific* was again captured by the French. A note in the customs records says that this time she was burned. This seems disputed, however, by a report in the *Gazette* of September 4, 1798:

> . . . Arrived ship Pacific, 32 days from St. Kitts; sailed from St. Vincent's, under convoy, fell to leeward, and was captured by a French privateer on the 23d July, who, after coming along side, commenced firing grape-shot and musket-balls into the ship, but happily did but little damage; took out the Captain, Perkins Salter, and four hands; on the 24th was retaken by the British sloop of war *Favorite*, and carried into St. Kitts.

Subsequent events lend the *Gazette* version more credibility. On May 31, 1799, for example, the death of William Fernald, 21, "of this town" was reported. Fernald was killed in a fall on board the ship *Pacific*. Again, the *Pacific* was reported at Hull, England, later in 1799, under Salter.[6] If the master was Perkins Salter, he was then only 24 years old, and died at the age of 31 in 1806.

Tryal

Specifications: Built in 1793. Burthen, 190 tons; length, 76.9 feet; beam, 24.1 feet; depth, 12.05 feet. Owner, January 25, 1794, Joseph Woodward of Boston.

Statira

Specifications: Built in 1795. Burthen, 235 tons; length, 85.6 feet; beam, 25.2 feet; depth, 12.6 feet. Owner, November 24, 1795, Thomas Manning.

Although customs records don't list a builder for the *Statira*, it is fair to speculate that William Badger had a hand in her construction. Manning and Badger became acquainted during the Revolution, and Manning, as a seasoned mariner, could appreciate Badger's ability.

Like so many vessels, before and since, the *Statira* was named for someone dear to the owner; in this instance, his wife. Statira Manning was 54 when she died in 1807. The obituary said that the day before her death, "at a few moments past 11, in the forenoon, she was seized with a paralytic affection of the right side, and less than 24 hours suffering, concluded the solemn scene."[7]

The *Statira* made three voyages to Europe before 1800. Her first master was William Edwards, who brought her in from St. Ubes on October 15, 1796. John Seaward was next, coming in from St. Ubes in September 1798 after a 50-day passage. Thomas Manning sold the ship in Boston in 1800.

Florenzo

Specifications: Built in 1796. Square stern, billet head. Burthen, 210 tons; length, 78.4 feet; beam, 24.5 feet; depth, 12.2 feet. Owner, May 7, 1796, Stephen Chase.

Joseph Chase sailed the *Florenzo* out of Portsmouth on her maiden voyage to the United Kingdom.[8] Chase returned to Portsmouth in October 1796 in 47 days from St. Ubes. He reported that English consuls had been ordered to leave Spain with war expected at any time. On his passage, the captain saw a fleet of 150 merchantmen heading for the United Kingdom under the protection of a 74-gun warship and two East Indiamen.[9] Nathaniel Currier was the next master of the *Florenzo*, sailing her to Surinam and returning May 11, 1798. Joseph

Starks then took the *Florenzo* to Surinam, returning May 28, 1799. Stephen Chase then advertised her for sale:

... She has only performed three voyages, and was sheathed before any worm had touched her bottom—a very fast sailing ship, and calculated to stow well, now lying at the Long Wharf [Foot of old Jefferson Street] in Portsmouth, N.H.[10]

Chase also sold off the cargo the *Florenzo* had brought in from Demerara: "79 Hhds. Sugar, and 18 Puncheons Rum..." Exactly what quantity of rum was available in a puncheon can't be determined; it could vary from 72 to 120 gallons.

Samuel Ham became the owner of the *Florenzo* on August 9, 1800. She then sailed for the Cape of Good Hope in August with Asa Bodwell, master.[11] She returned to Portsmouth in April 1801. An advertisement appeared in the *Gazette* on April 21:

Just Landing, and for sale, on Rindge's Wharf [In the North End], part of the cargo of the Ship *Florenzo* viz.

Fifty Leaguers [A leaguer was a wine cask of uncertain capacity] of Cape Wine; 6 do. Arrack; 1000 Ox Hides; 15 chests of Suochong Tea; 16,000 Morocco skins; a quantity of Camwood.

Likewise—The above ship, if applied for soon...

In March 1802, it was reported that the *Florenzo*, under Ham, "who left the Vineyard on Friday previous, bound to Portsmouth, was drove on shore at Marshfield—a Vineyard pilot and three of the crew lost."[12] If the report was true, it is obvious that the *Florenzo* was gotten off, relatively unscathed, because Ham advertised her auction on June 29, 1802.[13] Ham agreed to take notes of "2, 4, & 6 months." Her new owners, Nathaniel and John Haven, registered her on July 9th. Lewis Barnes became master and took the *Florenzo* to Demerara, whence he returned in March 1803. Barnes was master in March 1805 when she was advertised for auction.[14] Although the sale was to be held in the offices of the New Hampshire Fire and Marine Insurance Company, the *Florenzo* was in Scituate Harbor, Massachusetts. The Customs record lists her as cast away in 1817 while still owned by the Havens.[15] Yet there are no references to her after March 1805 in the marine news or customs entries. It would seem possible that she had had another mishap on the Massachusetts coast and was sold as she was.

The *Journal*, on May 22, 1824, published the following:

INFORMATION WANTED

JOSEPH GARLAND, a native of Dundee in Scotland, left that place as a sea-faring man, and arrived at Portsmouth, N.H. about the month of September, 1804, at which time he boarded with Robert Colman—he afterwards went to sea with Captain Lewis Barnes, and was discharged at this place at the termination of the voyage—since which he has not been heard of.—Any information respecting said Garland furnished the printer of the Portsmouth Journal, will be promptly communicated to his brother in Scotland, who feels much anxiety on his account.

What happened to Joseph Garland is as much lost in history's dust as is the exact fate of the *Florenzo*. It can be noted, however, that there are a lot of Garlands living in the New Hampshire seacoast area.

Caroline

Specifications: Built in 1800 by William Hackett. Burthen, 190 tons; length, 77 feet; beam, 24 feet; depth, 12 feet. Owner, December 3, 1800, Thomas Manning.

Having named one ship for his wife, there is a possibility that Thomas Manning had a daughter named Caroline. At any rate, she was one of three merchant vessels built by the famous William Hackett at Newmarket. She was, however, the only one that was three-masted and ship-rigged. Hackett's reputation had been established by his work on the Revolutionary War frigates, *Raleigh* and *Ranger*. The late Howard Chapelle wrote of him:

William Hackett was born at Salisbury, Massachusetts, May 1, 1739; he became an apprentice to his father and uncle about 1751... Sometime prior to 1774 he and his cousin James operated the yard together... As a boy William Hackett saw the British 44-gun ship *America* built at Portsmouth, and it is possible that his elders worked on this ship. By the end of the Revolution William Hackett acquired a great reputation as a ship designer in New England...[16]

When William Hackett built the *Caroline*, he was 61 years old and had reached the peak of his career during the hasty buildup of United States naval forces during the Quasi War with France. He had also teamed with cousin James Hackett in building the second *America*, a 74-gun warship presented to France by a grateful United States Congress. The gift deprived John Paul Jones, the Revolutionary naval hero, of command of the *America*.

The *Caroline* was William Hackett's last venture in building bigger vessels. She made at least three voyages, two of them to the Isle of May. The *Gazette*, on March 9, 1802, reported:

> A letter from Capt. [John] Bowles, master of the ship *Caroline* of this port, mentions the deaths of five of his crew out of seven; viz. David Briard, aged 19, son of Mr. Robert Briard of Kittery, died at Trinidad; and four others died on the passage from Demerara to Charleston, viz. Thomas Hoskie, Thomas Mastin, Samuel Rowe, and John Nepton, all of Yellow Fever.

Captain Bowles was in from the Isle of May in August 1802[17] He brought with him the report that salt "was very scarce at the Isle."[18] In 1804, Thomas Manning was advertising "Salt for sale on board the ship *Caroline* at Portsmouth Pier."[19] A customs note says she was cast away later that year.[20]

Patriot

Specifications: Built in 1801 by John Shute. Square stern, billet head. Burthen, 256 tons; length, 90.2 feet; beam, 25.5 feet; depth, 12.75 feet. Owner, March 20, 1802, Thomas Manning.

Thomas Manning was the patriot who urged the renaming of Portsmouth's King Street to Congress Street after the public reading in Market Square of the Declaration of Independence.

If, however, Manning was hoping some of the aura of the name would bring the *Patriot* good fortune, he was mistaken. She made a successful voyage to St. Ubes with John Seaward, master, in 1802. Seaward was in command when the *Patriot* foundered. He survived and was later master of the brig *Dian* and the ship *Tom*. Seaward died in 1843 at the age of 68.

Lewis

Specifications: Built in 1802 by William Badger. Burthen, 234 tons; length, 83.3 feet; beam, 25.5 feet; depth, 13.4 feet. Owners, Ebenezer, John and Richard Breed and Daniel Orr, all of Boston.

This vessel is notable in that she was the only one in the nineteenth century that Badger built away from his cozy little yard on Badger's Island.

Governor Gilman

Specifications: Built by Samuel Cottle in 1802. Square stern, male figurehead. Burthen, 316 tons; length, 96.6 feet; beam, 27.4 feet; depth, 13.7 feet. Owners, December 28, 1802, Samuel Ham and Jonathan Clark.

John T. Gilman of Exeter, both a politician and businessman, had been governor for seven years when the *Governor Gilman* was launched and would continue in office two more years, terms being annual in those days. Asa Bodwell was master when the *Governor Gilman* cleared for Calcutta early in 1803.[21] Bodwell returned in May 1804.[22]

A month after her arrival, June 26, 1804, the *Gazette* published an advertisement for the sale of the *Governor Gilman* in Boston on July 3rd. The advertisement indicates the sale was compelled to meet "the payment of Mariner's wages." Exactly what was entailed wasn't spelled out. What happened to the *Governor Gilman* after that isn't known either.

Jason

Specifications: Built in 1804 by Benjamin Remick. Square stern, billet head. Burthen, 242 tons; length, 85.6 feet; beam, 25.6 feet; depth, 12.8 feet. Owners, February 7, 1805, George F. and Oliver C. Blunt. Sold in Portland in 1805.

James Cook

Specifications: Built in 1804 by William Shute. Burthen, 254 tons. Owner, William Charles Neil.

The *James Cook* was named to honor the memory of the great English explorer of the South Pacific, James Cook. Three voyages by the *James Cook* are on record, all of them were to Liverpool under William Cox. She was captured by a privateer in 1810. The United States wasn't at war, but those were perilous times for seamen. No nationality was given for her captor, but her name was *Wagram*, and that was the name of the locale of one of Emperor Napoleon's victories. So the implication is strong that the *Wagram* was French and operating out of the West Indies.

Watson

Specifications: Built in 1805 by Zechariah Beal. Square stern, billet head. Burthen, 214 tons; length, 81.6 feet; beam, 24.7 feet; depth, 12.35 feet. Owners, March 21, 1806, Dudley Watson, Joshua Neal and Benjamin Swett.

Zechariah Beal, William Badger's stepson, had already built one ship, the *Isabella Henderson*, at Portsmouth three years earlier. The *Watson* was the only vessel he built on his home ground of Newfields, and she, obviously, was named for one of her owners.

Joshua Neal was master on her first voyage. He returned on July 16, 1807. Benjamin Swett sold out on the 20th to Edward J. Long. The service of the *Watson* was undoubtedly affected by the Embargo. If she was working, it was out of ports other than Portsmouth until 1810. In that year, William Cox brought her in from Liverpool on November 12th. It's of interest to note that Captain Cox had been master of the *James Cook* when taken by a privateer, and by November, he had another ship. Cox brought salt, coal and crates to Joshua Neal.

At the time of her sale in 1807, the *Watson* was advertised:

> One third of the ship Watson and appurtenances, at the Portsmouth Pier—is burthened 216 tons; 18 months old, can be fitted for sea in a few days... Terms liberal and made known at time and place of sale.[23]

The War of 1812 again interrupted the *Watson*'s career, but with the outbreak of hostilities, she made at least two voyages. The *Gazette* reported on July 30, 1811:

> Ship *Watson* of Portsmouth, from LaGaius, in the Gulph of Mexico, and 19 days from the Coast, with logwood to owner, ar. at New York 23d inst.

In March 1812, Henry Sherburne brought the *Watson* in from St. Ubes, having left there on January 6th.[24] Early in 1814, the ownership changed again. Theodore Chase and Neal bought out the others, and they were still owners when the *Watson* foundered. The *Gazette* reported on October 28, 1817:

Loss of the Ship Watson. —The French ship *Amitie*, has ar
at New York from Bordeaux. —Oct. 1 . . . fell in with ship *Watson*,
Capt. Nathaniel Kennard, of Portsmouth, 34 days from Havre,
with plaster and dry goods, bound to Philadelphia, in distress,
having lost her fore and mizzen masts in a severe gale—took off
the crew, the *Watson* foundered soon after.

Manning

*Specifications: Built in 1805 by John Shute. Burthen, 267 tons; length,
90.4 feet; beam, 26.1 feet; depth, 13.05 feet. Owner, January 7, 1806,
Thomas Manning.*

Having named one of his ships for his wife, and another, in all probability, for a daughter, Thomas Manning apparently thought it was time
to honor himself: hence, the ship *Manning*. Manning put Henry Salter
in command, and he brought her in from the Isle of May on September
27, 1806. Captain Salter also made a voyage to Rotterdam and back in
1807. Then the Embargo Act gave the *Manning* a long rest. Not until
1810 did Thomas Manning take command of his own ship.

Manning made a voyage to the West Indies and came in from
Bonavista on August 8, 1810, with salt consigned to himself.[25] The
Manning was at New Orleans on March 2, 1811, on the first leg of a
triangular voyage.[26] Although there is no direct evidence of the fact, the
Manning probably beat her way across to Liverpool with cotton, then to
St. Ubes. She was home, with salt for the owner, in October.[27] Charles
Blunt made a voyage to the West Indies before she was idled by the War
of 1812.

With the war over, Manning sailed the *Manning* to the West
Indies, returning in November 1815 in 23 days from St. Bart's with
rum.[28] About this time, John Bowles bought an interest in the ship, and
Manning advertised her in December 1815 as sailing to Charleston
under Bowles in "ten to twelve days."[29] That trip around the triangle
brought the *Manning* home where she discharged her cargo and sailed
for the West Indies on her last voyage. Captain Bowles had the ship at
Pointe-a-Pitre, Guadeloupe, December 10, 1816.[30] A portent of bad
news to come, the *Manning* was reported ready to sail but couldn't. She
had lost the mate and half the crew to illness. Bowles finally recruited a
few hands and sailed for Portsmouth. The *Gazette* reported on June 17,
1817:

> The ship *Manning*, Bowles, from Point Petrie for this port,
> went ashore near Wellfleet, 8th inst. She had received on board a
> Cape Cod pilot, and endeavored to get into Provincetown harbor,
> but struck on a bar, when the main and mizzen masts were cut

away, she soon afterwards beat over, with loss of rudder and struck the shore, and has since bilged. Cargo saved.

Grand Turk

Specifications: Built in 1806 by George Hilton. Square stern, billet head. Burthen, 270 tons; length, 90.6 feet; beam, 26.2 feet; depth, 13.1 feet. Owners, December 20, 1806, Lewis Barnes and Oliver C. Blunt. Sold in New York soon after.

Eliza Sproat

Specifications: Built in 1807 by John Shute. Square stern, billet head; Burthen, 234 tons; length, 82.5 feet; beam, 25.8 feet; depth, 12.9 feet. Owners, James Sheafe, Matthew S. Marsh and Robert Lenox, 1807.

Little is on record about the *Eliza Sproat*. What success she had came in her first two years. She was cast away in the Orkneys, February 18, 1809.[31]

Merchant

Specifications: Built 1807 by Samuel Cottle of Eliot. Square stern, billet head. Burthen, 270 tons; length, 89.5 feet; beam, 25.1 feet; depth, 13.2 feet. Owners, Jacob Sheafe, Charles Neil and George Hilton. Captured by the British.

Trajan

Specifications: Built in 1810 by Benjamin Remick of Kittery. Square stern, billet head. Burthen, 238 tons; length, 87.5 feet; beam, 25.1 feet; depth, 11.9 feet. Owners, February 22, 1811, Samuel Sheafe, Charles March and Robert Benson.

The *Trajan* took her name from the Roman emperor who flourished around 98–117 A.D., and that may have been the most distinctive thing about her.

Despite her launching date of 1810, Portsmouth customs records list no entries about her until November 12, 1818. That was when Joshua Neal arrived from Russia with a cargo of hemp, iron and duck, the latter being a strong fabric.[32] The cargo was consigned to John Langdon, Jr., Jacob Cutter and the master.[33] William Briard was the *Trajan*'s next master, clearing for Charleston, January 25, 1819. On March 9th, the *Oracle* also reported that a young seaman named Henry McDonough had drowned. The *Trajan* didn't return home until May

1820, a lapse of time that hints she went to Europe from Charleston and then to Rio de Janeiro. On May 20, the *Oracle* noted the *Trajan*'s arrival and said that on her way north, she had loaded with salt at Turk's Island. She made that leg in 22 days.

There's unfortunately a lapse of three years in the records. The *Trajan* was probably sailing out of other ports, having cleared from Portsmouth in December 1820 for New Orleans under a Captain Langdon (Perhaps Woodbury, John Langdon, Jr.'s brother).[34] Her next recorded entry took place October 1, 1823, from Stockholm under John G. Pray. Following that, her master was Pierpont Hammond. He had the quarterdeck in the last years of her Portsmouth ownership. The *Journal*, on July 17, 1824, reported the arrival of the *Trajan* from Havana via Norfolk. Six persons died on the passage between Havana and Norfolk. One was John Seaward of Portsmouth, 16; another was John Kimball of Newburyport. Captain Hammond made three more voyages in the *Trajan*, all of them to Rio de Janeiro. The *Trajan* was sold in Portland, July 11, 1827.

Rockingham

Specifications: Built in 1811 by Samuel Morrell. Square stern, billet head. Burthen, 359 tons; length, 105 feet; beam, 27.8 feet; depth, 12.2 feet. Owners, December 20, 1811, Clement March, Jr., and F.C. Tucker. Sold in New York, March 27, 1813.

Lycurgus

Specifications: Built in 1821 by George Hilton. Square stern, male bust figurehead. Burthen, 252 tons; length, 87.3 feet; beam, 25.8 feet; depth, 12.9 feet. Owners, February 9, 1821, Thomas Sheafe and Charles Coffin.

Though what inspired it is not known, the owners named the *Lycurgus* after a legislator in ancient Sparta. The figurehead must have been some artisan's concept of what a Greek lawgiver might look like. It might be more remarkable to note that the *Lycurgus* was the first ship built in Newmarket in a decade. In fact, in the 10 years between 1811 and 1821, only one vessel of any description was built there: the 242-ton brig *Criterion* in 1814.

John B. Haley, Jr., of Auburn Street (Richards Avenue), was the first master of the *Lycurgus*, going to "sea in the new and elegant ship" on February 21, 1821. She went to New Orleans for cotton, thence to Liverpool. Then her orders took her to St. Petersburg. She returned to Portsmouth, September 23, 1822, via Cronstadt, with iron, duck and hemp to Sheafe & Coffin.[35] Captain Haley also had her on a passage from Hamburg when she was struck by lightning, which killed a seaman named John Sumter. She was 52 days on a passage to New York with heavy weather all the way.[36] From New York, she went on the triangular circuit, coming to Portsmouth, September 16, 1824, from St. Ubes. She continued in the triangle trade, under various masters, one being Thomas Sheafe Coffin, son of one of the owners. Under Captain Coffin, the *Lycurgus* had one of her great adventures:

> The ship *Lycurgus*, Coffin, Liverpool, bound to N. Orleans, put into Charleston, July 5th, for a supply of water. The L. was detained by calms and light southerly and westerly winds, on and about the Bahama Banks for 30 days. June 14 was chased by a piratical sch'r of about 60 or 70 tons, (shewing American colors) from the Bahama Banks to 10 miles south of the Orange Keys—the chase lasted three days, when we lost her by tacking in the night. Next day heard the report of a gun, about 10 miles to the windward, supposed she was bringing a brig to, that was in co. the day previous. 3d inst. lat 23 31, lon 79, 30, [About off Miami] fell in with a herm. brig, showing American colors half mast as a decoy, she had two quarter boats which would carry 20 men each, and a small boat at the stern, had a great many men about her deck, and one on each mast head looking out. She chased us about five hours...[37]

Later that year, she recrossed the Atlantic, arriving September 1, 1830, in Liverpool.[38] In 1831, she was sold and entered New York on September 26th with 101 passengers. Her last days were reported:

> Formerly from this port, from Rum Key for New York, with main and fore mast gone, and spars hanging to the vessel was seen the 20th lat, 39, lon 70. She was abandoned apparently in a sinking condition. Another ship was close to the windward, with foremast and bow sprit carried away. Showed no signal of distress and soon stood up to the east. It was a northwest gale, and she had probably run afoul of the *Lycurgus*.

Izette

Specifications: Built in 1822 by William Shute. Square stern, billet head. Burthen, 275 tons; length, 93 feet; beam, 26 feet; depth, 13 feet. Owner, December 20, 1822, Abraham Shaw.

Abraham Shaw's pride in his new vessel was evidenced by the name he gave her—Izette, for his wife:

> Saturday, Sept. 7—Came down the River, the beautiful new ship Izette, of 280 tons. The *Izette* was built at New-Market

by Messers Shute and Tarlton, and was launched the 3d inst. She is owned by A. Shaw, Esq., and is intended for the Southern and Liverpool trade, and is considered a first-rate ship.

Thomas M. Shaw, the owner's brother, sailed the *Izette* on her maiden voyage in January 1823, and, nine days out of Portsmouth, a seaman jumped overboard and was drowned "in an apparent fit of insanity."[39] Five days before Christmas in 1823, the *Izette* entered Boston after a voyage of 50 days from Bristol. The *Izette* continued to serve, working between Baltimore and European ports, and, occasionally, as on November 6, 1830, coming home.[40]

In January 1831, she sailed for Salem and was sold to become a whaler.[41] There had been previous efforts to sell the *Izette*. In May 1829, she was put on the block at Samuel Larkin's auction store on State Street:

> As she came from the sea at Baltimore... Six years old, built of the best materials; sails well and carries a large cargo; and was coppered in London 12 months ago.[42]

Parties from Salem bought the *Izette*, and she was described as being the first whaler to operate out of that port. J.S. Osgood was the purchaser. Osgood, for reasons of economy, changed her rig to that of a bark. Between 1831 and 1842, she made four whaling voyages, earning a total of $94,717, which could be a million dollars or more by today's values.

Nile

Specifications: Built in 1825 by Joseph Coe of Durham. Square stern, billet head. Burthen, 403 tons; length, 113 feet; depth, 14.1 feet. Owners, November 5, 1825, Putnam & Cheevers, et al. of Danvers, Massachusetts.

The largest ship Joseph Coe ever built, the *Nile* went at once to Salem where she was registered. It isn't known why Coe elected to leave his yard in Durham to build the *Nile*. Her size probably had nothing to do with it because his ship *Montgomery*, built in Durham the next year, rated only four tons smaller. After she sailed from the Piscataqua, only one mention was made of her locally. She arrived in New York in May 1827. On May 3rd, she "fell in with numerous islands of ice," and on the 5th saw an iceberg, judged to be five or six miles long, 200 feet high.[44] It is probable that she was in the triangle trade until sold to become a whaler.

In her whaling days, the *Nile* was owned in Greensport, New York, by Ireland, Wells & Carpenter. Three whaling cruises are on record. Two of these voyages were to the northwest coast of the United States, and one to the Arctic.[45] The longest voyage was for 43 months and was also her most successful as she brought in 316 barrels of sperm, 2,305 of whale oil, and 43,692 pounds of bone. In 1857, being 32 years old, she was broken up. At least she was spared an ignominious role in the Stone Fleet.

Minerva

Specifications: Built in 1828 by John Shute. Square stern, billet head. Burthen, 352 tons; length, 109.2 feet; beam, 26.8 feet; depth, 13.4 feet. Owners, Ebenezer Dodge, et al. of Salem.

Although owned outside the Portsmouth District, the *Minerva* came back occasionally. She left under the command of a Captain Rice, heading for Mobile.[46] She took 15 days to come from Liverpool in August 1828 and headed back to Mobile in November.[47] And there her Portsmouth record ends.

Elizabeth Frith

Specifications: Built in 1828 by Dudley Chase. Square stern, female figurehead. Burthen, 355 tons; length, 108 feet; beam, 27 feet; depth, 13.5 feet. Owners, March 2, 1829, Henry and Alexander Ladd and William Briard.

Quite often, one of the most difficult things to learn about an old vessel is the source of her name. Good fortune prevailed in the case of the *Elizabeth Frith*. Elizabeth Frith was the maiden name of the wife of the first master of the *Elizabeth Frith*, William Briard. They were married in New York.[48] They made their home at what was then 23 Middle Street, at the corner of Summer, which is now owned by Dr. George Patten.

Briard took the *Elizabeth Frith* to Savannah and Europe in January 1829, returning on September 7, 1829, from St. Ubes with salt for the owners. In early December, Briard took her out again, heading for New Orleans and another voyage around the triangle. As so often happened, she put into Charleston on the way south, found a cargo, and went to England. She was at Gravesend, March 3, 1830.[49] She arrived in New York from London on June 1st and was sent to Leghorn, Italy.[50] Her return cargo, however, was loaded at Cadiz and taken to Charleston where she arrived February 18, 1831.[51] In her next venture to Europe, she went to Hampton Roads from Charleston and then to Cowes, England, arriving October 11 with some storm damage, including the loss of boats.[52] It was October 1823 before she came into Portsmouth again, bringing salt from the Isle of May.

The *Elizabeth Frith* cleared out in January 1833 with Charles H. Ladd of Portsmouth as a passenger. He was, no doubt, a member of the Ladd family going to New Orleans to check on Ladd interests.[53] In August, the *Journal* reported the *Elizabeth Frith* had left for Boston on June 19. In October, coming from Cork, she was fully engaged in the triangle service, arriving in New York, April 7, 1834, with 142 steerage passengers.[54] Pierpont Hammond became master and brought the ship in from Liverpool in mid-October 1834 with salt and copper for the owners and hardware for Richard Jenness.

Right after Christmas 1834, the *Elizabeth Frith* sailed for New Orleans to load cotton for Edward F. Sise of Portsmouth. She brought 1,060 bales when she docked at the end of April 1835 in 19 days from New Orleans—very good time.[55] Sise, acting as agent for the mills on the Cocheco and those on the Salmon Falls River in South Berwick, transferred the cotton on smaller river craft like gundalows. She sailed for Hampton Roads again on July 1st and left there on August 28th for London, arriving there on October 10th. Early in 1836, she was at Bristol, England, and sailed from there for Philadelphia. In August 1837, she was signalized as being for Boston or Portsmouth.[56] She entered the latter port on September 15th, 70 days from Liverpool, with a thousand sacks of fine salt and 370 tons of coarse for Henry Ladd.[57] In April 1839, she arrived at Mobile from Portsmouth but had to go on to New Orleans to find a cargo. In August, she passed the Rock of Gibraltar on her way to Trieste, Italy.

William Briard was again master when the *Elizabeth Frith* returned to Portsmouth in September 1840 with salt for the Ladds. Briard continued as master until 1843, when he took command of the *Harriet Rockwell*. He was succeeded by a captain by the name of Pearce, probably Oliver P. About this time, the *Elizabeth Frith* suffered the indignity of being re-rigged as a bark. Until September 1845, she continued in the triangle trade and then was sold at Sag Harbor for service as a whaler.[58] Owned by Post and Sherry, she made two whaling voyages of record under John Bishop. The first ran from March 3, 1843, to May 20, 1848. Out on the northwest coast, her catch was 100 barrels of sperm, 2,000 of whale oil, and five tons of bone. In her second, to the same area, she was gone less than two years, coming in with 95 barrels of sperm, 2,700 of whale oil and 35,000 pounds of bone.

What she did in the next few years isn't known, but she sailed to California in 1860 and was caught in a savage gale off the South American coast. She was driven ashore, February 15, 1861, at a place then called Monte Quesmario. The wreck ended the 33-year career of the *Elizabeth Frith*, the last full-rigged vessel built in Newmarket. Her launching had marked the end of an era in that town.

IX *Other Towns*

FIRST, LET IT BE KNOWN there is no intent by the author to denigrate the contributions of other towns to the story of shipbuilding in the Port of Portsmouth between 1783 and 1829. There were four of these communities: Hampton, Hampton Falls, Somersworth and Stratham. They were put in a common chapter simply for packaging. The quartet produced 10 three-masted, square-rigged vessels in the study period. One each came from the Hamptons and Stratham, with seven from Somersworth. The total ship tonnage was 2,319, an average per vessel of 228.5 tons. Considering that most of them were constructed in the years before the War of 1812, they were of a respectable size for their era.

THE HAMPTONS

Although neither of the Hamptons is located on the Piscataqua River or any of its tributaries, they were assigned to the Portsmouth Customs District. Both had proud records for shipbuilding in colonial times. Besides each producing a ship, the two towns built 15 schooners with a combined tonnage of 747. An historian wrote:

> It is known that vessels were owned in Hampton within a few years after the settlement was begun [1638]. Some of them were probably for the fishing business... The larger vessels usually sailed from the place known as the *The Landing*, through the many windings of Taylor's River, and so on down through the main river and over the bar. On the banks of Taylor's River, at a

place still known as *The Ship Yard*, numerous vessels were built, some of them ships of many tons burthen. One of the bends in thus river was called *The Mooring Turn*, where our records state the vessels "do usually ride at anchor."[1]

Christopher Toppan was probably the greatest entrepreneur in the Hamptons in the years after the Revolution. His shipyard was within the bounds of Hampton Falls, and his significance is such that a history of Hampton Falls opens its shipbuilding section as follows:

> Hon. Christopher Toppan of Hampton, who was born in Hampton in 1735 and died in 1818, was somewhat extensively engaged in shipping, both as an owner and builder. His yard was situated at the turnpike near the river. The Toppan pasture, nearly opposite where Arthur Chase now lives, situated partly in Hampton and partly in Hampton Falls, was purchased and used by him for a shipyard...[2]

If the building of major vessels had continued in the Hamptons, it would be useful to tell more of the Toppan story. The heyday of the Hamptons as the home of ship-rated vessels expired, however, shortly after the Revolution. But two ships were built in the Hamptons within a dozen years of the end of the Revolution, and it is more than likely that Toppan had a hand in the construction of both of them.

Nancy

Specifications: Built in 1786. Burthen, 203 tons. Owner, December 3, 1789, Nathaniel Folsom.

It isn't known where the *Nancy* was, or what she was doing, from the date of her construction until 1789. The official customs records didn't start until the year when Folsom registered her. It is probable she was engaged in trading to Europe because John Wardrobe brought her in from France on November 27th. Wardrobe was then 27 years old and one of the rising young shipmasters in the Port of Portsmouth. Her next master was James Sellers who made a voyage to the West Indies, returning from Guadeloupe in November 1790. In January 1791, Wardrobe took the *Nancy* to the West Indies, bringing her back in October.[3] In 1792, Wardrobe bought the *Nancy* and kept her until she was sold in Norfolk in 1795. She was put up for auction while lying at Richard Hart's Wharf, and the advertisement for sale hints she might already have been used for whaling:

> The Ship NANCY, with all her stores and Whaleing materials, as she came from the sea.—Her Stores and materials may be

viewed any time previous to the sale by applying to Capt. ELIJAH HALL, or Capt. JOHN WARDROBE.[4]

Two Brothers

Specifications: Built in Hampton Falls in 1795. Burthen, 243 tons; length, 85.3 feet; beam, 25.7 feet; depth, 12.85 feet. Owner, July 20, 1798, Nathaniel A. Haven.

As in the case of the *Nancy*, it isn't known where the *Two Brothers* was during the three years between launching and her registration by Haven. An advertisement in the *Gazette* of February 27, 1798, however, indicates her first owner or her builder had run into financial problems, because she had been "taken in execution" of an attachment and was being auctioned by Deputy Sheriff Edward Hart:

> The good ship *Two Brothers* and her appurtenances, now lying at Portsmouth Pier, burthen 247 tons, not two years old, sails fast and stows well; built in a workman like manner, and of the best materials.

Nathaniel Haven captured the bid and sent her to sea under Peter Turner, who came home from Liverpool on November 30, 1798. Turner sailed to Hamburg and back in 1799 and went to Tobago early in 1800, returning April 10th. Two months later, the *Two Brothers* was sold to John Skinner of Boston and disappeared from Portsmouth ken.

SOMERSWORTH

Like the neighboring towns of Berwick and Dover, Somersworth enjoyed its great moments in the story of post-Revolutionary shipbuilding. Of note is the fact that the yard in Somersworth produced the most deadly vessel, the *Mentor*, ever to navigate the Piscataqua's fast-flowing waters, albeit through no fault of her own. The shipwrights in Somersworth built ships with a total of 1,567 tons between 1796 and 1806. Although the figures and descriptions are confused in the customs records, seven appears the probable number of ships.[5] Moreover, between 1783 and 1818, Somersworth produced 3,581 tons of shipping of all descriptions. In 1818, the building of vessels ceased with the construction of a brig, the *Florida*, built by Hugh Paul for Edmund Roberts, Jacob Cutter and Charles Cushing. She was lost at sea shortly after leaving Portsmouth on her maiden voyage.

Mentor

Specifications: Built in 1796. Burthen, 213 tons; length, 80.5 feet; beam, 24.9 feet; depth, 12.45 feet. Owner, April 12, 1800, James Sheafe.

Although the customs records don't say so, the *Mentor* was owned during her first voyages by Thomas Sheafe, brother of James. This is ironic in itself because two of Thomas Sheafe's children were victims in the yellow fever epidemic that swept Portsmouth's North End shortly after the *Mentor*'s arrival. No vessel ever came into Portsmouth Harbor more laden with the potential to kill. She had come in under John Flagg, July 28, 1798, from the Caribbean. Besides her nominal cargo, she brought mosquitoes laden with the germs of yellow fever. Before the chill winds of November put an end to their depredations, the winged killers had claimed 55 victims. Outbreaks of yellow fever were frequent in northern ports during the summer months when vessels from the West Indies came in, their damp, steamy holds serving as incubators for the mosquito eggs. Medical science was far enough advanced to recognize it as a tropical affliction, sometimes called "Barbados Distemper." The *Mentor* came into Portsmouth with two sick men on board, but no one paid much heed:

> Who would have known what to look for? Within a few days, stevedores who had unloaded the *Mentor* were taken ill, and two young sons of the owner, Thomas Sheafe, who had played on board her, were stricken and died. Their deaths brought the medical men and town officials to the realization that the fearsome West Indies killer was loose in their midst...[6]

No one blamed the *Mentor* or her master for the problem. How could they? John Flagg had no idea that his stowaway mosquitoes were carriers of death. Such an understanding was another century in developing. Flagg was no novice to West Indian voyages; he had come from Grenada in March 1797 with no problems. Then he went out again, returning with a mosquito-laden vessel. Despite the loss of his children, Thomas Sheafe sent the *Mentor* south again in 1799. He had full confidence in John Flagg who had established himself a year before:

> Arrived here the ship *Mentor*, Capt. Flagg, in 22 days from St. Thomas; Feb. 25th he was brought too by a French privateer, and had his papers, &c. examined; but being from a neutral port, they permitted him to proceed on his voyage. Capt. Flagg saw on board of her three American masters that had been taken...[7]

Flagg continued in Sheafe's service, and the latter advertised on January 22, 1800, that he had for sale in his store in the North End, "adjoining the Town Wharf," part of the cargoes of the brig *Harmony* and the ship *Mentor*:

Russia and Swedes Iron; bar and sheet Lead; dry white do.; kegs of do. ground in oil; red and yellow Ochre; red lead.

Liverpool cream color'd, blue and white Ware in crates; Liverpool Salt; House and Hearth Brushes; No. 2, 4 and 6 Canvas; 10 by 8 and 7 by 9 Glass; Cordage, Cod Lines; Nets; Bank Hooks; Sewing Twine.

Best rose Blankets; Flemish Linens; 10 d, 20d & Clout and Pump Nails; long and short handle Tar Brushes; a few casks Burton ALE, and London PORTER; also, 10 hhds, Tobago Rum.

The list of English goods available at Thomas Sheafe's and all other Portsmouth stores emphasizes the dependency Amerians still had on the mother country for manufactured goods early in the nineteenth century. The rupture of trade caused by the War of 1812 increased their independence, but it took a long time.

But for the *Mentor*, time was running out. Flagg turned her over to Richard Shapley, and he sailed for Argentina, April 15, 1800.[8] In October, the following news item appeared:

French Amity

Captain Richard Shapley, late master of the ship *Mentor*, arrived here on Wednesday evening last, via Newport, from Rio de Janeiro.

Capt. Shapley sailed from this port in the fine ship *Mentor*, on the 15th of April last, for the River La Plate, at the entrance of which... he was taken by 3 French frigates in company, viz., the *La Concorde*, Capt. Landolph; the *Medee*, and the *Francaise*; after plundering Capt. Shapley of every article they could, and him and all his hands on board the different frigates, they sold his ship and cargo at sea to a Spanish merchant, then on board *La Concorde*, for $12,000 when in fact, she was worth above $40,000. And after cruizing 35 days on the coast of Brazil, and capturing many Portuguese vessels, sunk, burnt and destroyed them all.

After this, fell in with the outward bound British East India fleet, convoyed by the *Belliquex*, Commodore Rowley Bulteel, which captured *La Concorde* and *Medee* after one hour's engagement, (Capt. Shapley being on board *La Concorde*) after this the whole British fleet and their prizes went into Rio de Janeiro; from whence Capt. Shapley took passage in the ship *Fabius*, Capt. Dailey, for Philadelphia, and arrived here as above.[9]

Eagle

Specifications: Built in 1799. Burthen, 185 tons; length, 76.6 feet; beam, 23.8 feet; depth, 11.9 feet. Owner, May 11, 1801, John Rollins.

To the *Eagle* goes the distinction of being the smallest ship built in Somersworth. Again, it isn't known where she was until after John Rollins registered her. Under Rollins' ownership, she went to Liverpool with Abraham Shaw as master, returning home on October 19, 1801. While still owned by Rollins, Thomas Shaw took her to the West Indies, returning on March 6, 1802. After his brother's return, Abraham Shaw sailed the *Eagle* to Hamburg, coming home on September 12, 1802.

Two months later, in company with James Drisco, Abraham Shaw bought the *Eagle*, registering her on November 22, 1802. Less than a month later, James Drisco and his son, James, Jr., bought out Shaw. The Driscos had a wharf in 1813 near the foot of Court Street. They converted the *Eagle* into a two-masted square-rigger—a brig. Under that rig, William Trefethen made a voyage in her to the West Indies, re-entering on April 8, 1803. Shortly thereafter, the *Eagle* was sold in New York.

Magnet

Specifications: Built in 1801 by Moses Paul. Square stern, billet head. Burthen, 207 tons; length, 79.9 feet; beam, 24.65 feet; depth, 12.3 feet. Owners, January 21, 1802, Clement Jackson, Hiram Rollins and Martin Parry.

At one time or another, several members of the Paul family were building ships in Somersworth. When Moses Paul was constructing the *Magnet*, James Paul was working on the *Howard* in a Kittery yard, but, as will be seen, seven years later he built a ship in Somersworth. As will also be seen, Stephen, the most prolific of the family, also built one ship in Somersworth. Nathaniel Kennard was master on the *Magnet*'s maiden voyage, coming in from Grenada on June 4, 1802. A week after her arrival, Martin Parry acquired Jackson's interest, which was sold, after his death, to Thomas Sheafe. Her first voyage was Kennard's only one in her, but he undoubtedly followed his custom of importing 100 to 300 gallons of rum on every trip he made. This he sold on his own account, as did most of the shrewder merchant captains of the time. That was one of the ways in which they, too, became merchants. The *Magnet* was the tenth vessel he had commanded, although she was still his first ship. All but one or two of his voyages were to the West Indies, which enabled him to make two or three a year.

Charles Treadwell followed Kennard as master, coming into

Portsmouth from Havana on May 4, 1803. In December 1803, he completed a voyage to Russia. Then there is a lapse of four years in local records; at which time John Bowles came in from Russia. A marine news item in February of 1805 said:

> The ship *Magnet*, Coffin, of this port, is ashore near Robin's Reef.—She was bound to Philadelphia, with linens, iron, and glass; and left Tonninges 28th October. On the 8th inst. lighters were sent down to her from New York; she lied on a sandy bottom, did not leak and had six feet of water around her at low tide.[10]

It is known, from subsequent marine news items, that the *Magnet* was in Russia in 1807 under John Bowles.[11] She undoubtedly suffered through the rough times of the Embargo Act. In 1809, Joseph Swett brought her in from Trinidad. She was lost at sea in 1817.

Four Sisters

Specifications: Built in 1803 by Stephen Paul. Square stern, billet head. Burthen, 204 tons; length, 81.2 feet; beam, 24.1 feet; depth, 10.9 feet. Owner, December 6, 1803, Ebenezer Ricker of Somersworth.

The *Four Sisters* was the first of 10 ships built by Stephen Paul but the only one he launched in Somersworth. Little is known about the *Four Sisters* because Ricker sold her to Elisha Hill, who sold her in New York in 1804. News items, however, lead to a bit of speculation. In April 1804, it was reported that the *Four Sisters* was ashore on Sandy Hook, and it is possible she was sold as she laid on the beach.[12]

Roberts

Specifications: Built in 1806 by Stephen Tobey. Burthen, 230 tons; length, 85.3 feet; beam, 25.4 feet; depth, 12.7 feet. Owner, March 18, 1807, Edmund Roberts.

Stephen Tobey built only one of his nine ships at Somersworth; all the rest he constructed in Dover yards, as related earlier. At the time he was building the *Roberts*, he had the much larger *Brutus* on the stocks in Dover.

Much more is known about Edmund Roberts than about the ship which bore his name. Apparently the only master of the *Roberts* during Roberts' ownership was William Shackford. The Embargo Act was in full effect in her first years, but she was advertised for New Orleans in Decemeber 1808.[13] She came up from New Orleans on September 10, 1809, presumably with cotton.[14] In October, she cleared for Cuba.[15] She returned from that voyage by way of Cork on August 4, 1810. She left Portsmouth again in April 1811, heading for New York and returned September 19, 1811, from Havana "in the remarkable passage of 10 days."[16] Shackford and Roberts became partners in the *Roberts* on November 1, 1811. Six days later, Shackford cleared for the West Indies. The partners finally sold the *Roberts* in 1813 "to a foreigner."[17]

Commerce

Specifications: Built in 1809 by James Paul. Square stern, billet head. Burthen, 292 tons; length, 95.7 feet; beam, 26 feet; depth, 13 feet. Owner, April 18, 1809, Abraham Shaw. Sold in New York in 1809.

Atlantic

Specifications: Built in 1795. Square stern, billet head. Burthen, 199 tons; length, 78.4 feet; beam, 24.3 feet; depth, 12.15 feet.

Chronologically, the *Atlantic* should have headed the roster of Somersworth ships, but there was an unusual twist in her story. Ships were often converted into barks or brigs, but rare indeed is the brig that was changed into a ship. Such was the case with the *Atlantic*. Once again, it isn't known where she was and what she did between her launching in 1795 and her registration by Abel Harris in October 1800. After Harris bought her, he sent her to sea under William Thompson, and she returned from Liverpool on November 25, 1801. Abel Harris was joined in ownership in 1809 by Robert Harris, but nothing else is known of the *Atlantic*.

STRATHAM

The building of vessels in Stratham followed an irregular pattern over the years between 1785 and 1815. A schooner, the *Sally*, 36 tons, was built in 1785. In 1794, the *Deborah* was listed to Richard Hart of Portsmouth, and John Marble was master on voyages to the West Indies. Three years later, the brig *George* was built for James and Thomas Sheafe. She made several voyages to England with John Moore as master. With that, as far as customs records show, no vessels of any description were built in Stratham until 1811, when the ship *Niagara* was launched. She was the last vessel built in the town.

Niagara

Specifications: Built in 1811 by William Dutch. Square stern, billet head. Burthen, 343 tons; length, 101 feet; beam, 27.8 feet; depth, 13.6 feet. Owner, November 10, 1815, Andrew Bell.

The name of William Dutch has an Exeter ring to it, and he may have been from that town. It is possible Dutch had the *Niagara* on his hands for four years because of the War of 1812. When Andrew Bell put her into service, Nathan Stoodley took her to Charleston on the first leg of the familiar triangle. That was on November 21, 1815.[18] More than 18 months passed before the *Niagara* arrived in Boston in 40 days from Liverpool with salt, crockery and earthenware. She returned to Portsmouth on July 18, 1817, with salt for Andrew Bell. On that passage, the *Niagara* collided with a brig, the *Maria*, of Cork carrying 140 passengers and already short of provisions. The *Niagara* took off 19 of the passengers and supplied provisions. A hint of the suffering undergone by immigrants in that era is indicated from charges by the passengers that the *Maria*'s captain "had been most shamefully oppressive toward them."[19] The *Niagara* dropped the passengers in Boston and continued to Portsmouth.

The *Niagara* had problems of her own three years later in New Orleans where she had arrived with passengers. Coming from Greenock, Scotland, she was lying at the Pine Street Wharf, having discharged 40 steerage passengers. The passengers hadn't been a problem, but the crew had. They rioted. Observers heard shouts of "Murder!" and "Throw him overboard!" Police officers finally subdued the riot but two men were missing.[20] No one knew, nor cared, what happened to them. After that, Nathaniel Gookin was master of the *Niagara*, and he had her for at least three more voyages. The *Niagara* gave good service for several more years and was condemned abroad in 1829.

X Portsmouth

PJ, November 25, 1826

FOR THOSE IMBUED with the belief that Portsmouth, the largest of the Piscataqua communities, was always in the forefront of shipbuilding activities, the truth will come as a shock. The fact is that between 1783 and 1829, Portsmouth produced only 14 of the more than 200 ships built in the Portsmouth Customs District. Various explanations come to mind as to the cause of this seeming contradiction. Basically, ships were framed, planked and decked in the upper Piscataqua Valley towns because timber was close at hand, being easily floated down the streams or hauled to landings on the Great Bay. Second, these vessels were small, and large gangs of workers weren't needed. A third factor, of course, was the construction of the bridge between Portsmouth and Kittery (1820–21), which left only a narrow passage for vessels. As modern pilots can testify, navigation on the Piscataqua is difficult, even with the use of powerful tugs, but long ago, everything depended on the luck and skill of the pilot.

Although it may seem a defense of Portsmouth's stature as a ship-building center, it has to be emphasized that yards in Kittery were producing full-rigged ships in this period and early town directories indicate that artisans from Portsmouth rowed across the river daily to work on the ships being built in Kittery.

Furthermore, as was noted in the discussion of Newmarket, the ships were floated to Portsmouth where they were rigged and prepared for sea. The reasons for this were simple. For one thing, it meant less weight in the vessel, thus making it easier to bring them down tricky rivers like the Cocheco. Moreover, big fighting ships were being constructed on Badger's Island and at the Navy Yard, which meant shears and other equipment for masting were available along with trained riggers. Then, too, shipbuilders were dependent on imported hemp and canvas for the rigging of their vessels. Those materials were handled by Portsmouth merchants. As a later volume in this series will show, the shipbuilding industry had moved down the river to Kittery and Portsmouth by the 1830s.

So who were these post-Revolutionary shipwrights on the lower Piscataqua? If Reuben Shapley wasn't a shipwright himself, he certainly inspired the work of others. As indicated in earlier chapters, customs regulations at first apparently made no requirement of recording builders' names. After 1800, they were listed as a matter of course. The first builder of record in Portsmouth was Enoch Bagley, and, about the same time, James Paul, Jr. Others who built in Portsmouth in the first two decades after the Revolution included Samuel Cottle, Zechariah Beal, William Hanscom, Nathaniel Knight, Ebenezer Thompson and Jacob Remick.

Portsmouth shipwrights in the 1783–1829 period produced almost 10,000 tons of vessels. Only a third was in ships, and the tonnage for the 21 brigs built nearly equaled the ships. In addition, Portsmouth shipwrights produced 24 schooners, one snow and three sloops. And it must be noted that Portsmouth produced the first ship-rigged vessel in the period under study.

Marchioness de Lafayette

Specifications: Built in 1783. Burthen, 173 tons. Owner, in 1789, A. Comerais & Company.

It is no challenge to the imagination to guess that the *Marchioness de Lafayette* was named for the wife of America's young French hero, Marie Joseph Paul Yves Roch Gilbert du Motier, the Marquis de Lafayette. The young aristocrat had fought gallantly in America's War for Independence and was a trusted subordinate of George Washington. The Marquis may even have seen his wife's namesake launched because he was in Portsmouth during that period, visiting with officers in the French fleet then anchored in the Pool.

Little is known about the career of the *Marchioness de Lafayette*. Customs records show her being brought in from the West Indies on September 25, 1789, only a bit more than a month before President George Washington paid a four-day visit to Portsmouth. So perhaps he, too, saw this vessel named for the wife of a dear young friend.

Mary

Specifications: Built in 1784. Burthen, 199 tons. Owner, in 1789, Jacob Sheafe.

The *Mary* was the second and last built in the new era until 1791, a span of seven years. Like the *Marchioness de Lafayette*, it isn't known what finally happened to her. She made five voyages under Richard Salter Tibbetts, all but one of them to the West Indies. The exception, in 1790, came when the *Mary* arrived from London on October 23rd. In other voyages, William Rice was master, arriving from Hamburg, May 10, 1797.[1] Titus Salter became master, coming in from Grenada in 23 days, November 28, 1798.[2] The last note about her was in April 1802, when she was at St. Ubes loading salt.[3]

The brief story of the *Mary*, however, offers the chance to say a little more about Richard Salter Tibbetts, her master on five voyages. Few Port of Portsmouth masters had more adventurous careers than Tibbetts. Born in Portsmouth, May 10, 1762, he died in Jacmel, on the south coast of Haiti, in October 1821.[4] In his 59 years, Tibbetts packed enough dangerous living to fill the lifetimes of two ordinary men. The *Salter Genealogy* says, in part:

> His uncle, Captain John Salter, took him, when a boy, to London to be educated. Later the nephew accompanied the uncle to sea as an apprentice. In 1775 he was in the ship *Crisis* when captured. Tibbetts subsequently made a successful cruise in a privateer. On June 14, 1780, he was captured in a letter-of-marque brig *Aurora*, Capt. Samuel Gerrish, and committed to Old Mill Prison, Plymouth, England, where he was confined for more than a year....[5]

While in prison, Tibbetts passed the hours by keeping track of all the men held, their vessels and date of capture. One imprisoned with him was Andrew Sherburne of Portsmouth, who later became an itinerant Baptist preacher. Tibbetts taught Sherburne how to read, write and figure. When he got out of the Old Mill Prison, Tibbetts became master of a letter-of-marque brig, the *Scorpion*. She was captured by the 40-gun British ship *Amphion*, and Sherburne was among those taken prisoner. In his memoirs, years later, Sherburne wrote:

> Our Captain Tibbets and three others continued on board the *Scorpion*, which was afterwards cast away, but I believe no lives were lost. Thirteen of us were put on board the *Amphion*, and two weeks later we arrived at the prison ship [British] in New York.

Returning to Tibbetts and the ship *Mary*: after she came home in March 1792, Tibbetts became master of the Kittery-built ship *Lydia* (q.v.). On a passage from North Carolina to Lisbon, Tibbetts and the *Lydia* were pursued by an Algerine pirate as they neared the coast of Portugal but escaped through superior speed. She loaded with salt at St. Ubes and returned home. Tibbetts' career wasn't limited to the merchant marine:

> Captain Tibbetts was one of the first officers selected for the new navy of the United States. Entering the service in December 1798, he was commissioned a lieutenant by President John Adams in January, 1799, and ordered to report immediately on board the ship *Portsmouth*, commanded by Captain Daniel McNeill. The *Portsmouth*, 24 guns, was built in Portsmouth, carried a crew of 220 men.[6]

It is impossible to give the details of Tibbetts's life, but he commanded, at various times, many of the ships built in the Port of Portsmouth. He made his home in a house on Pleasant Street that became part of the Jacob Wendell estate.

Fame

Specifications: Built in 1791. Burthen, 210 tons; length, 80 feet; beam, 24.8 feet; depth, 12.8 feet. Owner, December 8, 1791, Thomas Dickerson.

The *Fame*'s bid for fame was brief. The third ship built after the creation of the Portsmouth Customs District, she sailed for Europe but was lost in the North Sea on that passage.

Lydia

Specifications: Built in 1793. Burthen, 240 tons. Length, 86.5 feet; beam, 25.3 feet; depth, 12.25 feet. Owner, January 11, 1794, Reuben Shapley.

While direct evidence is lacking, the odds are that the *Lydia* was built on Shapley's own ways on Shapley's Island. He built other vessels there.

The *Lydia* became a transporter of salt. In October 1795 under Robert Blunt, she came in from Liverpool with salt for the owner. In March 1796, it was reported that the *Lydia* had been "left at Kingston, Jamaica, by the schooner *Industry* [built in Newmarket in 1792], Captain William Trefethen. Captain Blunt had five men impressed by a 40-gun English warship. Three of the men belonged in Portsmouth— Edward Nutter had a wife and several children; John Libbey and Richard Howe also had families." Two other men were from York, Maine. The Englishman had impressed 40 other men from American vessels at Kingston.[7] It was reported the next year that the *Lydia* had arrived in 118 days from St. Ubes.[8] She had left at St. Ubes, "ship *Randolph*, Captain Greenough, of this port..."

Final word on the *Lydia* was in the *Gazette* on September 8, 1801:

> Capt. Smith of the ship *Lydia*, burnt at sea on the 24th July, states that himself and crew were taken up from their boats on the 26th by the Danish brig *Ryhersteg*, Capt. Cornelius Luyte Corneliesson, from St. Thomas for Hamburg; that on the 28th they spoke the brig *Maria Jane*, John Bowles, from the Isle of Wight for Portsmouth, who very humanely took Capt. Smith and two of the crew on board the vessel, though short of provisions, and then on allowance; that on the 6th August they spoke ship *Amarhyst* ___ Capt. Rogers,, who very politely neglected to assist or supply them with provisions; that on the 12th they spoke ship *New York*, Capt. Leonard of New York, from Hamburgh for Philadelphia, who kindly supplied them with beef, pork, pease, candles, spirits, bread and herrings, with other articles, for which he refused to accept pay.

Friendship

Specifications: Built in 1795. Burthen, 177 tons. Owner, August 18, 1795, Henry Kermith, New York.

The *Friendship* has to be rated as one of the smallest of the post-Revolutionary ships. And that's all that can be said of her.

Nancy

Specifications: Built in 1795. Square stern, billet head. Burthen, 220 tons; length, 82 feet; beam, 25 feet; depth, 12 feet. Owner, January 20, 1796, Reuben Shapley.

Reuben Shapley entrusted the *Nancy* to James Orne, who brought her in from St. Ubes in April 1797.[9] Orne was master through the *Nancy*'s next three voyages. She came in from London on November 2, 1798. In September 1799, the *Gazette* reported the *Nancy* had been brought in on August 31, 60 days from London to Charleston. Orne brought her into Portsmouth from Liverpool in 35 days in July 1800.

Richard Shapleigh, with what kinship he might have held with Reuben Shapley not being clear, became a part owner in 1805, and the two of them kept their interests until 1808 when Clement March bought in. An item in the *Gazette* indicates she was working in 1806 when Richard Shapleigh came home on November 29th in 75 days from

Liverpool. As late as July 10, 1807, the *Nancy* was active under Shapleigh and in port in Russia.[10] Customs records show her as lost at sea.

Murdock

Specifications: Built in 1796. Burthen, 232 tons; length, 86.2 feet; beam, 24.5 feet; depth, 12.45 feet. Owner, January 17, 1797, James Sheafe.

James Sheafe immediately sent the *Murdock* to the East Indies, an area that was only beginning to open up to American merchants. Under Robert Treadwell, the *Murdock* was one of the first Port of Portsmouth vessels to enter the trade. Salem merchants were already sending their ships in that direction. Matthew S. Marsh was the first Portsmouth trader to send a vessel there. He sent his brig, the *Augustus*, built in Newmarket in 1794, to the East Indies under the same Captain Treadwell. The *Augustus*, all 95 tons of her, was condemned in 1800, but it is unclear whether she was unseaworthy or captured by one of the pestiferous privateers.

Treadwell confirmed Sheafe's faith in him by bringing the *Murdock* into Portsmouth on June 7, 1798, from Calcutta. Before being sold in Baltimore in 1801, the *Murdock*, under Thomas B. Stevens, made two voyages to South America, returning from the second in November 1800.

Wonolansett

Specifications: Built in 1799. Square stern, billet head. Burthen, 184 tons; length, 75.3 feet; beam, 24 feet; depth, 12 feet. Owner, March 14, 1800, Reuben Shapley.

The last ship built in a Portsmouth yard in the eighteenth century, the *Wonolansett* was typical of the three-masters being built in the Port of Portsmouth at the time. She was barely three times as long as she was wide, and her depth of hold was minimal. She was a useful, hardworking vessel, to which goes the sad distinction of being one of the few Portsmouth vessels to burn at her wharf and that within an hour of her arrival time.

Before that last fateful evening in August 1811, the *Wonolansett* sailed the oceans, returning to Portsmouth at least five times. The first four of these entries were under Reuben Shapley Randall, who lived on Gates Street in Portsmouth, a friend of the owner. The *Wonolansett* cleared for London on March 19, 1800, and re-entered on October 7th in 66 days from St. Petersburg. This was a passage made in heavy weather but she escaped damage.[11] She came in from Rotterdam in September

1803 and late in 1804, came from Madeira via Boston. Randall sailed for the East Indies on December 30, 1805, returning on July 5, 1806.[12] After that return, there is a four-year gap in the records which may well be explained by the Embargo Act. She arrived from St. Petersburg on Friday, November 9, 1810, in a passage of 100 days.[13] An earlier report, conveyed by the ship *Miranda*, placed the *Wonolansett* at Gottenburg, Sweden, in September.[14]

That was Randall's last voyage in her and his last sea command. He turned the *Wonolansett* over to John Seaward, who sailed, February 11, 1811, for New Orleans.[15] The *Wonolansett's* last passage, north from New Orleans, was eventful. Two passengers, Nicholas Grace of Portsmouth and Nathaniel Fernald, died on the way, perhaps of yellow fever. Then on July 3rd, the *Wonolansett* met a ship, the *Alde Baron* of New Orleans bound for Baltimore, which had lost her captain and mate and had no one left to navigate. So the mate of the *Wonolansett*, a man named Walker, took command of the *Alde Baron*, while the *Wonolansett* proceeded to Portsmouth. On August 20, 1811, the *Gazette* reported:

> FIRE!—On Tuesday evening at 8 o'clock the inhabitants of this town were alarmed by the cry of Fire which had accidentally caught in the ship *Wonolansett*, owned by Reuben Shapley, Esq., which had arrived but one hour previous, from New Orleans, via Boston. From a report that there was a large quantity of Powder on board, a great proportion of the citizens were deterred from affording that assistance ever ready to offer in similar situations.
>
> Every exertion to scuttle the ship proving ineffectual, in order to save the other shipping and the stores on the wharf she was cut adrift, and ran on Sunken Rocks, where, after cutting away the masts to save the sails and rigging, she was entirely consumed with her cargo of Hemp, Cotton, Molasses, Naval stores and Flour. The principal sufferers are Reuben Shapley, owner, Seth Walker, John Langdon, Jr., and Capt. Seaward. The fire caught from striking a light in the steerage near the bulk head against which a quantity of hemp was stored.

The term "naval stores" lent substance to the fears of the volunteer firefighters that gunpowder might detonate as they worked to save the ship. The *Gazette* item makes it obvious that only a gutsy few fighting a losing cause braved that peril. This stirred the wrath of owner Reuben Shapley who advertised in the *Portsmouth Oracle* complaining of the way the fire was handled. His protest prompted a statement from the Board of Firewards:

> RESOLVED unanimously, that in the opinion of this Board the Card in the *Oracle* of Saturday last, signed "Reuben Shapley," stating that some of the Firewards prevented his friends from saving his ship and cargo from fire on Tuesday

evening last, reflects a gross calumny, is wholly destitute of truth and is an illiberal, unjust and ungentlemanly attack on this board.

St. Cuthbert

Specifications: Built in 1802 by Enoch Bagley. Square stern, billet head. Burthen, 387 tons; length, 105 feet; depth, 14.5 feet. Owners, April 12, 1802, James Sheafe and Matthew S. Marsh.

Why did the owners, or builder, seize on the name of an obscure Scottish monk for the name of their vessel? Sir Walter Scott, in *Marmion*, written in 1808, gave the monk lasting fame:

On a rock of Lindisfarn
St. Cuthbert sits, and toils to frame
The sea-horse heads that bear his name.

The *St. Cuthbert* bears another distinction: she was one of the first ships known to have been built on Pierce Island. In later years, others, such as the clipper *Charger*, were built there; also the Floating Dry Dock for the Portsmouth Navy Yard.

Not much is known about the *St. Cuthbert*'s career. The *Gazette*, on June 26, 1804, reported her at Calcutta on February 15th. She apparently returned to the United States in 1806.[16] Her destination was New York, and she was sold there on July 18, 1806.[17]

Isabella Henderson

Specifications: Built by Zechariah Beal in 1811. Square stern, billet head. Burthen, 289 tons; length, 95.1 feet; beam, 26.3 feet; depth, 12 feet. Owner, April 14, 1815, James Sheafe.

The nine-year gap between the launching of the *St. Cuthbert* and the building of the *Isabella Henderson* emphasizes the problems facing shipwrights and owners in the period between 1800 and 1812. It is quite possible the *Isabella Henderson* laid idle all through the war. She wasn't registered by James Sheafe until 1815, after the news of the Treaty of Ghent had reached Portsmouth. She sailed, under a Captain Dame in late April 1815 for Norfolk on the start of a triangular voyage.[18] The lack of Portsmouth District entries indicates the *Isabella Henderson* worked out of ports other than Portsmouth. Various news items confirm this. In August 1817, she arrived in New York in 45 days from St. Ubes.[19] In December 1818, she came into New York in 147 days from

Bombay. In 1819, the *Isabella Henderson* was sold in New York and went back to the East Indies. In 1821, on a passage from Savannah to Liverpool, it was reported that John S. Dennett, 21, of Portsmouth and Moses Rackcliffe of Eliot had died. And that was the last note on the *Isabella Henderson.*

Neptune

Specifications: Built by Ebenezer Thompson in 1816. Square stern, male figurehead. Burthen, 337 tons; length, 104.2 feet; beam, 27 feet; depth, 13.5 feet. Owners, September 26, 1816, John Langdon, Jr., and Jacob Cutter.

The *Neptune* first caught the public eye by the way of an advertisement published in the *Gazette* in August 1816. Ebenezer Thompson was in a financial squeeze, and the hull that became the ship *Neptune* was auctioned off on September 5th. At the time, she was tied up at Ayer's Wharf, which was about a 100 feet north of the Shaw Wharf in what is now Portsmouth's Prescott Park. The *Neptune* went into the salt trade.

John S. Place was the *Neptune's* first master, bringing her in from the Isle of May on March 16, 1818, in 29 days. She experienced "very heavy gales from the southwest in the Gulf Stream."[20] Place's next two voyages were to Liverpool, perhaps by way of southern ports. John Langdon, Jr., sold his two-thirds interest in 1822.[21] It should be noted again that John Langdon, Jr., was the nephew and not the son of Governor John Langdon. His interest was bought by Henry and Alexander Ladd. They sold out to Jacob Cutter the next year. Nathan Walden commanded the *Neptune* when she came in from St. Ubes on December 3, 1824. Walden was relieved by George Langdon, then only 24 years old. He took her on two triangle voyages. George Langdon died in California in 1858.[22]

Captain Langdon had a rough passage with the *Neptune* when he brought her home from Liverpool in February 1826. She had sailed on January 12th "and encountered a succession of heavy westerly gales, until 2d February when a heavy sea struck the ship when lying to, stove in the headlights, destroyed cabin furniture, damaged a quantity of bread, and left four feet of water in the cabin."[23] Another tremendous gale swept the *Neptune* on February 14th, and everything movable on deck went overboard. She tried to reach the Azores but was driven past them. The *Neptune* finally reached port but was getting short on rations. In another passage from Liverpool in that same year, she came in with salt and coal for Jacob Cutter and hardware for Sherburne & Blunt. During the passage, she had aided a wrecked schooner, taking off the master, mate and three seamen. Four men had perished in the wreck.

Sailing for New Orleans in March 1827, she completed the triangle in late August and went out again in January 1828. She was at Poverty Point in the Mississippi River in 23 days from Portsmouth, fairly good time. She was advertised for sale in the *Journal* on October 6, 1829. In part, the advertisement said:

> ...Built in Portsmouth, copper fastened and new coppered with heavy copper in August last at Havre de Grace [France]; is a first rate sailing Ship for a merchantman, carries well, stowed under deck last voyage from New Orleans, 441,000 lbs. cotton. She has 4 Anchors, 1 Chain Cable 90 fathom, 1 Hemp Cable, 90 fathom, 1 Stream do. and is otherwise well found, and can be put to sea for a small expence. She would answer well for a whaleman or freighting ship.

William Lambert had brought the *Neptune* into Portsmouth for her last call, and he took her on Sunday, December 20, 1829, to Sag Harbor, New York, where she was turned over to her new owner, Benjamin Huntley, for use as a whaler. Lambert later commanded such Port of Portsmouth ships as the *Isaac Newton* and *William Badger*. During her years as a whaler, the *Neptune* made 11 cruises between 1831 and 1849. She brought in a total of 24,310 barrels of whale oil, an average of 2,210 per voyage. Her longest whaling voyage was her last and the best when she arrived with 2,700 barrels of oil and 17,000 pounds of bone, for a total value of $38,609.[24]

In 1849, the *Neptune* went the way of so many ships, around Cape Horn to California with men and goods for the gold fields.

Factor

Specifications: Built in 1822 by Ebenezer Thompson. Square stern, billet head. Burthen, 333 tons; length, 103.6 feet; beam, 23.9 feet; depth, 13.45 feet. Owner, John Dike, et al.

The *Factor*, which was never a factor in shipping annals of the Portsmouth District, went to sea, "new and elegant" on November 12, 1822, under William Haskell, heading for Charleston.[25] When Captain Haskell arrived in Charleston in the respectable time of 15 days, he reported that he had been chased by a pirate in latitude 33°. The pursuit lasted about 24 hours, and Haskell believed that a brig he had seen earlier fell victim to the pirates.

When the *Factor* was launched, the *Journal* showed its increasing awareness of the importance of shipbuilding. It devoted a paragraph to the event:

Yesterday was launched at Col. Thompson's ship yard in this town, the beautiful ship *Factor*, of 340 tons, owned by William Haskell and John Dike of Salem. This ship is considered one of the best ever built here, being constructed of white oak, long decked. She is intended for the European trade, and to be commanded by Captain Haskell.[26]

As so often happened to ships her size, the *Factor* became a whaler. For two cruises, she was owned in Poughkeepsie, New York. The first lasted only 15 months, and she brought in, on September 8, 1840, 250 barrels of sperm, 2,950 barrels of whale oil, and 15 tons of bone. Her second cruise, to New Zealand waters, lasted nearly three years. On April 5, 1844, her catch was 700 barrels of sperm, 1,600 barrels of whale oil, and 13,000 pounds of bone with a total value of $40,921.

After that voyage, she was sold in New Bedford, then the whaling capital of the New World. She went to the Indian Ocean, returning with 585 barrels of sperm; and 4,136 barrels of whale oil with a value of $65,330. The next time out, she was condemned, on July 2, 1847, at Taihaita in the Pacific.

America

Specifications: Built in 1823 by Reuben Shapley. Square stern, billet head. Burthen, 346 tons; length, 107 feet; beam, 26.9 feet; depth, 13.45 feet. Owners, March 13, 1824, Thomas W. Penhallow, Oliver Penhallow, William Jones and Samuel Pray.

The *America* is credited to Reuben Shapley, and there is little doubt she was built in his yard on Shapley's Island. Shapley was, however, more a merchant than a shipwright, and it is reasonable to believe that the talented William Hanscom was the master builder. Hanscom had built at least five smaller vessels on Shapley's Island before the *America*'s launching. In 1824, Hanscom went up river to build the *Marion* in a Berwick yard.

The *America* left for Charleston in March 1824, not long after her launch. Samuel Pray was her first master. Her owners put her into the triangle trade, and she came frequently into Portsmouth with salt from St. Ubes. A marine note in the *Journal*, October 9, 1830, records her arrival at New York in 54 days from Cadiz with salt.

T.W. Penhallow sold his interest to Samuel Hale of Dover. The latter held it when the *America* came in 1831 with salt for her owners and sheet iron and hardware for Richard Jenness. Like other Portsmouth-built vessels of the period, the *America* went to other southern ports when unable to find a cargo at Charleston. After Samuel Pray, she was commanded by Thomas Kitson, who had her on at least one run to

Liverpool. On this passage, Kitson lost his first mate, George Clark Fiske, 29, of Boston, who had been on the ship several years. In the *America*'s first year, she lost John Adams of Kittery, Maine, when he drowned in New Orleans. While he was at sea, 10 years later, Captain Kitson's 17-year-old daughter died, a loss he didn't hear about for many months.

In 1836, the *America* was put up for sale.[27] Joseph G. Sise, one of her owners, signed the advertisement, describing her in part "...she carries and sales well, and is a very desirable vessel for the whaling business." Apparently there were no purchasers at that time, because the next year Sise advertised 1,400 hogsheads of salt for sale on board the *America*. During one period, the *America* was commanded by John S. Place, who had her on a couple of voyages to Turk's Island for salt. It appears that the *America* was still Portsmouth-owned in 1840, with Samuel Handy the master. In March of that year, bound from New Orleans for Europe, she ran aground on the Florida Reef but was able to get off before the wreckers from Key West could get to her. What finally happened to the *America* isn't known. It can be strongly speculated she became a whaler. She was of a size well liked in that industry, and, by the 1840s, larger vessels were driving the older ones out of the freighting business. Another possibility is that she was chartered into the gold rush madness in 1849.

Sarah Sheafe

Specifications: Built in 1824 by Jacob Remick. Square stern, billet head. Burthen, 402 tons; length, 112.6 feet; beam, 28.25 feet; depth, 14.25 feet. Owners, December 21, 1824, James Sheafe and Robert Lenox.

The *Sarah Sheafe* was the first of two ships built by Jacob Remick in his yard on the North Mill Pond near Rindge's Wharf. He had built three brigs in the 250-ton range before laying the keel of the *Sarah Sheafe*. There is a strong possibility that a young George Raynes was then employed in the Remick yard. It is known that Raynes worked for Remick before branching off on his own to build the brig *Planet* in 1828.

The *Sarah Sheafe* was one of the first vessels to become part of a trend, in that, once she cleared Portsmouth Harbor, she never returned. In the next decades, as Portsmouth faded as a competitive, commercial seaport, that became a standard procedure: big ships rarely returned. The *Sarah Sheafe* went into the cotton trade, working back and forth between Liverpool and Savannah. On one such voyage, she arrived at Savannah on December 7, 1828, with salt. Going up river two days later, she collided with a brig, suffering damage to her rigging.[28]

At some point in her career, the *Sarah Sheafe* went into the whaling business, working out of New Bedford. She made two cruises to the Pacific between 1851 and 1859. The second lasted 44 months, and she returned to New Bedford with a cargo valued at $59,970. What finally happened to her isn't known, but she didn't become one of the Stone Fleet.

Ann Mary Ann

Specifications: Built in 1828 by Jacob Remick. Square stern, billet head. Burthen, 380 tons; length, 110.2 feet; beam, 27.8 feet; depth, 13.9 feet. Owners, March 10, 1828, Samuel Hale and Ichabod Rollins.

Only four ships were built in the Town of Portsmouth in the 1820s, and the *Ann Mary Ann* was the last of them. After Jacob Remick launched the *Ann Mary Ann*, he moved his operations to Kittery. A new ship-building era was dawning in Portsmouth, one that will be discussed in a later volume. For the moment, it suffices to say that George Raynes, described in the 1821 *Town Directory* as a "boat builder," was ready to come on stage as a master shipwright, one who would, in the next quarter century, rank among the great American shipbuilders. In fact, as Remick moved out of his North Mill Pond yard, Raynes was building his brig *Planet* there.

Thomas B. Clark took the *Ann Mary Ann* on her maiden voyage. Her destiny was the cotton trade. She cleared at Savannah, January 1, 1829, for her first transatlantic crossing, and Clark was master through six more of them. Nothing was more unpredictable in sailing days than the length of a passage. There were so many variables: weather, crew proficiency, the master's ability, the vessel's design, and so on. On the *Ann Mary Ann*'s first east-to-west crossing, headed for Charleston, she was 50 days out when a passing vessel had to supply her with provisions, and she was another six days in making port. Typical of the cargoes she brought into Portsmouth was one in August 1833. The manifest included 513 tons of coarse salt, 200 bags of fine salt, and one roll of carpeting for William and Samuel Hale.[29] Back and forth she went, sometimes going directly back to southern ports for more cotton, at other times coming to Portsmouth with assorted cargoes, although salt from Cadiz or Liverpool was the main item. The salt loaded at Liverpool came from Cheshire.

The uncertainty of seafaring life in the 1830s was well illustrated by an incident on the *Ann Mary Ann* in August 1832 after her arrival in Boston from Liverpool:

On Saturday afternoon, a man named John Rohl, a

foreigner, cook on board the ship *Ann Mary Ann*, of Portsmouth, which arrived on Tuesday from Liverpool, died on board the vessel where he was gathering up his clothing. The cause of his death appears to have been a pulmonary complaint, as he had been much troubled with a cough on the passage. He had been from the vessel carousing, and wet his feet in the shower of Friday afternoon, and complained of severe pain in the chest. In the morning he said he had been to a doctor, who gave him some pills, after which he vomited. The pain in his chest continuing, Captain Clark gave him 30 drops of laudnum, but he died soon after. Captain C. was not aware of his being dangerously ill, but thought he had only taken a violent cold. He has a wife and family in Portsmouth, N.H.—Boston Pat.[30]

John Rohl left a wife and family in Portsmouth. The *1834 Town Directory* listed Rebecca Rohl as a widow, living on Liberty Square, an area in the vicinity of the Liberty Pole in present-day Prescott Park. Widow Rohl was then operating a boarding house. The *1839–40 Town Directory* has no mention of her, so she could have moved, remarried or died.

In 1835, the *Ann Mary Ann* came into Portsmouth from Cadiz with her usual cargo of salt. One day, while she was tied up at a wharf, her chief mate, James Chick, was working in the main top when he saw a man fall from the wharf into the swirling waters of the Piscataqua. Chick scampered down and out of the rigging and dove into the river. Although the man, James Marden, had gone to the bottom, Chick found him, brought him up and got him ashore, but Marden died shortly thereafter. Chick was later master of the *Ann Mary Ann* on several voyages before she was sold for a whaler in 1842.[31]

The *Ann Mary Ann*'s new owners were Mulford & Sleight of Sag Harbor, N.Y. Her new master, Captain Winters, made two voyages in her in pursuit of the elusive whale. Her first voyage lasted from November 25, 1842, until May 27, 1845, and she brought home 75 barrels of sperm, 2,600 barrels of whale oil, and nearly 12 tons of bone, for a total value of $36,896. Her second cruise was of the same duration and earned $31,381, although she had none of the prized sperm oil on board.[32] After her sale as a whaler, the *Ann Mary Ann* disappeared from the marine news columns of Portsmouth newspapers. What finally became of her isn't known for certain. In 1849, there was a report that under a Captain Desing, she had left Sag Harbor for San Francisco.[33]

And with the *Ann Mary Ann* came the end of an era in Port of Portsmouth shipbuilding. Local merchant firms would prosper for a few years, but gradually, the shipbuilders began catering to purchasers from Boston and New York. But that is a story yet to be told.

Notes

Key to abbreviations in notes and captions

MLH: Moffatt-Ladd House, MHS: Massachusetts Historical Society, MM: Mariner's Museum, NHG: *New Hampshire Gazette*, NHHS: New Hampshire Historical Society, PM: Peabody Museum, Salem, MA, PA: Portsmouth Athenaeum, PHS: Portsmouth Historical Society, PJ: *Portsmouth Journal*, SB: Strawbery Banke.

Chapter 1

1. National Archives.
2. *Customs Records*, vol. II, p. 46.
3. *American Merchant Marine*, p. 116.
4. *They Came to Fish*, vol. II, p. 175.
5. *Merchant Sail*, vol. II, p. 1128.
6. Ibid., p. 757.

Chapter 2

1. Boyd Correspondence. NHHS Collections.
2. *The Ladd Family*, p. 47.
3. *Rambles*, First Series, p. 240.
4. *The Ladd Family*, p. 48.
5. Ibid.
6. *New Hampshire Gazette* (NHG), October 21, 1807.
7. Ibid., February 9, 1808.
8. *Customs Records*, vol. III, p. 160.
9. *Haven Memoir*, p. xii.
10. *NHG*, August 21, 1784.
11. *They Came to Fish*, vol. I, p. 88.

12. *Customs*, vol. III, p. 133.
13. *Portsmouth Journal*, November 1, 1845.
14. *Customs*, vol. III, p. 132.
15. Ibid., p. 135.
16. Ibid., p. 137.
17. *Journal*, January 31, 1829.
18. *Customs*, vol. III, p. 137.
19. *NHG*, January 10, 1784.
20. *Customs*, vol. III, p. 286.
21. Ibid., p. 296.
22. *The Blunts*, p. 33.
23. *NHG*, September 2, 1799.
24. *Customs*, vol. III, p. 34.
25. Ibid., p. 3.
26. Ibid., p. 6.
27. *NHG*, November 1, 1830.
28. *Customs*, vol. III, p. 7.
29. *Journal*, July 4, 1856.
30. *Customs*, vol. III, p. 23.
31. Ibid., p. 41.
32. *NHG*, October 5, 1793.
33. Ibid., July 16, 1816.
34. Ibid., January 4, 1797.
35. Ibid., November 7, 1800.
36. Ibid., January 3, 1784.

37. Ibid., March 23, 1801.
38. *Customs*, vol. III, p. 70.
39. Ibid., p. 72.
40. *NHG*, February 12, 1800.
41. *Customs*, vol. III, p. 70.
42. Ibid., p. 72.
43. Ibid., p. 74.
44. *Rambles*, Second Series, p. 149.
45. *Customs*, vol. III, p. 91.
46. Ibid., p. 101.
47. *NHG*, May 20, 1793.
48. *Customs*, vol. III, p. 122.
49. Ibid., p. 124.
50. Ibid., p. 131.
51. *NHG*, November 6, 1790.
52. *They Came to Fish*, vol. II, p. 162.
53. *Customs*, vol. III, p. 150.
54. *Portsmouth Chronicle*, November 8, 1856.
55. *NHG*, September 9, 1808.
56. *Journal*, May 24, 1849.
57. *NHG*, November 6, 1796.
58. Ibid., March 17, 1801.
59. *They Came to Fish*, vol. II, p. 125.
60. *Rambles*, First Series, p. 354.
61. *NHG*, February 4, 1785.
62. *They Came to Fish*, vol. II, p. 126.
63. *NHG*, September 11, 1784.
64. Ibid., May 27, 1785.
65. *Journal*, November 17, 1855.
66. *Customs*, vol. III, p. 203.
67. *Journal*, February 24, 1821.
68. *They Came to Fish*, vol. II, p. 163.
69. *NHG*, December 24, 1793.
70. Ibid., August 3, 1802.
71. Ibid., February 3, 1797.
72. *Customs*, vol. III, p. 256.
73. *They Came to Fish*, vol. II, p. 178.
74. *Customs*, vol. III, p. 270.
75. *NHG*, August 5, 1806.

76. Ibid., August 20, 1813.
77. *Customs*, vol. III, p. 277.
78. *Journal*, April 30, 1859.
79. *NHG*, March 12, 1825.
80. Ibid., May 28, 1825.
81. Ibid.
82. St. John's Lodge *Trestleboard*, March, 1976.
83. *NHG*, July 12, 1786.
84. *Customs*, vol. III, p. 316.
85. Ibid., vol. III, p. 321
86. *Rambles*, First Series, p. 137.
87. *Customs*, vol. III, p. 244.
88. Ibid., vol. I. p. 6.

Chapter 3

1. *NHG*, December 17, 1796.
2. Ibid., November 7, 1798.
3. *Quasi War*, vol. IV, p. 452.
4. *NHG*, October 1, 1799.
5. Ibid., January 18, 1803.
6. Ibid., February 26, 1805.
7. *Customs*, vol. IV, p. 10.
8. *NHG*, December 5, 1798.
9. Ibid., April 2, 1811.
10. Ibid., May 11, 1713.
11. Ibid., March 11, 1816.
12. Ibid., May 30, 1809.
13. *Customs*, vol. IV, p. 18.
14. *NHG*, November 5, 1816.
15. *Customs*, vol. IV, p. 18.
16. Ibid.
17. *NHG*, December 12, 1815.
18. Ibid., March 5, 1816.
19. Ibid., October 17, 1817.
20. *Customs*, vol. II, p. 164.
21. *Journal*, March 7, 1829.
22. *NHG*, July 11, 1816.
23. Ibid., March 11, 1817.
24. *Customs*, vol. II, p. 214.
25. *NHG*, February 26, 1828.
26. *Customs*, vol. II, p. 155.
27. *NHG*, May 15, 1827.
28. *Journal*, March 23, 1833.

29. Ibid., April 23, 1842.
30. Ibid., November 14, 1846.

Chapter 4

1. *NHG*, November 23, 1791.
2. Ibid., December 17, 1796.
3. *Customs*, vol. IV, p. 34.
4. Ibid., p. 35.
5. *NHG*, March 19, 1800.
6. Ibid., March 11, 1797.
7. Ibid., April 3, 1799.
8. Ibid.
9. Ibid., November 14, 1816.
10. Ibid., September 30, 1817.
11. Ibid., November 2, 1802.
12. Ibid., August 16, 1803.
13. Ibid., May 14, 1805.
14. Ibid., June 12, 1804.
15. Ibid., May 22, 1804.
16. Ibid., July 3, 1810.
17. Ibid., August 21, 1810.
18. Ibid., March 12, 1811.
19. *Customs*, vol. IV, p. 44.
20. *Journal*, February 27, 1836.
21. *NHG*, December 28, 1813.
22. *Customs*, vol. IV, p. 44.
23. *Readers Encyclopedia*, p. 45.
24. *NHG*, October 7, 1811.
25. *Readers Encyclopedia*, p. 806.
26. *NHG*, November 4, 1811.
27. *Customs*, vol. IV, p. 46.
28. *NHG*, March 4, 1817.
29. *Customs*, vol. II, p. 175.
30. *NHG*, February 28, 1815.
31. *Customs*, vol. IV, p. 47.
32. *NHG*, November 7, 1815.
33. *Oracle*, October 14, 1820.
34. *Customs*, vol. II, p. 219.
35. *NHG*, August 8, 1826.
36. Ibid., July 14, 1812.
37. Ibid., October 15, 1817.
38. Ibid., March 24, 1818.
39. *Customs*, vol. II, p. 219.
40. Whitehouse Collections.
41. *NHG*, April 6, 1819.
42. Ibid., January 31, 1835.
43. *Journal*, August 24, 1861.
44. Whitehouse Collections.
45. *Oracle*, February 21, 1821.
46. *Chronicle*, April 9, 1889.
47. *Customs*, vol. II, p. 175.
48. *Journal*, September 28, 1833.
49. *Customs*, vol. II, p. 175.
50. *Journal*, November 25, 1837.
51. *Customs*, vol. II, p. 157.

Chapter 5

1. *History of Durham*, p. 341.
2. *NHG*, November 6, 1790.
3. Ibid., October 21, 1800.
4. Ibid., February 17, 1801.
5. Ibid., October 9, 1798.
6. Ibid., February 10, 1795.
7. *Customs*, vol. IV, p. 67.
8. *NHG*, May 31, 1799.
9. *Readers' Encyclopedia*, p. 815.
10. *NHG*, September 14, 1802.
11. Ibid., August 29, 1802.
12. *Customs*, vol. IV, p. 70.
13. *NHG*, December 6, 1825.
14. Ibid., May 15, 1810.
15. Ibid., October 17, 1815.
16. *Oracle*, April 4, 1811.
17. *NHG*, October 9, 1810.
18. Ibid.
19. Ibid., November 27, 1810.
20. Ibid., August 20, 1810.
21. Ibid., April 27, 1813.
22. *Oracle*, February 9, 1819.
23. *Journal*, December 16, 1823.
24. *NHG*, September 25, 1815.
25. *Chronicle*, November 8, 1856.
26. *NHG*, September 5, 1815.
27. Ibid., November 4, 1817.
28. Ibid., January 13, 1818.
29. Ibid., March 21, 1815.
30. Ibid., April 21, 1818.
31. Ibid., January 13, 1813.

32. Ibid., January 5, 1819.
33. *Oracle*, November 18, 1820.
34. *NHG*, March 18, 1825.
35. Ibid., June 21, 1825.
36. Ibid., February 14, 1826.
37. Ibid., January 1, 1828.
38. Ibid., January 20, 1816.
39. *Customs*, vol. II, p. 156.
40. *Readers Encyclopedia*, p. 1138.
41. *Journal*, March 1, 1834.
42. Ibid.
43. *NHG*, September 11, 1827.
44. *Journal*, January 12, 1833.
45. *Customs*, vol. IV, p. 77
46. *NHG*, June 1, 1824.
47. *Customs*, vol. II, p. 178.
48. *Journal.*
49. *Oracle*, December 9, 1820.
50. Ibid., November 13, 1821.
51. Ibid., January 19, 1822.
52. *NHG*, November 6, 1827.
53. *Journal*, May 17, 1823.
54. *NHG*, September 30, 1823.
55. *Journal*, December 6, 1823.
56. *NHG*, April 21, 1829.
57. *Customs*, vol. II, p. 154.
58. *NHG*, April 21, 1829.
57. *Customs*, vol. II, p. 154.
58. *NHG*, April 21, 1829.
59. Ibid., August 3, 1824.
60. Ibid., April 29, 1828.
61. Ibid., September 9, 1830.
62. *Journal*, July 27, 1833.
63. Ibid., November 15, 1834.
64. *NHG*, January 4, 1825.
65. *Journal*, January 22, 1831.
66. Ibid., April 1831.
67. Ibid.
68. *NHG*, November 11, 1828.
69. *Journal*, June 15, 1833.
70. Ibid., November 25, 1826.
71. Ibid., October 6, 1832.
72. Ibid., October 10, 1840.

73. *They Came to Fish*, vol. II, p. 442. (First Edition)
74. *Dictionary of American Fighting Ships*, vol. V. appendix 1.
75. Ibid.
76. *NHG*, February 13, 1827.
77. *Journal*, September 11, 1837.
78. Ibid., October 5, 1839.
79. Ibid., February 29, 1840.
80. *NHG*, September 28, 1828
81. *Customs*, vol. II, p. 184.
82. *Journal*, December 16, 1837.
83. Ibid., October 13, 1838.
84. Ibid., August 7, 1841.
85. Ibid., October 9, 1841.
86. Ibid., June 24, 1843.
87. *Salter Genealogy*, p. 19.
88. Ibid.
89. *Journal*, September 13, 1834.
90. Ibid., October, 1837.
91. Ibid., April 22, 1843.
92. Ibid., February 17, 1849.

Chapter 6

1. *History of Exeter*, p. 336.
2. *Customs*, vol. IV, p. 111.
3. *The Ladd Family*, p. 47.
4. *Swazey Genealogy*, p. 144.
5. *Customs*, vol. IV, p. 98.
6. *The Salters of Portsmouth, N.H.*, p. 11
7. *NHG*, June 8, 1816.
8. Ibid., May 21, 1792.
9. *History of Exeter*, p. 338.
10. *Customs*, vol. IV, p. 101.
11. Ibid., vol. I, p. 142.
12. Ibid., vol. IV, p. 105.
13. *NHG*, November 3, 1803.
14. Ibid., September 12, 1809.
15. Ibid., April 2, 1811.
16. *Customs*, vol. IV, p. 107.

17. Ibid., p. 108.
18. *NHG*, February 11, 1811.

Chapter 7

1. *NHG*, December 18, 1790.
2. *Customs*, vol. IV, p. 123.
3. *NHG*, October 18, 1792.
4. Ibid., March 19, 1793.
5. Ibid., October 1, 1793.
6. Ibid., September 15, 1807.
7. Ibid., September 26, 1809.
8. Ibid., November 18, 1817.
9. *Oracle*, December 17, 1818.
10. Ibid.
11. *Customs*, vol. IV, p. 140.
12. *NHG*, July 10, 1810.
13. Ibid., October 21, 1817.
14. Ibid., August 17, 1819.
15. *Customs*, vol. IV, p. 141.
16. *Oracle*, November 11, 1820.
17. *NHG*, May 15, 1810.
18. *Customs*, vol. III, p. 46.
19. Ibid., vol. IV, p. 143.
20. *NHG*, April 23, 1811.
21. Ibid., August 20, 1811.
22. *Reader's Encyclopedia*, p. 671.
23. *NHG*, May 8, 1810.
24. Ibid., September 24, 1811.
25. Ibid., December 19, 1815.
26. Ibid., May 6, 1817.
27. *Customs*, vol. IV, p. 146.
28. *NHG*, January 29, 1811.
29. Ibid., December 12, 1815.
30. Ibid., October 8, 1811.
31. Ibid., December 15, 1812.
32. Ibid., November 14, 1817.
33. *Oracle*, November 2, 1819.
34. Ibid., August 26, 1820.
35. *Journal*, September 14, 1822.
36. *NHG*, August 12, 1823.
37. Ibid., January 30, 1827.
38. Ibid., April 9, 1811.
39. *Journal*, June 1, 1822.
40. *NHG*, July 18, 1825.
41. Ibid., November 21, 1826.
42. Ibid., September 11, 1827.
43. *Journal*, September 18, 1830.
44. Ibid., November 10, 1832.
45. *Customs*, vol. II, p. 157.
46. *Journal*, April 21, 1829.
47. Ibid., December 19, 1829.
48. Ibid., January 8, 1831.
49. Ibid., January 10, 1829.
50. Ibid., September 29, 1829.
51. *Customs*, vol. IV, p. 160.
52. *Journal*, January 5, 1833.
53. Ibid., April 13, 1839.
54. Ibid., September 10, 1842.
55. Ibid., February 10, 1844.
56. Ibid., May 11, 1844.
57. Ibid., August 30, 1845.
58. *American Neptune*, vol. XXXII, No. 1, p. 34.
59. Ibid., p. 57.
60. *Journal*, October 9, 1827.
61. Ibid., May 2, 1829.
62. *Customs*, vol. IV, p. 161.
63. *Journal*, June 9, 1832.
64. Ibid., May 2, 1829.
65. Ibid., May 12, 1832.
66. Ibid., April 18, 1835.
67. *Customs*, vol. II, p. 159.
68. *Journal*, May 9, 1829.
69. Ibid., June 22, 1833.
70. *Customs*, vol. II, p. 159.

Chapter 8

1. *Hazlett*, p. 572.
2. *History of Newfields*, p. 336.
3. *NHG*, July 16, 1792.
4. Ibid., November 2, 1795.
5. Ibid., September 30, 1794.
6. Ibid., September 1799.
7. Ibid., June 9, 1807.
8. Ibid., May 14, 1796.
9. Ibid., October 22, 1796.
10. Ibid., May 31, 1799.
11. Ibid., August 12, 1800.

12. Ibid., March 9, 1802.
13. Ibid.
14. Ibid., March 12, 1805.
15. *Customs*, vol. IV, p. 238.
16. *Chapelle*, p. 68.
17. *NHG*, August 24, 1802.
18. Ibid.
19. Ibid., September 4, 1802.
20. *Customs*. vol. IV, p. 239.
21. *NHG*, January 11, 1803.
22. Ibid., May 22, 1804.
23. Ibid., October 6, 1802.
24. Ibid., March 12, 1812.
25. Ibid.
26. Ibid., April 2, 1811.
27. Ibid., October 29, 1811.
28. Ibid., November 21, 1813.
29. Ibid., December 22, 1815.
30. Ibid., January 7, 1817.
31. *Customs*, vol. IV, p. 243.
32. Ibid., p. 224.
33. *Oracle*, November 17, 1818.
34. Ibid., December 4, 1820.
35. *Journal*, September 28, 1822.
36. Ibid., March 27, 1824.
37. *NHG*, November 13, 1810.
38. Ibid., October 16, 1830.
39. *Journal*, June 25, 1823.
40. *NHG*, July 20, 1830.
41. *Journal*, January 27, 1831.
42. Ibid., May 9, 1829.
43. *Customs*, vol. II, p. 158
44. *NHG*, May 2, 1827.
45. *Customs*, vol. II, p. 158.
46. *NHG*, January 1, 1828.
47. *Journal*, January 2, 1829.
48. Ibid., August 4, 1829.
49. Ibid., April 24, 1830.
50. Ibid., November 15, 1830.
51. Ibid., March 5, 1831.
52. Ibid., December 10, 1831.
53. Ibid., January 12, 1833.
54. Ibid., April 18, 1834.
55. Ibid., May 2, 1835.
56. Ibid., August 29, 1837.
57. Ibid., September 16, 1837.
58. Ibid., September 27, 1845.

Chapter 9

1. *History of Hampton*, p. 33.
2. *History of Hampton Falls*, p. 399.
3. *NHG*, October 13, 1791.
4. Ibid., November 7, 1794.
5. *Customs*, vol. IV, p. 342.
6. *They Came to Fish*, vol. I, p. 88.
7. *NHG*, March 22, 1797.
8. Ibid., April 22, 1800.
9. Ibid., October 28, 1800.
10. Ibid., February 18, 1805.
11. Ibid., September 15, 1807.
12. Ibid., April 24, 1804.
13. Ibid., December 6, 1808.
14. Ibid., September 12, 1809.
15. Ibid., October 17, 1809.
16. Ibid., September 29, 1811.
17. *Customs*, vol. IV, p. 339.
18. *NHG*, November 28, 1815.
19. Ibid., September 16, 1817.
20. Ibid., July 20, 1818.

Chapter 10

1. *NHG*, May 10, 1797.
2. Ibid., November 28, 1798.
3. Ibid., November 6, 1802.
4. *The Salters of Portsmouth, NH*, p.13.
5. Ibid., p. 14.
6. Ibid.
7. *NHG*, March 26, 1796.
8. Ibid., March 22, 1797.
9. Ibid., April 15, 1797.
10. Ibid., July 29, 1800.
11. Ibid., October 7, 1800.
12. Ibid., January 1, 1805.
13. Ibid., November 13, 1810.
14. Ibid., November 6, 1810.

15. Ibid., February 12, 1806.
16. Ibid., February 11, 1806.
17. *Customs*, vol. IV, p. 258.
18. *NHG*, April 24, 1815.
19. Ibid., September 2, 1817.
20. Ibid., March 17, 1818.
21. *Journal*, November 30, 1822.
22. Ibid., March 20, 1858.
23. *NHG*, April 4, 1826.
24. *Customs*, vol. II, p. 158.
25. *Journal*, November 19, 1822.
26. Ibid., October 5, 1822.
27. Ibid., September 10, 1836.
28. Ibid., December 18, 1828.
29. Ibid., August 17, 1833.
30. Ibid., September 1, 1832.
31. Ibid., September 19, 1835.
32. *Customs*, vol. II, p. 134.
33. *Journal*, November 10, 1849.

Bibliography

Books

Bell, Charles H. *History of Exeter.* Exeter, New Hampshire. Boston: J.E. Farwell & Co., 1888.

Blunt, Roscoe C., Jr. *The Blunts: A History.* By the Author, No date.

Brewster, Charles W. *Rambles About Portsmouth.* Portsmouth, New Hampshire: Lewis W. Brewster, 1859.

Brighton, Ray. *They Came to Fish.* Portsmouth, New Hampshire: Portsmouth 350, Inc., 1973.

Brown, Warren. *History of Hampton Falls.* Manchester, New Hampshire: John B. Clarke Company, 1900.

Chapelle, Howard I. *The Baltimore Clipper.* Salem, Massachusetts: The Marine Research Society, 1930.

                          , *The Search for Speed Under Sail.* New York: W.W. Norton Company, 1967.

Dictionary of American Naval Fighting Ships. Washington, D.C.: Naval History Division, 1959.

Dow, Joseph. *History of Hampton.* Hampton: 1983.

Emery, William M. *The Salters of Portsmouth, N.H.* New Bedford, Massachusetts: 1936.

Fairburn, W.A. *Merchant Sail.* Center Lovell, Maine: Fairburn Marine Educational Foundation, 1944.

Fitts, James Hill, Reverend. *History of Newfields.* Concord, New Hampshire: 1912.

George, Nellie Palmer. *Old Newmarket.* Exeter, New Hampshire: News-Letter Press, 1932.

Hazlett, Charles A. *History of Rockingham County*. Chicago, Illinois: Richmond-Arnold Publishing Company, 1915.

Johnson, Allen, ed. *Dictionary of American Biography*. New York: Charles Scribner & Sons, 1957.

Ladd, Warren. *The Ladd Family*. By the Author, 1890.

Marvin, Winthrop L. *The American Merchant Marine*. New York: Charles Scribner & Sons, 1902.

The Reader's Encyclopedia. New York: Thomas Y. Crowell, 1955.

Salter, W.T. *John Salter, Mariner*. By the Author, 1910.

Scales, John. *History of Dover, N.H.* Dover City Council, 1923.

Stackpole, Everett S. and Thompson, Lucien. *History of the Town of Durham*. Town of Durham.

Tarleton, C.W. *The Tarleton Family*. Concord, New Hampshire: 1900.

World Atlas. International ed. New York: Rand McNally & Company, 1929.

World Atlas. New Census ed. New York: Rand McNally & Company, 1961.

Magazines

American Neptune (Salem, Massachusetts: Peabody Museum).
Granite State Monthly (Concord, New Hampshire).
The Old Eliots (Eliot, Maine).

Newspapers

The New Hampshire Gazette (Portsmouth, New Hampshire).
The Portsmouth Chronicle (Portsmouth, New Hampshire).
The Portsmouth Herald (Portsmouth, New Hampshire).
The Portsmouth Journal (Portsmouth, New Hampshire).
The Portsmouth Oracle (Portsmouth, New Hampshire).

Manuscript Collections

Portsmouth Customs Records. Portsmouth Athenaeum.
Whitehouse, Robert, An unpublished, untitled manuscript history of Cocheco River shipping.

Documents

Portsmouth Directories.

Index

Ray Brighton, a retired newspaper editor, is a researcher and writer of Portsmouth history. Among his previous books are *They Came To Fish; Frank Jones, King of the Alemakers;* and, for the Portsmouth Marine Society, *The Prescott Story; The Checkered Career of Tobias Lear* and *Clippers of The Port of Portsmouth and the Men Who Built Them.*